Edition KWV

Die „Edition KWV" beinhaltet hochwertige Werke aus dem Bereich der Wirtschaftswissenschaften. Alle Werke in der Reihe erschienen ursprünglich im Kölner Wissenschaftsverlag, dessen Programm Springer Gabler 2018 übernommen hat.

Weitere Bände in der Reihe http://www.springer.com/series/16033

Sebastian Rothe

Portfolio Analysis of Power Plant Technologies

A Simulation Approach to Rebalance Fuel Mix Strategies

 Springer Gabler

Sebastian Rothe
Köln, Germany

Bis 2018 erschien der Titel im Kölner Wissenschaftsverlag, Köln
Dissertation Universität Hamburg, 2011

Edition KWV
ISBN 978-3-658-24378-4   ISBN 978-3-658-24379-1   (eBook)
https://doi.org/10.1007/978-3-658-24379-1

Library of Congress Control Number: 2019935541

Springer Gabler

This Springer Gabler imprint is published by the registered company Springer Fachmedien Wiesbaden GmbH
part of Springer Nature
The registered company address is: Abraham-Lincoln-Str. 46, 65189 Wiesbaden, Germany

Foreword

In recent years, there has been renewed interest in the fuel mix strategy of utility firms. The nuclear catastrophe in Japan demonstrated that existing power plant technologies carry risks which have not been adequately priced yet. In addition, energy consumption in the world is soaring. As a result new power generation capacities are needed. The emission reduction objectives of the European Union as well as the finiteness of fossil fuels require investments in new power plant technologies; moreover European utilities do have to replace over aged power plants in the near future. As a consequence, a wave of replacements and investments in power generation capacities is expected within the next years accompanied by a shift in the energy fuel mix.

The most efficient composition of power plant technologies, however, has hardly been an issue in the relevant academic literature so far. Sebastian Rothe aims to close this gap. To derive such a composition, he mainly draws on the traditional portfolio approach of financial theory. In this respect, the analysis sheds light on the determinant factors that result in an economically efficient portfolio and that help assemble an efficient power plant mix over time.

Furthermore the analysis takes the change of the CO_2 emission regulation into account.

The work of Sebastian Rothe contributes to the academic literature, as based on the work of Roques et al. (2008), Sebastian Rothe has managed within his doctoral thesis to handle an extremely complex and actual topic. His findings and recommendations are valuable not only for scientists but also for practitioners.

Hamburg, October 2011   Alexander Bassen

Acknowledgements

I worked on this thesis during my time as an academic assistant at the Chair of Capital Markets and Management of Alexander Bassen at the University of Hamburg. Looking back feels good not only due to the fact of having finished my thesis but also, as I used to work with great people in an inspiring environment.

First of all, I am greatly indebted to my first supervisor, Alexander Bassen, for his motivating support, encouragement and advice. In addition, I would like to thank him for giving me the freedom and having the confidence in my work which evolved in a unique atmosphere at his Chair. Specifically, I thank him for his granting of a short-term leave and the Kyungpook National University, Korea, for providing me a position as a Visiting Scholar.

Secondly, I would like to thank Ingrid Größl for being my second supervisor. Furthermore, I thank Manfred Sommer and Horst Zündorf for their acceptance to be further members of my final examination committee.

I benefited a lot from my colleagues. For this reason I wish to thank Ana Maria Kovacs, Hidajet Ramaj, Barbara Roder, Daniela Senkl, Christine Zöllner, Houdou Basse Mama and Nicolas Koch.

It was great having a secretary like Sabina Gorrissen Salazar who looked after us all and managed to create a warm and friendly atmosphere. I thank her for accurately proofreading most parts of my thesis for language as well as the biggest birthday cake I have ever received.

I am grateful for support provided by our student assistants Patricia Schmiß, Bettina Luft, Christoph Hörbelt and Thomas Rewel.

I gained a lot of my motivation from students who were taking my courses at the School of Business, Economics and Social Sciences. Therefore, I would like to thank them.

Finally, I could always rely on the support of my friends and family. They encouraged me a lot to keep track on my schedule in particular at the end of my work and to finally succeed. Therefore this thesis is dedicated to the people I love.

Cologne, October 2011   Sebastian Rothe

Table of contents

List of abbreviations

AAU	Assigned Amount Unit
APT	Arbitrage Pricing Theory
APX	Amsterdam Power Exchange
Bn	Billion
BnetzA	Bundesnetzagentur
CAGR	Compound Average Growth Rate
CAPM	Capital Asset Pricing Model
CARMA	Carbon Monitoring for Action
CCGT	Combined Cycle Gas Turbine
CDM	Clean Development Mechanism
CER	Certified Emission Reduction
CH_4	Methane
CHP	Combined Heat and Power
CITL	Community Independent Transaction Log
CML	Capital Market Line
CO_2	Carbon dioxide
DCF	Discounted Cash Flow
DWD	Deutscher Wetterdienst
EAT	Earnings after Taxes
EBITDA	Earnings before Interest, Taxes, Depreciation and Amortization
ECX	European Climate Exchange
EDF	Électricité de France
EEFA	Energy Environment Forecast Analysis
EEG	German Renewable Energy Act
EEX	European Energy Exchange
EnWG	Energiewirtschaftsgesetz
ERU	Emission Reduction Units
e.g.	for example

etc.	et cetera
et al.	et alli
ETS	European Trading Scheme
EU	European Union
EUA	EU Allowance
EWI	Energiewirtschaftliches Institut der Universität zu Köln
FCF	Free Cash Flow
G	Gram
GDP	Gross Domestic Product
GER	Germany
GMRP	Global Maximum Return Portfolio
GMVP	Global Minimum Variance Portfolio
GT	Gas Turbine
GW	Gigawatt
HFC	Hydrofluorocarbon
IAEE	International Association of Energy Economics
IEA	International Energy Agency
ICE	Intercontinental Exchange
i.e.	id est
JI	Joint Implementation
K€	Thousand Euro
LNG	Liquefied Natural Gas
MRP	Market Risk Premium
M&A	Mergers and Acquisitions
NAP	National Allocation Plan
N_2O	Nitrous oxide
NBP	National Balancing Point
NL	The Netherlands
NPV	Net Present Value
O&M	Operation and Maintenance
OLS	Ordinary Least Squares

OMEL	Operador del Mercado Ibérico de Energia
OPEC	Organization of Petroleum Exploring Countries
OTC	Over the Counter
p.	Page
pp.	Pages
PFC	Perflurorocarbon
PV	Photovoltaic
SML	Security Market Line
SF_6	Sulphur hexafluoride
Std. Dev.	Standard Deviation
s.t.	subjected to
T	Ton
TTF	Title Transfer Facility
TSO	Transmission System Operator
TV	Terminal Value
UBA	Umweltbundesamt
UK	United Kingdom
UN	United Nations
US	United States of America
VBA	Visual Basic for Applications
VER	Voluntary Emission Reductions
WACC	Weighted Average Cost of Capital

List of symbols

α	Alpha
$\&$	And
$\bar{r}_F$	Average realized yield of fund F
$\bar{r}_f$	Average risk-free interest rate
D_{base}	Base load
β_i	Beta coefficient of asset i
L	Cholesky's matrix
$c_{O\&M}$	Cost of operation and maintenance
ρ	Correlation coefficient
σ_{ij}	Covariance between two random variables i and j
D_t	Depreciation
$\$$	Dollar
$E[.]$	Expectation operator
μ	Expected return/ value
c_{fix}	Fixed generation costs
$\bar{P}_t^E$	Fixed remuneration of generated electricity for renewable energies in period t
g	Growth rate
δ	Horizontal distance to the efficient frontier
A	Initial matrix
I	Investment
λ	Lambda
τ	Marginal tax rate
D_M	Market value of debt
E_M	Market value of equity
b	Maximum value
a	Minimum value
m	Mode

D_{peak}	Peak load
%	Percent
Z_i	Performance ratio of portfolio i
p	Probability
ϕ	Probability space
Q_t^C	Quantity of carbon in period t
Q_t^F	Quantity of fuel in period t
Q_t^E	Quantity of generated electricity in period t
S	Supply
σ_ε	Random error
r_i	Return of asset i
r_f	Risk-free interest rate
σ_i	Standard deviation of a random variable
E	Technical efficiency
L^T	Transpose of Cholesky 's matrix
w^T	Transpose matrix of portfolio weights
TV	Terminal value
$\tilde{P}_t^C$	Uncertain price of a carbon in period t
$\tilde{P}_t^E$	Uncertain price of electricity in period t
$\tilde{P}_t^F$	Uncertain price of fuel in period t
V	Value
σ^2	Variance of a random variable
S	Variance-covariance matrix
η	Vertical distance to the efficient frontier

$\tilde{Q}_t^E$	Volume risk of generated electricity from renewable energies in period t
w_i	Weight of asset i

Energy units and conversion factors

Work

kWh	Kilowatt hour
MWh	Megawatt hour
GWh	Gigawatt hour
TWh	Terawatt hour
Btu	British thermal unit
MMBtu	1,000,000 Btu
t.c.e.	ton of coal equivalent
t.o.e.	ton of oil equivalent

Power

kW	Kilowatt
MW	Megawatt
GW	Gigawatt
TW	Terawatt

Conversion factors

Coal	1 t.c.e = 8.14 MWh
Gas	1 BTU = 0.0293071MWh
Oil	1 t.o.e. = 11.63 MWh
Barrel	158.988 l
	1 Barrel oil = 147 kg

List of tables

List of figures

1 Introduction

As evidenced in many reports of the International Energy Agency (IEA), by 2030 power consumption in the world will be twice as much as the current level at the end of 2009. While in Asia the need for investments in generation capacity is driven by the soaring demand for electricity, the growth-rate in Europe is rather moderate. However, huge investments in generation capacity are still required, as the European power plant park is aging. Most of the power plants, which were built up during the 1970s have to be replaced shortly.[1] Energy market experts predict that the investments for replacements amount to between 300 and 600 GW of installed generation capacity in Europe.[2] Indeed, most of the thermal power plants from German utility firms are already older than 30 years which requires replacements of 40 GW until 2020.[3]

As a consequence, investments in generation capacity are necessary in order to provide a reliable supply for customers. The liberalization of electricity markets, however, has changed the European market structure and therefore shifted these issues from a country basis down to a firm level.

1.1 Motivation

Liberalization goes along with increased competition and uncertainty, which requires European utility firms to adapt their business strategies.[4] Alongside the demand for replacements of power plants, tightening environmental standards force utilities to reassess their generation mix and investment planning. Even though a shift in utilities' fuel mixes towards low emitting electricity power plants is very likely, new conventional thermal power plants are still needed. The volatility of electricity generated by renewable energies as well as a lack of power storage require a back-up from reliable, steady, quick and flexible sources such as conventional power plants. Hence, from a utility's perspective different power plant technologies do exist with individual merits very similar to ordinary financial assets. However, the issue arises of how utilities should combine different power plant technologies.

---

[1] See IEA (2008a) pp. 88-89.
[2] See Weber/ Swider (2006), pp. 1-2.
[3] See UBA (2005), p. 107.
[4] See Dyner/ Larsen (2001), pp. 1145-1154; Felder (1996), pp. 62-67.

© Springer Fachmedien Wiesbaden GmbH, part of Springer Nature 2011
S. Rothe, *Portfolio Analysis of Power Plant Technologies*, Edition KWV,
https://doi.org/10.1007/978-3-658-24379-1_1

Power plants are real assets and as a consequence the power plant park of a utility firm equals a portfolio of different generation assets. Hence, utilities operating a power plant efficiently in terms of return and risk are better off compared to competitors. Traditional capital market theory might assist to solve this trade-off.

1.2 Previous research

Mean-variance portfolio theory originally refers to the work of *Markowitz* (1952, 1959) who has developed the first analytical framework for selecting financial securities to optimize portfolios. Meanwhile such theoretical frameworks have been established in different business fields. In particular the Markowitz approach has become a useful instrument for appraising the return and risk for energy investments.[5] In the following section previous research will be briefly introduced.

Related research can be distinguished in two major fields. While the first group explores the national generation mix of an economy (henceforth: *macro level*) in terms of efficiency and social welfare, the second group studies the efficiency from an investor's or company's perspective (henceforth: *micro level*). The former has spurred extensive research during the time period before liberalization and therefore the interest in cost efficient energy supply from a welfare perspective. However, the structural change by opening European electricity markets to competition in the last decade has caused a need for further research by taking the micro level perspective. In addition the introduction of the European Emission Trading Scheme (EU ETS) will force utility firms to reassess their investments in generation capacity and as a consequence to refine existing theoretical models.

In particular, cutting-edge research on a macro level refers back to the contributions of *Awerbuch*. Evaluating the generation mix of the European Union (*Awerbuch/ Berger*, 2003), Ireland (*Awerbuch*, 2004) the United States and Mexico (*Awerbuch*, 2006), the cost based study analyses the effect of adding renewable energies to the existing generation portfolios in order to fulfill regulatory targets. In particular wind, geothermal energy and other renewable energies are considered to enlarge the diversity of the generation mix. Following *Awerbuch*, national generation mixes are better off if renewable energies are added.

---

[5] See Sunderkötter/ Weber (2009), p. 2.

Although renewable energies are costly on a stand-alone basis, including them in a generation portfolio shrinks generation costs and enlarges energy security. The mean-variance approach is not limited to fuel cost analyses, however. According to *Jansen et al.* (2006), *Awerbuch/ Berger* (2003), it is also suitable to explore the incorporation of other sources of risk in terms of operation, maintenance and construction time risks. In addition, another study by *Krey/ Zweifel* (2008) has applied the framework towards different national markets in order to identify efficient generation portfolios, namely those of Switzerland and the United States, and alongside has refined the application by econometric estimations of the underlying covariance matrix. A time varying covariance matrix was first introduced by *Humphreys/ McClain* (1998) to improve the existing analysis framework. Finally, *Bar-Lev/ Katz* (1976) rely on the mean- variance framework to optimize power industries' fuel mixes on a cost-based. Moreover they suggest ratios which allow comparing the performance of regulated utilities in different regions of the United States.

For the German power market, *Sunderkötter/ Weber* (2009) have recently presented an analytical approach by linking elements of mean-variance and of peak load pricing theory. They take two different kinds of gas plants, gas turbine and *combined-cycle gas turbine* (CCGT), as well as lignite, coal, nuclear and existing renewable technologies into account. They find that in contrast to the current German fuel mix, an efficient national generation portfolio should consist of more nuclear and lignite generation capacity based on historically CO_2 prices in comparison to coal generation capacity. However, any restrictions from national energy policy regarding the amount of these generation capacities will change the efficiency of the national energy mix. In that case coal plants turn out to be the most economical technology.[6] The issue arises whether the results and economic implications hold, if their objective function of minimizing costs changes towards the perspective of a utility firm.

In this respect, *Roques et al.* (2008) explore optimal generation portfolios for the power market in the United Kingdom (UK). The analyses focus on base load technologies in order to study the impact of different uncertain variables, namely fuel, electricity and CO_2 prices on generation portfolios. The authors rely on a *discounted cash flow* (DCF) valuation approach and simulate expected *net present values* (NPV). To account for risk a Monte Carlo simulation is used. Within their study they identify the advantages of gas-fired power plants compared to other base load technologies.

---

[6] See Sunderkötter/ Weber (2009), p. 26.

As gas and electricity are highly correlated, power plant portfolios that are dominated by gas plants, hedge themselves. Nevertheless, the question arises, whether gas fired plants are able to run base load in the long run. The gas conflict[7] between Ukraine and Russia about transmission services in winter 2008/2009 raises concerns in the EU, whether the reliability of the gas supply is guaranteed.[8]

While *Roques et al.* (2008) conduct the study from an investor's point of view, *Madlener et al.* (2009) choose a company's perspective. The second study conducts portfolio analyses of the E.ON generation capacity operating in the UK and Sweden. Instead of focusing on one certain type of plant technology, they consider the actual generation mixes of these two E.ON subsidies which are evaluated separately. According to their preliminary results the generation portfolios of the E.ON business units are inefficient. The authors advise investing more in renewable energies in both power markets in order to reach an efficient generation mix. The proper investment timing of the new plants remains unanswered, though.

Existing studies (e.g. *Roques et al.* 2008, *Madlener et al.* 2009) assume that the feasibility set and therefore the generation assets remain constant, as power plants are solely valued with respect to their specific economic life-time. In fact, a utility firm which opts for an efficient fuel mix has to take its existing power plants and their respective age structure as well as new investments due to power plant replacements into account. Exploring how a utility firm can realize to operate an efficient power plant park in a target year therefore requires an alternative approach. Otherwise the need for replacements over time would be neglected. In contrast to a static optimization, we define a *dynamic approach* as one which takes the change of a utility's power plant park through time into account. This allows specifying an investment strategy to rebalance a generation portfolio towards efficiency. However, referring to previous research this kind of a multi-period approach has not been taken yet. To fill that gap we develop a dynamic simulation model to conduct a comprehensive portfolio analysis for utilities competing on liberalized markets.

---

[7] See Bettzüge/ Lochner (2009), pp. 26-27.
[8] See Krey (2008), pp. 114-115.

1.3 Objectives and methodology

Motivated by the work of *Roques et al.* (2008), we refine their approach from a static to a dynamic analysis. Therefore, the main objective of the thesis is to identify efficient target generation portfolios by taking the perspective of a utility firm which operates on European electricity markets. Hence, we are confronted with picking generation assets which cause operating efficient portfolios not only from an economic but also from a technical point of view. Our challenge is to develop a simulation model which allows rebalancing generation portfolios from a base year towards a target year by conducting the research on a power plant level.

Against this background, we determine the degree of efficiency for generation portfolios. By measuring the degree of - what we call - *relative efficiency* of power plant portfolios, the implications can be used to optimize investment programs. Here, we aim to specify these investment strategies. The tightening emission allocation represents an another interesting issue to our research, as our goal is to measure the impact of value and risk for conventional power plant technologies and therefore generation portfolios. Since major utility firms have started to hold generation assets also in non-domestic electricity markets, we shed light on international diversification effects.

Based on the objectives introduced above, the following research questions have been derived in order to achieve the aims of the thesis:

- Which power plant technologies represent an efficient generation portfolio not only from an economic but also from a technical point of view?
- What does an efficient generation portfolio within a target year look like?
- How can an efficient generation park be realized over time?
- What does a proper investment strategy to optimize expected return and corresponding amount of risk look like?
- How does the change of the emission allocation process affect the profitability of power plant technologies and as a consequence impact the value and risk of generation portfolios?
- Does the operation on international power markets pay off in terms of value and risk?

The contribution of this thesis to the literature is mainly threefold: Firstly, we conduct a comprehensive portfolio analysis from a utility's perspective. Hence, instead of taking single power plants into account (e.g. *Roques et al.*, 2008), we consider a whole power plant park operating with different kinds of fuel technologies. As a consequence, we analyze not only the crucial conventional thermal and non-conventional thermal but also renewable energy power plants. Secondly, we show how to rebalance a generation portfolio in order to operate an efficient power plant park over time. Therefore we develop a dynamic simulation model on a plant basis including the respective age structure and as a consequence a feasibility set which consists of the existing generation capacity on the one hand and new generation capacity on the other hand. To the best of our knowledge, the analysis of a dynamic power plant park that covers existing power plant technologies towards the merit order has hitherto been neglected.

Thirdly, instead of separately valuing European markets on a stand-alone basis, we turn the lens on the exploration of international diversification effects by conducting a cross-national analysis. All in all, we investigate not only the composition of an efficient fuel mix but also *how* efficient European generation portfolios are. Here, we are interested to explore the degree of efficiency of generation portfolios that are actually planned by a utility firm operating on liberalized electricity markets. While utility firms benefit from this approach to measure the performance of generation portfolios and as a consequence be able to optimize their investment program, financial analysts get insights into the degree of efficiency for stock-traded generation business.

Against this background, the thesis relies on the following methodology to respond to the aforementioned research questions: We start in Chapter 2 analyzing the impact of structural changes to the European energy industry. For this purpose, we briefly review the liberalization process and present how investments in generation capacity are affected thereby. As a consequence, we introduce common power plant technologies to detect specific technical and economic merits as these generation assets represent our feasibility set. Irrespective of the kind of technology, power plants operating on competitive markets are already faced with uncertainties, and the introduction of the EU Emission Trading Scheme is a new source of uncertainty. In order to understand these uncertainties which mainly materialize as price risks, we analyze commodity prices, driving forces and mutual dependencies.

Within Chapter 3 in a first step we present the traditional portfolio-valuation theory. Here we briefly review the fundamentals of a discounted free cash flow valuation methodology and show how to combine this traditional valuation concept with a Monte Carlo simulation to account for uncertainties. To solve the risk-return trade-off, we describe the portfolio approach developed by *Markowitz* (1952). However, in comparison to these traditional approaches for financial assets, in a second step we adjust these concepts for generation assets. Therefore we derive, based on the findings of *Roques et al.* (2008), the requirements for our theoretical model. In addition, we derive ratios to determine the degree of efficiency for generation portfolios following capital market theory. The theoretical part of this thesis closes with deriving underlying hypotheses.

Chapter 4 develops a dynamic simulation model for analyzing generation portfolios. Based on the foregone analyses stochastic distributions are presumed for the risky parameters, which have an impact on power generation assets value. In this respect, electricity, fuel and carbon prices as well as meteorological data are defined as exogenous and uncertain variables. Alongside underlying technical and costs assumptions for power plants, we present non-linear commodity price developments for these uncertain variables as well as projected remunerations for renewable energies. Having defined these input variables, we devote the modeling procedure to dynamize a power plant park. Combining the simulation with a DCF approach determines the expected *net present value* (NPV) of a generation asset. While the expected NPV per capacity unit in MW measures the return of a plant, the corresponding standard deviation of the expected NPV serves as measure of risk. The results of the Monte Carlo simulation are used to determine efficient generation portfolios, whereas we distinguish between technical and economic efficiency.

Chapter 5 delivers the empirical simulation results of the analyses. Specifically, we rely on real power plant data provided by *Platts*, commodity prices from European Energy Exchanges and meteorological data from *Deutscher Wetterdienst* (DWD). We test an initial investment strategy leading to a target fuel mix communicated by a European utility firm for efficiency. Our results are presented first on a single power plant basis as well as for portfolios of affiliated technologies. Second, we determine the efficient frontiers before providing results for the country-specific generation portfolios. At last, based on our findings we demonstrate how to rebalance generation portfolios by adjusting the initial investment strategy.

This thesis closes in Chapter 6 with a conclusion, implications not only for management but also for research practice and gives an outlook for further research.

2 Economics of energy markets

The purpose of this section is to illustrate the main risk factors that have an impact on the profitability of power plants. Therefore, the outcome of liberalization and differences to regulated electricity markets are presented first. Secondly, the variety of power plant technologies is introduced to highlight individual merits regarding market, operational and other risk factors. Thirdly, we describe the European Emission Trading Scheme (EU ETS), as carbon prices affect the profitability of conventional thermal power plants. Furthermore electricity, carbon, coal and gas are introduced in order to point out the distinctive characteristics of these risk factors in comparison to ordinary assets. Ultimately, the interaction among these commodities is analyzed.

2.1 Liberalization and fuel mix

The European Union (EU) stipulates the legal framework of the energy policy. Hence, the member states have to adapt their national energy policy in order to fulfill the goals of the EU. The key objective of the EU is an economic, reliable and environmentally friendly energy supply. To achieve this, the energy markets have been opened to competition. Since this thesis deals with an appraisal of generation assets from a portfolio perspective, just the fundamental legal framework is introduced, which affects the power plant planning process.

2.1.1 Legislation and market design

To achieve the overall aim of a well functioning European electricity market the development of a common European energy policy is required to improve grid interconnections and as a consequence the level of trade between national markets.[9] Therefore, the EU developed common rules in their energy policy and reached an agreement on the electricity market liberalization, namely *EU-Directive (96/92/EC)*. The latter has been the starting point to gradually open national electricity markets to competition.[10] Therefore, member states of the EU were obligated to transfer the directive into national law. Key factors of the directive are the separation of business activities of a utility firm. According to this directive generation activities, network

---

[9] See Cornwall (2008), p. 98.
[10] See Cornwall (2008), p. 111.

© Springer Fachmedien Wiesbaden GmbH, part of Springer Nature 2011
S. Rothe, *Portfolio Analysis of Power Plant Technologies*, Edition KWV,
https://doi.org/10.1007/978-3-658-24379-1_2

business and sales have to be unbundled from a legal, accounting, operational and informational perspective.[11]

Instead of realizing a harmonization of national electricity markets, the first directive caused significant differences between the degrees of liberalization within the European member states. This was mainly due to the market concentration of larger utility firms which were able to exercise their market power.[12] As a consequence, the second *EU-Directive (2003/54/EC)* concerning common rules for the internal market in electricity was adopted by the EU Council and Parliament on 16 June 2003. Member states had to transfer the directive to national law by July 2004. In order to diminish these discrepancies the directive postulates, the creation of non-discriminatory network access, the development of interconnection infrastructure, security of supply and an effective regulation. These measures were supposed to lead to a downward pressure on network charges, stimulate cross-border trade and promote fair competition and economic efficiency.[13]

Besides, the *EU-Directive (2003/54/EC)* forces the member states to establish a national regulator[14] that enables network access for third parties in order to strengthen the liberalization processes. The directive points out that a competitive market requires a network access which is fair, transparent and adequately priced.

The market design can be characterized by the following major elements, *wholesale trade, power exchanges*, and *transmission system operators*:[15] Firstly, energy wholesale trade mainly takes place through bilateral and over-the-counter (OTC) markets. Secondly, the establishment of European power exchanges causes higher price liquidity and transparency. These market places facilitate short-term physical transactions of electricity by improving market information, competition and liquidity.[16]

---

[11] The national government of Germany, for instance, passed the law "Gesetz über die Elektrizitäts- und Gasversorgung (Energiewirtschaftsgesetz-EnWG) on 24th of April 1998 to reconstruct the national power market.
[12] See Arocena (2008), p. 40.
[13] See Cornwall (2008), pp. 113-114.
[14] Referring to the Directive, Germany founded a national regulatory authority, namely the Bundesnetzagentur (BNetzA).
[15] See Cornwall (2008), p. 105.
[16] See Fiorenzani (2006), p. 5.

Since the Scandinavian countries first opened their electricity markets, the power exchange *Nord Pool* is the largest exchange in terms of traded power volumes. The *European Energy Exchange* (EEX) in Germany, however, is the predominant market place for electricity in Central Europe reaching a traded volume in 2005 of 89 TWh and 1,044 TWh in the spot and future market, respectively.[17] Other major power exchanges are the *Amsterdam Power Exchange* (APX) of the United Kingdom and Spanish *Operador del Mercado Ibérico de Energia* (OMEL) representing the largest spot market in Europe.[18] Thirdly, to manage network constraints and ensure system balance, so-called *transmission system operators* (TSO) are implemented. Ultimately, the establishment of competitive retail markets by July 2004 will cause benefits to all non-domestic customers.

The full liberalization of national electricity markets has taken more time, however, due to the existence of barriers to enter on the one hand and lack of grid interconnections on the other hand.[19] Officially, the electricity markets of the 25 member states of the European Union have been 100% open to competition since July 2007. Yet, the development of a single European electricity market has not been closed and due to the enlargement of the EU it will still demand further efforts.[20]

2.1.2 Investments in liberalized electricity markets

Before the liberalization of the EU electricity markets the investment program of a utility company was mainly based on load growth expectations, reliability standards or defined by social welfare criteria.[21] In comparison to competitive electricity markets the former monopolistic market structure used to guarantee stable prices, which were related to the cost of a utility firm.[22] Therefore, utilities were able to pass on their cost and cost changes directly to customers. As a consequence, these utilities invested in capital-intensive power plant technologies characterized by huge generation units rather than in small power plants.[23]

---

[17] See Burger et al. (2007), p. 35.
[18] See Madlener/ Kaufmann (2002), p. 12.
[19] See Cornwall (2008), p. 115.
[20] See Knight (2010), p. 6.
[21] See Botterud et al. (2005), p. 254; see Sun et al. (2006), pp. 2.
[22] While the regulatory authorities in Europe used to work with a "cost-plus" regime, the regulator in the USA used to set prices via "rate of return" scheme for utilities.
[23] See Averch/ Johnson (1962), p. 1063.

On liberalized markets, however, prices are based on market principles instead of prices set by a regulatory authority. Therefore, new market entrants as well as incumbent competitors are faced with the uncertainty of fluctuating electricity prices.[24]

Nowadays, utility companies are exposed to financial risks as markets are open to competition. As a consequence, the strategy for investments in electricity generation capacity has changed significantly.[25] In a competitive environment the choice of a specific plant technology depends on the market structure. Compared to the electricity generation planning within the regulation era, investment decisions on liberalized markets are based on future earnings rather than on system adequacy.[26] As long as revenues exceed costs adequately, investments in power plants are made.

In general, the motivations of utilities to invest in new generation capacity are threefold:[27] Firstly, the current level of capacity is lower than the target generation capacity. Secondly, there is a need for replacements as soon as power plants have reached the end of their economic life time. Finally, a change of market environment might make certain types of power plant technologies better suited leading to a shut-down of existing plants earlier than their useful life expectancy. However, investments in generation capacity are irreversible, immobile and bear a long economic life time.[28]

Capital-intensive industries like the power sector are characterized by investment waves. A lack of generation capacity causes soaring prices, which is the starting point for building up new power plants. Since electricity markets are not obligated to any coordinative institution, the likelihood of an oversupply of generation capacity increases, as investors do not take the decision of competitors into account.[29]

As a result of the liberalization process the risk of investments in generation capacity has shifted from customers to the utility firm.[30] Therefore, the latter has to consider different risk factors that have an impact on the profit of a power plant. From a long term perspective, the development of fuel prices could likely turn out to be the major market risk of a power plant investment, assuming the plant does not operate competitively after the construction period.

---

[24] See Takashima et al. (2008), pp. 1810-1811.
[25] See Dyner/ Larson (2001), p. 1145.
[26] See Sun et al. (2006), pp. 2-3.
[27] See Green (2006), pp. 26-30.
[28] See Chao et al. (2008), p. 58.
[29] See Green (2006), p. 35.; Ford (1999); also Ford (2001).
[30] See Deng/ Oren (2006), pp. 941.

Alongside the fuel price risk, demand is one of the most uncertain factors in the power plant planning process.[31] Investments in generation capacity are affected by an increase in consumer power as well as the possibility of market authorities tightening standards regarding climate policy standards.[32] Consequently, in order to invest in generation capacity a higher return is necessary during plant operation in order to compensate fuel price risk in the long run.[33] Hence, the cost of capital for power plant investment projects has turned out to be the key decision variable.[34] Therefore, the investment decision should capture the risk of fluctuating cost of fuel and the consequences for the existing generation mix.[35]

Generally, a utility firm is faced with a wide range of generation technologies. While electricity markets are dynamic and uncertain regarding future development, the life cycle of a power plant typically lasts more than decades. As a consequence, today's investors face the trade-off between high *flexibility* on the one hand and a high *heat rate* of the power generation asset on the other hand. The heat rate describes the ratio of generated electricity and fuel needed. Consequently, a lower heat rate goes along with more generated electricity for the same amount of fuel.

While investments in plant technologies were motivated by *economies of scale* and for this purpose preferred huge capacity power plants with high heat rates, nowadays power plant technologies with a quick start time dominate the investment planning and therefore represent the lion share of incremental investments.[36] The flexibility of a power plant has become more important, as it may benefit from volatile electricity prices.[37]

Since authorities have started to be promoting renewable energies in order to set incentives for investments to reach climate policy goals, the share of decentralized generation capacity out of renewable energies has significantly increased.[38] Due to the extension of generation capacity out of renewable energies like wind energy, conventional thermal power plants are necessary in times of lack of wind. Hence, the total power plant mix will increase.

---

[31] Hoffmann (2007); Yang et al. (2008).
[32] See Dyner/ Larsen (2001), pp. 1148-1152.
[33] See Weber/ Swider (2006), p. 15.
[34] See Glachant (2006), p. 73.
[35] See Awerbuch (2006), pp. 697-698.
[36] See Hansen (1998), p. 8.
[37] See Abadie/ Chamorro (2008), p. 7.
[38] Please refer to Table 2.1.

2.1.3 Fuel mix in competitive electricity markets

As stated in the previous section, utility firms are faced with uncertainties which mainly materialize as power, fuel and carbon price risks. The latter has a significant impact on the choice of a specific power plant technology.[39] However, this section analyzes whether the liberalization has caused any preference so far for a specific type of plant in Europe.

For this purpose, Table 2.1 represents the development of electricity generation in selected European countries between 2003 and the end of 2008. Even though coal and lignite power generation has diminished in *Germany*, these fuels still account, roughly speaking, for 44% of the total German electricity generation. In contrast, natural gas usage for power generation has increased by 5.3% on average per year and amounted to 12% in 2008. Alongside conventional thermal fuels, more than 20% or 148,495 GWh refer to nuclear power generation. Due to the promotion of renewable energies, wind power generation soared within this time period, so its share in 2008 was twice as high as in 2003. In addition, biomass and photovoltaic account for the increase (23.3%) of power generation from other renewable energies.

Within the *United Kingdom* (UK) natural gas dominates national power generation. While electricity generation out of coal diminished by 2% on average between 2003 and 2008, natural gas usage increased from 37.4% to 45.4% in the respective period of time. Nuclear power generation represented just half of the amount in 2008 compared to 2003. Nevertheless the share of nuclear power generation still amounts to more than 10% of total electricity generation. Even though wind power generation rose massively, reaching an average annual growth rate of 40%, total power generation of renewable energies represents just 6% in 2008.

Hard coal used to be the predominant kind of fuel for power generation in *Spain*. However, natural gas usage for electricity generation accounted for 39.1% in 2008 compared to 15% in 2003. In contrast, the proportion of hard coal decreased by 6.7% on average per year in the same time. Alongside conventional thermal, renewable energies – in particular wind energy –gained importance in Spanish power generation, which amounted to almost 20% in 2008.

---

[39] See Green (2006), pp. 30-31.

Compared to the fuel mix of the other European countries, the lion share of power generation in the *Netherlands* (NL) is made up by natural gas, which represented almost 60% of national power generation in 2008. In contrast, coal and oil power generation has been declining by 2.5% and 3.7%, respectively, on average between 2003 and 2008. While the share of nuclear power generation (3.9%) in the Netherlands is rather small in comparison to the aforementioned European power markets, renewable energies accounted for more than 10% of the national power generation in 2008.

Table 2.1 Development of electricity generation in selected European countries

Total electricity generation	2003 in GWh	in %	2008 in GWh	in %	CAGR
Germany					
Conventional thermal					
Hard coal	142,304	23.8%	124,617	19.7%	*-2.6%*
Lignite	164,277	27.4%	150,621	23.8%	*-1.7%*
Natural gas	58,505	9.8%	75,921	12.0%	*5.3%*
Oil	4,712	0.8%	8,604	1.4%	*12.8%*
Other	10,836	1.8%	28,137	4.4%	*21.0%*
Non-conventional					
Nuclear	165,060	27.5%	148,495	23.5%	*-2.1%*
Renewables					
Wind	18,859	3.1%	40,574	6.4%	*16.6%*
Hydro	24,440	4.1%	26,963	4.3%	*2.0%*
Other	10,144	1.7%	28,862	4.6%	*23.3%*
UK					
Conventional thermal					
Hard coal	138,305	34.7%	125,316	32.2%	*-2.0%*
Lignite	-		-		-
Natural gas	148,881	37.4%	176,748	45.4%	*3.5%*
Oil	4,594	1.2%	6,101	1.6%	*5.8%*
Other	3,800	1.0%	2,291	0.6%	*-9.6%*
Non-conventional					
Nuclear	88,686	22.3%	52,486	13.5%	*-10.0%*
Renewables					
Wind	1,285	0.3%	7,097	1.8%	*40.7%*
Hydro	5,961	1.5%	9,257	2.4%	*9.2%*
Other	6,692	1.7%	10,053	2.6%	*8.5%*
Netherlands					
Conventional thermal					
Hard coal	26,571	27.4%	23,469	21.8%	*-2.5%*
Lignite	-		-		-
Natural gas	55,009	56.8%	63,425	58.9%	*2.9%*
Oil	2,493	2.6%	2,065	1.9%	*-3.7%*
Other	3,419	3.5%	3,475	3.2%	*0.3%*
Non-conventional					
Nuclear	4,018	4.2%	4,169	3.9%	*0.7%*
Renewables					
Wind	1,318	1.4%	4,260	4.0%	*26.4%*
Hydro	72	0.1%	102	0.1%	*7.2%*
Other	3,898	4.0%	6,642	6.2%	*11.2%*
Spain					
Conventional thermal					
Hard coal	68,817	26.2%	48,714	15.7%	*-6.7%*
Lignite	5,905	2.2%	0	0.0%	*-100.0%*
Natural gas	39,368	15.0%	121,561	39.1%	*25.3%*
Oil	24,002	9.1%	18,002	5.8%	*-5.6%*
Other	2,615	1.0%	1,614	0.5%	*-9.2%*
Non-conventional					
Nuclear	61,875	23.5%	58,973	18.9%	*-1.0%*
Renewables					
Wind	12,075	4.6%	32,203	10.3%	*21.7%*
Hydro	43,897	16.7%	26,112	8.4%	*-9.9%*
Other	4,265	1.6%	4,036	1.3%	*-1.1%*

Source: Own table based on Eurostat data (2010).

Since passing the directive for a common energy policy, a technological switch to gas has been observed in electricity markets in Europe. This is especially true for countries in which coal used to be the predominant type of fuel. The increase in gas generation capacity is mainly a result of the comparative cost advantage of gas compared to other thermal fossil plants. Gas power plants used to be cheaper than other power plant technologies and cause for this reason a short pay-off time. However, the economic advantage of gas in operation compared to coal is not absolute; instead it is a relative advantage depending on future carbon prices. In addition, the reform bears the constraint of investing in efficient generation technologies. In the UK for instance, new gas power plants account for 75% of the total capacity change. In contrast, the Spanish electricity market has denoted a strong increase in generation capacity based on renewable energies and moderate investments in gas power plant technologies.[40]

When electricity prices reached high levels in Europe at the end of the 1990s[41], investors decided to build up additional generation capacity to enter the power markets. For this purpose, so-called combined-cycle gas turbines (CCGT) used to dominate new generation capacity in the UK, as their main merits were a higher efficiency and lower emissions compared to ordinary thermal fossil power plant technologies. However, the combination of plummeting stock markets and rising gas prices in 2001/ 2002 led not only to financial distress but also to bankruptcy of these generators in the UK.[42]

Against the background of this thesis the issue arises regarding the potential impact of gas power plants on the overall expected generation portfolio return and corresponding standard deviation. After having introduced the development of electricity generation capacity in European countries, we study in the following section the merits of specific power generation assets.

---

[40] See Glachant (2006), pp. 65-66.
[41] Further details are given in the following section.
[42] See Chao et al. (2008), p. 60.

2.1.4 Power plant technologies

In general, a great variety of power plant technologies exist in competitive electricity markets. However, the diversity of generation technologies in a specific electricity market depends on the availability of natural resources (e.g. lignite) and the objectives from national governments in energy policy (e.g. subsidies for renewable energies).[43] By setting the regulative environment, the latter shapes the supply side of the domestic power market.[44] In addition, the investor is faced with the trade-off between realizing *economies of scale* and minimizing *heat rates*.

For this purpose, we classify plants regarding market, financing and operating risks and evaluate, in this respect, power plants relative to each other. While the cost of fuel and carbon are attributed to market, operation risks comprise investment, fixed and variable operation and maintenance costs. Ultimately, these technology options are assessed from a technical point of view, which is flexibility on the one hand and availability on the other. Flexibility indicates the ability to switch between states of operation. Therefore a high flexibility goes along with a short ramp-up time, which is the time needed to start and terminate power generation. In contrast, the term availability stands for the likelihood of sudden shut-downs. The conversion of primary energy into electricity can be distinguished in three major groups of power plants: *conventional thermal, nuclear* and *renewable power plants*:

Conventional thermal power plants
Conventional thermal power plants dominate the electricity generation in Europe. *Coal power plants* are typically constructed as steam plants, where the burning of coal heats up water to run the plant's steam turbine. While the efficiency of coal power plants varies between 30% and 40%, state-of-the art plants are able to achieve an efficiency of 45%.[45] The efficiency describes the ability to generate an amount of MWh power out of one MWh of fuel. Therefore, the heat rate is reciprocal to power plant efficiency. However, since the ramp-up time is rather high and having in mind the aforementioned trade-off, the merit of a coal power plant compared to other technologies is to realize *economies of scale*.

---

[43] See Newbery/ Green (1996), p. 28.
[44] See Burger et al. (2007), p. 136.
[45] See Ströbele et al. (2010), p. 220.

Very similar to coal power plants, the combustion of lignite generates electricity in *lignite power plants*. These plants are usually constructed close to the lignite mine to minimize transport costs, as a lower heat value causes a higher need of input fuel. Since lignite resources are predominantly located in Central Europe, these countries rely mainly on lignite for electricity generation. In comparison to other thermal power plants, the costs of fuel are rather low. Yet high investment costs as well as higher specific CO_2 emissions neutralize this comparative advantage.[46] From a flexibility point of view, lignite power plants typically are less flexible compared to coal power plants.[47]

Investments in new generation capacity on European liberalized electricity markets are mainly based on *natural gas*.[48] The reasons for this phenomenon are threefold: Firstly, competitive electricity markets cause volatile electricity prices making flexible power plant technologies more attractive. Secondly, gas power plants emit less CO_2 per MWh. Lastly, the increase of renewable energy capacity gives rise to the need for *back-up technologies*, which particularly quick gas turbines meet. Natural gas stations typically reach an efficiency of 40% to 50%. Thanks to a heat recovery boiler, which uses the heat of the turbine operation, combined-cycle gas turbines (CCGT) can even reach an efficiency level of 60%. Besides, the main merit of gas power plants is their flexibility, as ramp up times are low.

In comparison to the conventional power plant technologies presented above, *oil power generation* in Europe is rather limited, due to environmental legislation.[49] In addition, oil prices are relatively higher than those of other fossil fuels. As a consequence oil power plant technologies serve solely for peak load or reserve capacity.[50]

Nuclear power plants

The use of nuclear power plants for electricity generation has been controversially discussed in literature as well as socially. Even though nuclear power seems like an attractive option to reduce carbon dioxide emissions, a few unresolved major issues

---

[46] See Burger et al. (2007), p. 138.
[47] See Ströbele et al. (2010), p. 220.
[48] Please refer to section 2.1.3 for further details.
[49] See Burger et al. (2007), p. 138.
[50] See Burger et al. (2007), p. 138.

are aligned with this kind of power plant. These issues mainly concern costs, safety, and waste.[51]

Nevertheless, nuclear power generation is still an important technology in Europe, although in some countries including Belgium, Sweden, Italy and Germany a nuclear phase-out has been approved and the governments of Austria, the Netherlands and Spain have rejected plans for new nuclear power stations by law. In contrast, France, Finland and the UK still regard nuclear power as an option to increase or maintain generation capacity. However, a few governments (e.g. Sweden, Switzerland and Germany[52]) have started to rethink their attitude towards this kind of power technology due to climate policy targets. The required heat for generating electricity with this type of power plant technology is provided by a nuclear fission reaction in the reactor.[53] While generating electricity the virtue of nuclear plants is the equal-zero-emission of CO_2 in comparison to conventional thermal power plants.[54] In addition, the costs of fuel as variable operating costs are rather low.

Therefore, nuclear power generation might appeal to investors, as it may serve as a hedge against volatile fuel and carbon prices.[55] However, investors in new nuclear power stations are faced with substantial risks that could cause financial losses.[56] This is due to high operation and maintenance costs as well as extraordinarily high investment costs. Besides, long planning and construction times trigger the profitability of nuclear power plant investment projects.[57]

As a consequence debt and equity holders claim a higher risk premium to finance this kind of fuel technology leading to higher cost of capital.[58] Hence, without government support future investments in nuclear power plants do not seem very likely to occur.[59] Finally, the unresolved issue of ultimate waste disposal limits this technology as an option for future power generation.

---

[51] See MIT (2003), p. 2.
[52] Germany has planned to prolong the operating life time for nuclear power plants according to the coalition contract in October 2009. New investments in nuclear, however, are still ruled out.
[53] See Burger et al. (2007), p. 138.
[54] The mining of uranium, however, causes emissions so that an appraisal of the impact on climate should take the whole value chain into account.
[55] See Roques et al. (2006), p. 9.
[56] See Atherton et al. (2009), pp. 2-3.
[57] See Atherton et al. (2009), p. 3; Burger et al. (2007), p. 138.
[58] See Tolley/ Jones (2004), p. 19.
[59] See Roques et al. (2006), p. 20.

Renewable energies

In contrast to conventional power plants, renewable energies are based on natural energy conversion (i.e. hydro, wind and photovoltaic power). Investments in renewable energies have been and are still subsidized by national governments. Due to fixed prices for *green electricity*, the extension of renewable plants has been soaring, particularly in Germany. The share of renewable energies amounted to almost 15 % of the total German electricity supply in 2008.[60]

A distinction is drawn between different types of *hydro power plants*. While run-of river power plants make use of height differences for generating electricity, storage-power plants are based on a water reservoir which drives a turbine below the respective water-storage. The utilization of both types of hydro power depend on regional and geographic characteristics, as the former is related to the natural flow rate of the river and the latter to natural water inflow to the reservoir. Besides, tidal and pump storage power plants do exist. The main merit of pump storage power plants is the ability of storing electricity indirectly in peak load times. However, the extension of hydro power plants is limited and the technical challenge causes high investment costs in comparison to other power plant technologies.[61]

Wind power plants are typically installed either *onshore* or *offshore*. Irrespective of the distinction made, turbines convert wind energy into electricity. While the marginal cost of electricity generation is rather low in comparison to other power plant technologies, the construction of wind power plants demands high investment costs in particular for *offshore* wind parks. This is not only due to network connections but also high costs of material. However, the power generation is hardly controllable due to the volatile wind supply so that back-up technologies are necessary in times of windless times.

Even though growth rates of *photovoltaic power plants* have been soaring, particularly in Germany, the impact on wholesale power prices is rather small.[62] Photovoltaic power plants are characterized by high initial investment costs, whereas variable generation costs are negligibly low.[63] The utilization rates of photovoltaic power plants depend mainly on the suitability of the location. Therefore the respective load factor

---

[60] See Ströbele et al. (2010), p. 196.
[61] See Burger et al. (2007), p. 139.
[62] See Burger et al. (2007), p. 140.
[63] See Ströbele et al. (2010), p. 198.

varies between 15% and 40% within one year due to seasonality and regional circumstances.[64]

Besides, *biomass*, *geothermal* and ocean *energy power plants* have been installed to generate electricity. However, the generation capacity does not play a major role in renewable energies and as a consequence its wholesale impact is very small.[65] These power plant technologies are therefore not further discussed and integrated in the following model simulation.

To sum up, Table 2.2 classifies the presented power plant technologies in market, operational and technical risks. Here, a comparative advantage is denoted by "+", whereas the sign "-" indicates a disadvantage in comparison to alternative power plant technologies.

Keeping the individual merits of these technologies in mind, we will now turn the lens on the virtue to combine these power plants.

---

[64] See Ströbele et al. (2010), p. 198.
[65] See Burger et al. (2007), p. 140.

Table 2.2 Classification of power plant technologies

Power plant technologies	Market risks		Operational risks			Technical risks	
	Cost of fuel	Cost of CO_2	Investment costs	Fixed O&M	Variable O&M	Flexibility	Availability
Conventional plants							
Coal plants	+	-	0	0	0	-	0
Lignite plants	+	-	0	0	0	-	-
Natural gas plants	-	+	+	+	-	+	+
Oil plants	-	-	+	+	+	+	+
Non-conventional plants							
Nuclear plants	0	+	-	-	-	-	0
Renewables							
Hydro power plants	+	+	-	-	+	+	-
Wind power	+	+	0	0	+	-	-
Photovoltaic plants	+	+	-	0	+	-	-

whereas "+", "-", "0" denote the degree of the comparative advantage, disadvantage or neutrality of the specific power plant technology, respecitvely.

Source: According to Ströbele et al. (2010).

2.1.5 Diversification of fuel mix

Since the liberalization of electricity markets in Europe, utilities have started not only to change their business strategy but also to *diversify* their mix of power plant technologies for generation.[66] As stated in the previous section a power plant investment is irreversible, long-lived and capital intense which strengthens the demand for an efficient composition within a competitive market environment. Hence, from a utility firm's point of view there is a need to minimize corresponding risks and as a consequence for diversification. Diversification means therefore to combine power plant technologies which depend on different kinds of fuel and operate not only in domestic but also in various markets to reduce risks.

According to the academic energy literature[67], however, diversification is usually related to the issue of security of energy supplies in the future. The peak of oil prices in middle of 2008 has recently revived the debate of alternative sources of energy to substitute diminishing reserves. Alongside energy supply, the realization of diversification improves not only financial but also environmental performance.[68] Indeed, diversification is not limited to energy security; in fact it is also a crucial application towards the composition of power plant technologies. In this respect, diversity is attributed to the number of available technology options, whereas the variety of options determines the strategic opportunities of response to market liberalization.[69] In addition, diversification of the fuel mix presumes that the universes of available power plant technologies are dissimilar. The dissimilarity of power plants is not only referring to the type of fuel but also to individual technical characteristics. As shown in the previous section, this is true for the universe of power plant technologies which has an impact on the European power market system.

According to *Stirling* (1994) the decision for a specific power plant technology which is more expensive and leads to higher generation cost compared to an alternative kind of fuel can be explained by a *diversity premium*.[70] In other words, the power generator should diversify the fuel mix as long as the marginal value of diversity is equal to the marginal cost of the respective investment. The simulation model will shed light on diversification benefits by taking different European power markets into account.

---

[66] See Stirling (1994), p. 197.
[67] Skea (2010); Constantini et al. (2007); Turton/ Barreto (2006).
[68] See Stirling (1994), p. 197.
[69] See Stirling (1994), p. 198.
[70] See Stirling (1994), p. 204.

In order to do so, however, we have to get first an understanding of the mechanism of power market systems which is developed in the upcoming section.

2.1.6 Power market system and merit order

In comparison to markets for other commodities, the system of electricity markets is intricate. Figure 2.1 simplifies and depicts the interaction of demand and supply on power markets and their respective driving forces, which have an impact on electricity prices.

The determinants of electricity demand are shown on the left hand side. Customer behavior and as a consequence the demand for electricity depends not only on the specific time of day but also on the season of the year. Therefore, meteorological conditions do have an impact on the demand (lightning, heating, cooling). However, long periods of heat-waves cause a lower water-level and in particular warms up river so that thermal fuel plants cannot operate with full capacity, as there is a lack of cooling water. Hence, plant availability as well as operation depend on weather conditions, which determine not only demand but also the generation supply of power systems. The latter depends on the total installed generation capacity of the power market which is a function not only of the number but also on the variety of power plant technologies.

Figure 2.1 Power market system

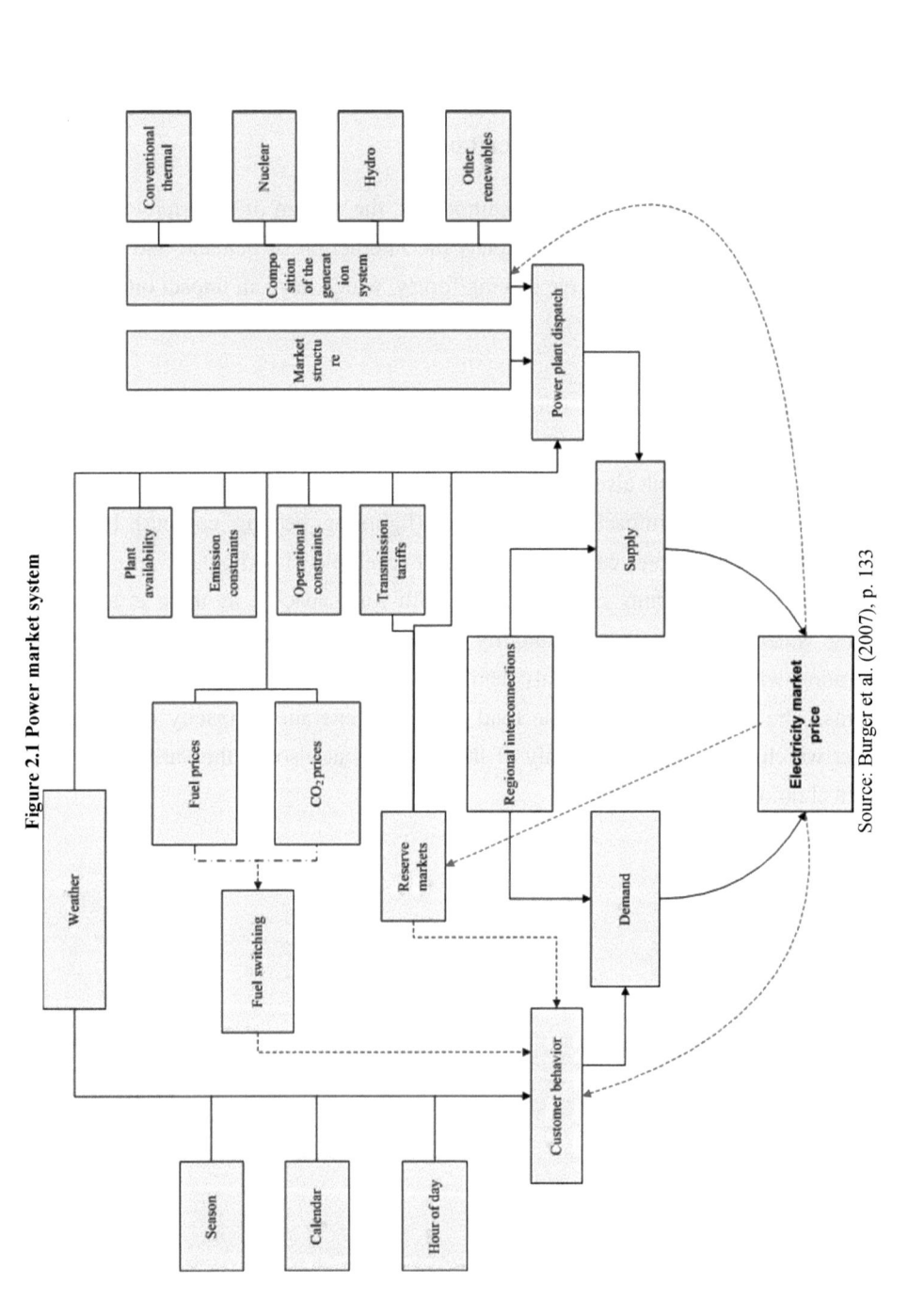

Source: Burger et al. (2007), p. 133

New power plants increase generation capacity and cause therefore lower power prices. Due to the limited interconnection capacities between different transmission areas of the power system, price differences between market regions occur. Interregional transmission flows can have an impact on the demand side as well as on the supply situation in any region. Finally, the dashed line in Figure 2.1 demonstrates the reverse effect from power prices to the composition of the generation system as well as the amount of reserve capacity. The latter has to secure the power supply in case of any shortage of the availability of the generation system. In contrast, high power prices are taken as a signal to invest in certain power plant technologies which affect the generation system. In addition, customers might be sensitive to certain price levels and change their consumption habits.

Following the classification presented above, the utilization rates of power plant technologies are related to the level of load in a particular hour. In general, load can be distinguished between different segments, base load, mid-merit and peak load, respectively. The separation refers to specific technical characteristics of a plant[71] and in particular to the ratio of variable costs to fixed costs.[72] Depending on the existing load level within each hour of the day different generation segments are running gradually starting with the lowest variable cost. This kind of ranking of power plants is called *merit order*. Therefore, the marginal cost of each plant determines the supply of capacity for the market. Consequently, the supply curve takes the form of a staircase (see Figure 2.2).

The electricity supply function depends on the specific characteristics of the generation technology that determine the system. As stated in the previous section, there is a wide variety of different technologies to generate power. This diversity is a result of regional supply of resources, the national energy policy and subsidies to promote specific generator technologies. Hence, a power system that is diverse in terms of plenty small generation units are in line with a continued process of the merit order. The following graph depicts the *merit order* of the existing capacity on the market in theory.

---

[71] Namely, capacity, heat rate, variable operation & maintenance costs, generation level, outages, ramp rates, start-up/ shut-down costs and runtime are the key technical parameters of a power plant. For a detailed description of technical characteristics of a power plant, which determine the cost of generation, please refer to Eydeland/ Wolyniec (2003).
[72] See Böske (2007), pp. 101-102.

Figure 2.2 Typical merit order on power markets

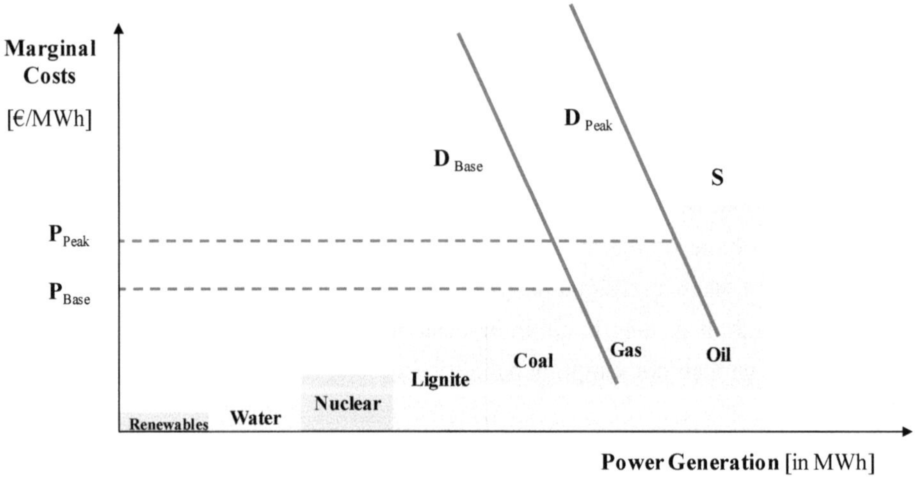

Source: According to Erdmann/ Zweifel (2007), p. 304.

Before examining the electricity price behavior, it is essential to get a clear insight into how prices are set in power markets by analyzing the characteristics of the aggregated demand and supply function. Generally, the interception of the system's merit order and the sum of the demand determines the marginal electricity price. Moreover, the merit order indicates the ability of the productive generation system to offer different quantities of electricity at different prices, in a given time. In other words; the merit order curve represents the *short-term aggregated supply function.*

However, wind and photovoltaic power plants cause significant adjustments of the power plant park. Since the power generation of renewable energies typically occurs far from the consumption, the integration requires a grid connection to transfer power to customers.[73] Additionally, as mentioned before, reserve capacity is needed to balance short-term load levels due to meteorological dependencies. Ultimately, the boost of the aforementioned technologies affects the merit order of the respective electricity market. Since these types of power plants must run due to limits of control and once their marginal costs of power generation turn to be competitive, the utilization rate of initial base load power plants (nuclear, lignite power plants) drops. Besides, conventional mid-merit power plants and flexible peak power plants (i.e. gas

---

[73] See Ströbele et al. (2010), p. 201.

turbines, GT) will gain importance as back-up technologies causing an increase of operating hours.[74] Figure 2.3 depicts these changes:

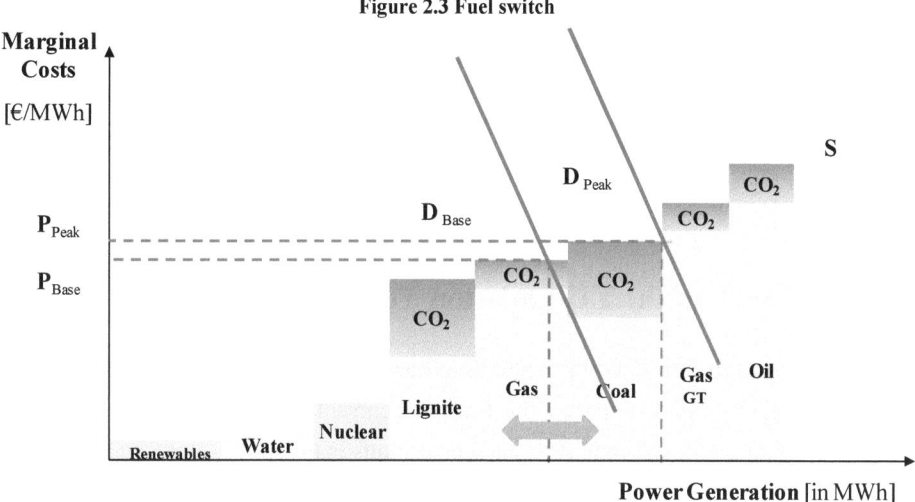

Figure 2.3 Fuel switch

Source: According to Ströbele et al. (2010), p. 225.

In addition, as can be seen in Figure 2.3, the introduction of the EU ETS has an impact on the respective merit order. In particular, utilities include the cost of carbon in their operative decisions for existing power plants.[75] Since a gas power plant emits less CO_2 compared to a coal fired plant, a power plant operator might be better off by switching from coal to gas. Depending on the price difference between coal and gas, the operating hours of gas plants increase compared to coal plants.

As mentioned above, the merit order illustrates the aggregated short-term supply curve, where the equilibrium electricity price is equal to the respective marginal cost for generated electricity of the power market system. In that case, CO_2 prices have a neutral impact on the profitability of a power plant and as consequence do not represent an additional source of risk for utilities operating on liberalized markets.[76]

Taking a long-term perspective, however, an increase of power prices causes a curb of power demand and therefore a new-equilibrium price is set, where these utility firms are better off which have changed their business strategy of electricity generation to a

---

[74] See Ströbele et al. (2010), p. 202.
[75] Delarue et al. (2008); Reinaud (2003).
[76] Bonacina/ Gulli (2007).

low-emitting power plant park. Therefore the EU ETS represents clearly a source of uncertainty for European utilities.[77]

Following the argumentation given, prices for emission certificates represent costs and therefore an additional price risk factor for operators' of conventional thermal power plants. As a consequence, we will present the legal framework of the EU ETS in the following section.

2.2 Framework of the EU Emission Trading Scheme

This section aims to introduce the regulative background of the EU Emission Trading Scheme (EU ETS) and to appraise the first and current trading phases. In addition, a future outlook of the development on carbon markets is given.

2.2.1 Historical emergence and objectives

Since the beginning of the 1990s the international community has been working on a climate policy convention to diminish the thread of global warming. Two years later the United Nations (UN) defined the climate policy objectives to reduce green house gas concentration in order to prevent the anthropogenic disruption of the climate system. However, binding emission reduction targets for countries had been missing.

Finally, the international community of states reached an agreement to globally reduce greenhouse gas emissions in Kyoto in 1997. The *Kyoto protocol*[78] determines the obligation for countries which ratified the agreement to cut emissions of 5.2% between the period of 2008 and 2012 compared to the base year 1990. To become effective, however, it was required that not only at least 55% of the industrialized countries (Annex I[79]) ratified the protocol but also that 55% of the emissions of the respective countries are covered.[80] Since the United States of America (US) as the biggest

---

[77] See Knight (2010), p. 4-5.
[78] The Kyoto protocol covers six greenhouse gases, namely carbon dioxide (CO_2), methane (CH_4), nitrous oxide (N_2O), hydro fluorocarbon (HFC), perfluorocarbon (PFC) and sulphur hexafluoride (SF_6). Since the conversion of fuel into electricity cause CO_2 emissions in particular, other gases will be neglected within the thesis.
[79] Annex I refers to countries, which have signed this obligation.
[80] See Wagner (2007), p. 9.

polluter of global emissions has not acceded to the Kyoto convention yet, it was necessary that Russia signed the protocol to fulfill these requirements.[81] Therefore it took a few years until the Kyoto protocol became effective on February 16th 2005 and will last in its current phase until the end of 2012.

The European Union (EU) proceeded during the Kyoto conference in order to reach an agreement. Consequently, the reduction targets for the EU are more ambitious compared to other countries. For this purpose the EU is obligated to cut back greenhouse gas emissions on average by 8% by 2012 compared with 1990 emission levels. However, depending on the economic capability of each European member state the *EU burden sharing* agreement defined national specific reduction targets. For instance, Germany is obligated to reduce their emissions level of 21% within the period 2008-2012 compared to 1990. In contrast, Spain, Greece and Portugal, however, are allowed to increase their total emissions in comparison to 1990 by 18%, 25% and 27%, respectively.[82]

In order to reach these objectives, the Kyoto protocol distinguishes between three flexible mechanisms; *International Emission Trading* (IET), *Joint Implementation* (JI) and *Clean Development Mechanism* (CDM). These instruments are visualized in Figure 2.4

Figure 2.4 Instruments of the Kyoto protocol

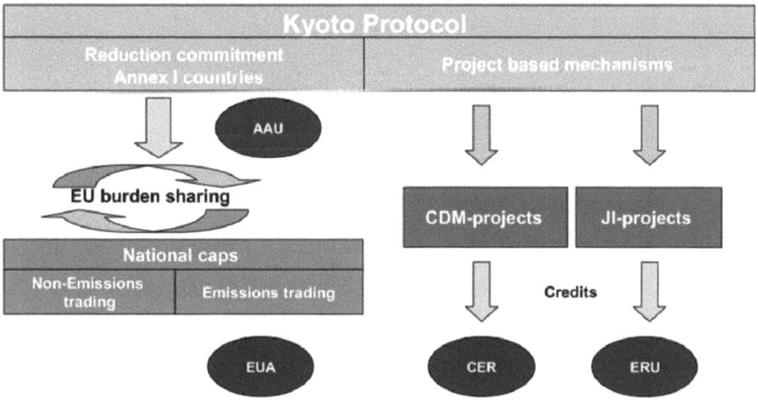

Source: EEX/ EUREX (2008), p.4.

---

[81] See Böhringer (2008), p. 236.
[82] See Böhringer (2008), p. 237.

Based on the reduction target of the individual country, the so-called *assigned amount* (AA) is approved, whereas the right to emit a ton of carbon is called *assigned amount unit* (AAU). As a consequence the AAUs are transferred on a national level in order to trade these allowances by establishing an IET.

Against this background, the EU launched the Emission Trading Scheme (EU ETS) in 2005, as part of a strategy aimed at cost-efficient reductions for companies and most importantly to fulfill the European climate objectives.[83] Here, an EU allowance (EUA) represents the right to emit a ton of carbon in the atmosphere, which can be either used for emission compliance or trade on carbon markets.[84]

According to article 6 of the Kyoto protocol, Annex I countries or companies that are investing in emission reduction projects of other Annex I countries gain *emission reduction units* (ERU) by JI. By investing in emission reductions projects in developing countries, article 12 of the Kyoto protocol, stipulates to receive so-called *certified emission reductions* (CER) by CDM for avoiding emissions. Very similar to the ERUs, the CERs are tradable on emission markets or used to fulfill firms' emission reduction obligations. While the latter is already accepted for trade and compliance since the beginning of the EU ETS in 2005, the generation of ERUs started in 2008.[85]

Since CERS and ERUs markets are still in its infancy in terms of liquidity and reliable prices, the remaining analysis focuses on EUAs.

2.2.2 Institutional framework

To transfer this scheme into national law, *national allocation plans* (NAP) have been passed to set up the reduction targets for specific industries. Each NAP determines the emission reduction on an industry sector level (macro plan), whereas the micro plan allocates the emissions for the plants covered under the *EU Directive (2003/87/EC)*.[86] The directive includes the following sectors: Energy industry, refineries, coke oven plants, steel, cement, glass, and ceramic, pulp and paper.[87]

---

[83] See Kara et al. (2008), p. 193.
[84] In the following we use carbon price and market as synonyms for the price and market of EU allowances (EUA).
[85] See Anger (2008), p. 2029.
[86] See Wagner (2007), p. 13.
[87] See Alberola et al. (2008), p. 5.

Whether an installation is obligated to the EU ETS regulation depends on the heat capacity of the plant, which is applicable to combustion facilities of more than 20 MW. Roughly, the power and heating industry accounts for 3,600 plants of the 10,000 plants covered within the scheme in total, whereas these installations emit almost 65% of the two billion tons of overall EU ETS emissions.[88]

Since the national regulator limits emissions by allocating certificates to industries, the EU ETS represents a *cap and trade* system.[89] Specifically, the EU ETS is a compliance market, which means that covered installations from CO_2-intensive emitting industrial sectors must surrender a number of allowances equal to its verified emissions each year on April 30th.[90] Here, the *community independent transaction log* (CITL) acts as an electronically database, in which the owners' of emission certificates and their respective transactions are collected. Generally, the allocation can be distinguished by three different options: Either the emissions certificates are grandfathered (allocated free of charge), auctioned or vended into the market. Obviously, a hybrid solution is also possible.[91]

As the emission certificates are traded on markets, they represent a value which has to be incorporated in operational decisions irrespectively of the method of allocation. If the holder of emission certificates actually emits fewer emissions than expected, he can sell the surplus of these emission certificates to parties in shortage. From a financial perspective the EUAs turn out, in that case, to be either an *asset* for selling emission certificates on the market or a *liability* to comply with produced emissions.[92]
The EU ETS distinguishes three different trading periods. The first trading period lasted from 2005 until 2007 (henceforth: *Phase I*). During this *trial period* the emission allowances were fully grandfathered based on historical emissions to the owner of the plants.[93] The current *Kyoto commitment phase* represents the second trading period, which started in 2008 and lasts to the end of 2012 (henceforth: *Phase II*). Carbon trading, however, is not just limited to companies which are part of the EU ETS. Investors can also participate in the market by speculating in emission certificates. In addition, the EU ETS stipulates the trades between countries, as emission certificates are valid in each European member state.

---

[88] See Oberndorfer (2009), p. 1117.
[89] See Wagner (2007), p. 11.
[90] See Ellerman/ Buchner (2008), p. 267.
[91] See Benz/ Trück (2009), p. 4.
[92] See Benz/ Trück (2009), pp. 4-5.
[93] See Wagner (2007), p. 14.

According to economic theory a price of an emission certificate has to be equal to the marginal abatement costs in market equilibrium. As long as prices of emission certificates exceed the marginal abatement costs, companies are better off by abating more CO_2 than needed. By selling the surplus of emission certificates in the market, companies would generate profits.[94]

Figure 2.5 illustrates theoretically the supply and demand in the European carbon market. The elasticity of demand is expected to be rather small, as the short-term reaction of market participants is limited due to the need of an adaption of plant technologies. However, the flexible instruments of the Kyoto protocol enable the regulator to expand the supply function by the CER certificates which should have a negative impact on the carbon price level of emission allowances.[95] As a consequence, the increase in emission allowances supply might push down prices. However, the validity of CERs and ERUs which can be used as substitute for compliance of a covered plant or trading is limited according to the EU Linking Directive.[96]

Figure 2.5 Supply and demand in European carbon market

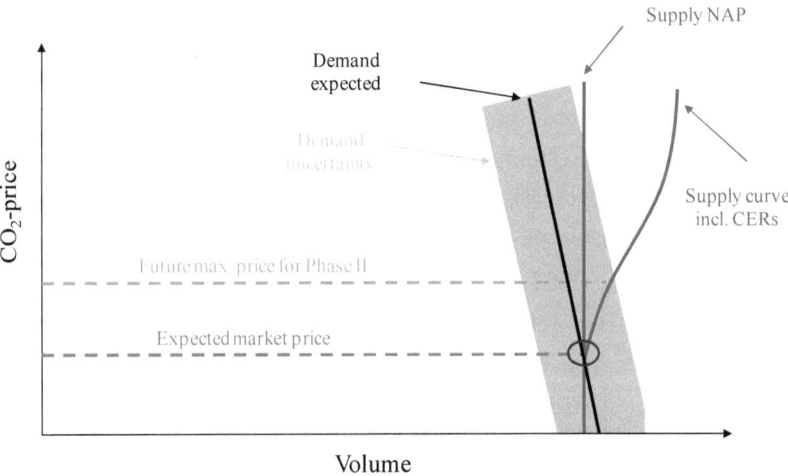

Source: Burger et al. (2007), p. 45.

---

[94] See Seifert et al. (2008), p. 182.
[95] See Burger et al. (2007), p. 45.
[96] See Wagner (2007), p. 15.

2.2.3 Appraisal of the first and second trading periods

Total emissions in the EU declined by 4.8% in 2007 compared to 1990 level. The reduction, however, is due more to the modernization of industrial processes in new member states (-23.5%) than to countries' individual energy policies. Thanks to the German reunification in 1990, which caused a replacement of old plants, Germany managed to decrease emissions by 18.8%. Otherwise, the German energy policy would have failed their climate objectives.[97]

Most member states, however, missed their reduction objectives which can be explained due to the individual national allocation of emission allowances.[98] Instead of taking historical emissions as a reference to limit the allocation budget, inflated business growth rate assumptions caused an oversupply of emission allowances in Europe. The following table summarizes the allocated carbon certificates vs. the emissions in 2005.

Table 2.3 Allocation vs. carbon emissions

EU Member State	Allocated CO_2 allowances (million tonnes in 2005)	Actual CO_2 emissions (million tonnes in 2005)	Short (-) vs. Long position (+)
Austria	32.4	33.4	-
Belgium	58.3	55.4	+
Czech Republic	96.9	82.5	+
Denmark	37.3	26.5	+
Estonia	16.7	12.6	+
Finland	44.7	33.1	+
France	150.4	131.3	+
Germany	495.0	474.0	+
Greece	71.1	71.3	-
Hungary	30.2	26.0	+
Ireland	19.2	22.4	-
Italy	215.8	225.3	-
Latvia	4.1	2.9	+
Lithuania	13.5	6.6	+
Netherlands	86.5	80.4	+
Luxembourg	3.2	2.6	+
Poland	143.1	115.1	+
Portugal	36.9	36.4	+
Sweden	22.3	19.3	+
Slovakia	30.5	25.2	+
Slovenia	9.1	8.7	+
Spain	172.1	182.9	-
United Kingdom	206.0	242.5	-
Total	**1,995.4**	**1916.2**	

Source: According to Wagner (2007), p. 12.

---

[97] See Ziesing (2009), p. 63.
[98] See Böhringer (2008), p. 238.

According to Table 2.3 solely six countries were short on emission based on 2005 data.[99] As a consequence the mechanism of *Phase I* has changed in the current trading period. Even though the majority of the certificates will still be grandfathered, the EU recommends now auctioning 10% of the total emission budget to minimize *windfall profits*.[100]

Besides, if a company uses less emission certificates for operation than budgeted, it is allowed to transfer the certificates to the next year within the same trading phase *(banking)*. In contrast, the compliance of allocated emission certificates within a trading phase earlier than the maturity is called *borrowing*. While banking was restricted in *Phase I*, the second phase facilitates the market participants to transfer emission allowances to the following year. Most likely the banking rule will stabilize the price level including future price expectations. In that case price volatility of emission certificates will decrease so that the transparency of the market increases, which causes a reduction of market risk for participants.[101]

2.2.4 Future outlook

Recently, the EU Directive (2008/101/EC) or *Phase III* has been approved so that it becomes clear how emissions in 2013 to 2020 will be regulated.[102] Irrespective, of other international conventions, the EU has agreed to cut greenhouse gas emissions by 21% until 2020 compared to 2005. If other countries adapt their own efforts, the EU will even intend to avoid 30%.[103]

Starting in 2013 the emission cap will decrease by 1.74% annually. In contrast to the first trading periods, the utility sector will have to purchase the emission certificates required for their electricity generation process. Yet, there are exemptions for Eastern European utilities in particular. Regulatory authorities are obligated to grandfather up to 70% of emission allowances to utilities, if one of the following two conditions is fulfilled: Either more than 30% of the national power generation is based on a single

---

[99] Namely, Austria, Greece, Ireland, Italy, Spain and the UK.
[100] Since emission certificates are traded on markets, they represent a value and therefore opportunity costs, irrespectively of the allocation mechanism. Charging these opportunity costs to customers, utilities generate so-called wind fall profits.
[101] See EWI/ EEFA (2008), p. 156; see Wagner (2007), pp. 15-16.
[102] See Bonacina/ Cozialpi (2009), p. 1.
[103] In addition, the EU aims to cover 20% primary energy consumption by renewable energies and to improve energy efficiency by about 20% as well. See Böhringer (2008), pp. 237-238.

fossil fuel or the gross domestic product per head is less than half of the average of the EU.[104]

For the other industries the regulative environment will be tightened as well. The EU plans to incorporate other industry branches like the shipping and the aviation industry in the ETS in the foreseeable future. Therefore it is very unlikely that the utility industry as well as other industries, which are part of the EU ETS, will be able to generate windfall profits.

Economically speaking, the demand side will soar in the next decade, while the supply side in terms of the total emission cap will decrease annually. The latter will limit the total amount of emission certificates on the market. As a consequence, the net effect in change of demand and supply will put pressure on emission certificate prices.

Emission regulators, however, have to establish a system which is reliable and will endure in order to avoid a lack of power supply, as investments in generation capacities require a long time period for designing, approving and construction.[105] The methods to reduce the total emission level from a utility's perspective are mainly investments in low carbon fuels (in particular gas, renewable or nuclear energies), improvement of energy efficiency by unaltered fuel technique, sequestration and capturing of CO_2 and demand side management.[106] Since we focus on the supply side of electricity generation, we prescind from demand side management and CO_2 capturing, which has not been approved in a legislative framework on a national level yet.[107]

To sum up, the tightening regulation in terms of full auctioning for emission allowances will have an impact on power plant mixes' of European utilities in the long run and therefore proper investment strategies are needed.[108] However, the issue arises in what ways European utilities will adapt their power plant parks. The decision to invest in a specific power plant technology depends on the future development of energy commodity prices. Thus, in the following section we turn the lens on

---

[104] See Kobes (2008), p. 3.
[105] See Milojcic (2009), p. 31.
[106] See EWI/ EEFA (2008), p. 146; MIT (2003), pp 1-2.
[107] The EU-Directive (2009/31/EC) came into force in June 2009 and has to be transferred to national law within two years.
[108] Please refer to section 2.1.6 for further details.

determinants and characteristics of energy commodities to gain an understanding for future price developments.

2.3 Determinants of energy commodities

Valuation techniques are based on capital market theory. However, energy commodities differ from financial assets, so that traditional financial engineering appears to be limited. Therefore, the determinants and price behavior of energy commodities will be analyzed, in order to adjust capital market valuation models to the distinctiveness of the commodities and take the respective long-term price risk into account. Since European power plant portfolios will be valued within a mean-variance-world, the focus of the following analysis will be on key value drivers for a power generator. Interactions between electricity, fuel and carbon will be studied separately.

Introductory, Figure 2.6 depicts the primary energy consumption by type of fuel in 2008.

Figure 2.6 Primary energy consumption by type of fuel in 2008
a) World b) European Union c) Germany

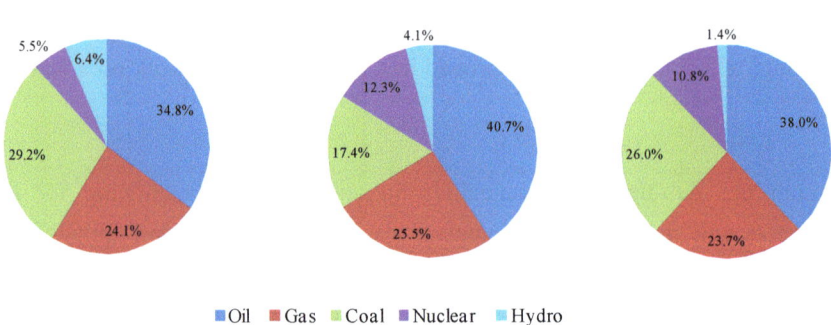

Source: Own graph, data based on BP Statistical Review of World Energy 2009.

2.3.1 Electricity

Electricity differs significantly from other commodities. Firstly, apart from hydro pumped plants, electricity is not technically storable. Secondly, electricity markets are regional markets as the commodity is restricted to a transmission network.[109] However, the power trade between neighboring countries has already improved[110] so that the permanent balance of supply and demand ensures to prevent black-outs. These characteristics have strong implications on the price behavior of electricity, which is highly volatile compared to other commodities.[111] Generally, the electricity market can be distinguished into the following three types:

- **Spot markets** in power exchanges comprise of day-ahead markets and intra-day markets. Market participants bid in day ahead markets for certain quantities expressed in MWh for each hour of the day. The interception of the bid and ask determines the price for the quantity, which will be delivered on a specific hour of the following day.[112] The intra-day market is a market place for short-term optimization, as the delivery date of the products is consistent with the day of the trade. Hence, this kind of market particularly serves the physical short-term need of producers as pure speculations.[113]

- **Forward** and **future markets** participants are able to hedge their open trading positions and use these markets efficiently for their risk management.[114] While one kind of futures includes the physical delivery of power, the other kind of futures covers only the financial risk.

- Crucial characteristic of electricity markets is the fact that supply and demand always have to be balanced. The opportunity to store electricity is still limited, so that a balancing and reserve service in electricity markets is required to prevent black-outs.[115] Being able to adjust the balance up to 15 minutes prior to delivery is a result of the **balancing** and **reserve market**, which provides flexibility to the electricity system. The structure of the market is obligated to

---

[109] See Burger et al. (2007), p. 27.
[110] Please refer to the previous section for further details.
[111] For instance, Simonsen (2005) studies the price behaviour of the Nordic power spot market. He computed a daily volatility of 16%; which equals an annual volatility of more than 300%. Please note, that the Nordic electricity market is less volatile compared to other power markets in Europe.
[112] See Fiorenzani (2006), p. 5.
[113] See Burger et al. (2007), p. 28.
[114] See Burger et al. (2007), p. 28.
[115] See Eydeland / Wolyniec (2003), p. 5.

the national transmission operator. Therefore, the structure of balancing and reserve market differs between countries in comparison to forwards and future markets, which are rather similar regarding their structure.

Generally, electricity markets distinguish between *base load* and *peak load* contracts. While base load contracts comprise a constant delivery of power over time, peak load contracts refer to specific hours of the day, which characterizes typically a high load level.[116] However, in comparison to the settlement of securities these power products stipulate a time period of delivery instead of certain times and voltage.[117]

Since electricity markets have started to be more competitive due to the liberalization process, forecasting models for electricity prices have gained in importance. The characteristics of the good electricity makes price predications more challenging compared to other commodities. The dynamics of electricity prices can be explained by the following determinants:

Firstly, seasonality, which restricts power plant operations in terms of lack of water level (e.g. cooling of nuclear plants), the wind and the water supply. For instance, in the summer price jumps in electricity exchanges refer mainly to a high usage of cooling goods (e.g. air conditioning) combined with a restriction operation of nuclear plants. Secondly, electricity prices are more volatile than that prevailing in other com modities or financial markets.

As stated in section 2.1.6 the electricity supply function and, therefore, electricity prices depend on the characteristics (regional supply of resources and national energy policy) of the respective generation system. Figure 2.7 depicts the base load price development of selected European power markets within spring 2005 until the end of 2009.

---

[116] See Burger et al. (2007), pp. 29-30.
 For instance, at the European Energy Exchange (EEX) in Leipzig the base load product "Phelix base" is the arithmetic mean of the 24 prices for each hour of the day. "Phelix peak" is the average price for the hours 9 am to 8 pm. See Härle (2006), p. 368.
[117] See Pilgram (2006), p. 315.

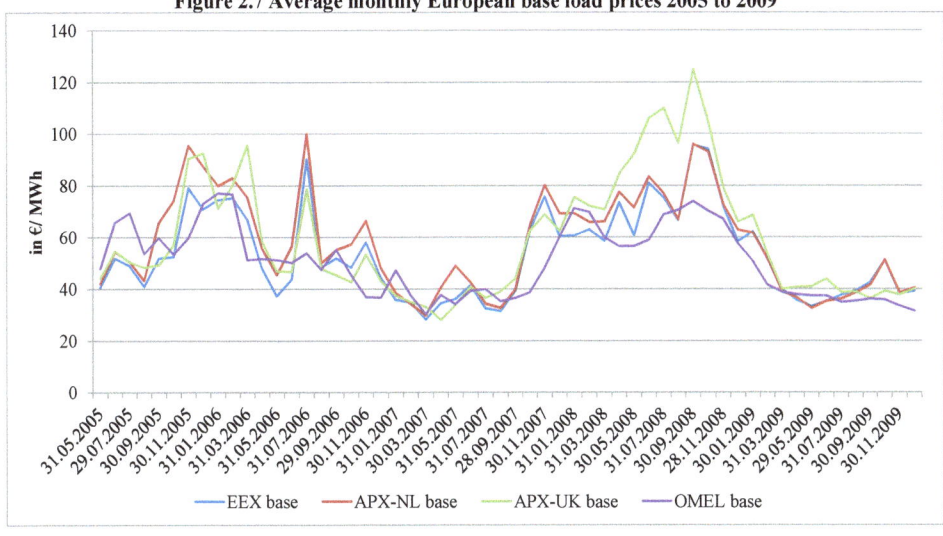

Figure 2.7 Average monthly European base load prices 2005 to 2009

Source: Own figure. Data gained from Thomson Data stream.

In comparison to financial markets electricity markets are rather decentralized. While the price of one Euro is independent of the geographical area, the price of one MWh includes the transmission costs. Hence, geographic contingencies are an important price factor of electricity.[118] Usually, electricity markets are regional markets. Differences between areas like the UK and South Europe refer to different technological methods of generating electricity, climatic conditions and specific demand and supply characteristics.[119]

While the liberalization of European power markets might push down electricity prices, increasing oil and gas prices on global markets affect European electricity prices. The latter effect is even strengthening through political conflicts, e.g. gas supply in Russia, or wars.[120] As evidenced by Figure 2.7, this especially true for base load prices of the UK and the Netherlands, due to the dominance of natural gas for power generation.[121]

Figure 2.8 depicts the shape of the hourly power price trajectory on the German electricity market. Since the demand for electricity is a function of daily routine of

---

[118] Transmission and distribution costs are part of the electricity price for customers. The wholesale price observed on energy exchanges does not captured these costs.
[119] See Clewlow/ Strickland (2000), p. 69.
[120] See Kanen (2006), p. 27.
[121] Please refer to section 2.1.3 for further details.

customers, electricity prices mirrors customers preferences for each hour of the day. Therefore different price levels are observable on working days, weekends and holidays.

Figure 2.8 EEX hourly spot price in 2009

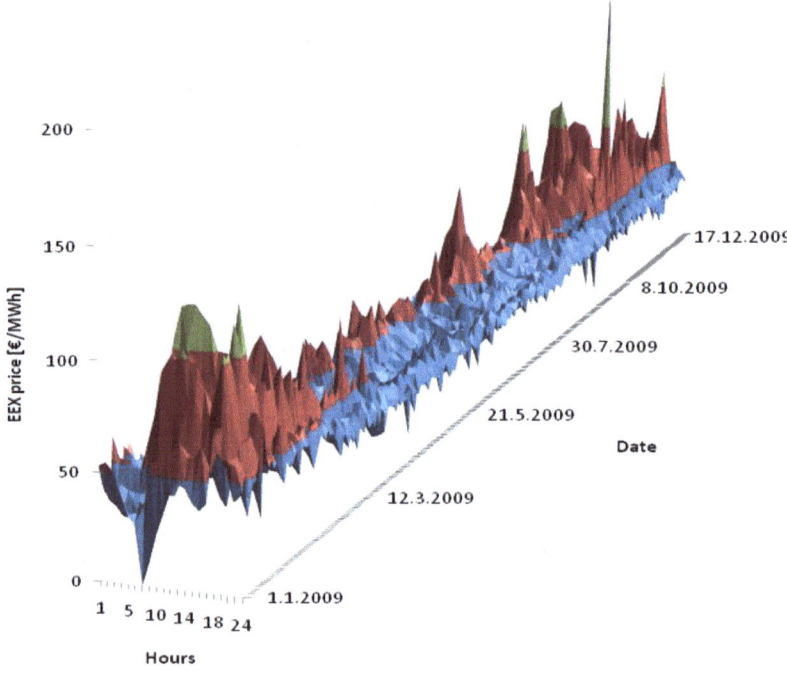

Source: Own figure based on EEX-data

On the whole, the power price is mainly determined by temperature, hours of sunshine, economic cycle, customer behavior, water inflow, fuel freight, wind supply, perception, cooling water, export and import electricity.[122] In addition, fuel and carbon prices which will be analyzed in the following sections.

---

[122] See Ulreich (2005), p. 283.

2.3.2 CO$_2$ emissions

The storage opportunity of EUAs in electronic accounts indicates similarities to other financial assets, however, the determinants of the former cause a diverging price development.[123] In economic theory, the value and as a result the demand of a financial security is based on expected future earnings. In contrast, EUA prices for carbon reflect the expected market scarcity which companies are able to control somewhat by investing in CO$_2$ abatement projects.[124] However, the annual quantity of emission allowances which serve for the allocation to the installations covered by the EU ETS is already determined by the country-specific NAP. In addition, the validity of an emission certificate is limited, as the certificates cannot be transferred towards trading phases. The EUA loses its value, only when the certificate is used for compliance or after trading phases.[125]

Carbon spot and future prices with maturity in 2010 between the first and current phases are depicted in Figure 2.9.

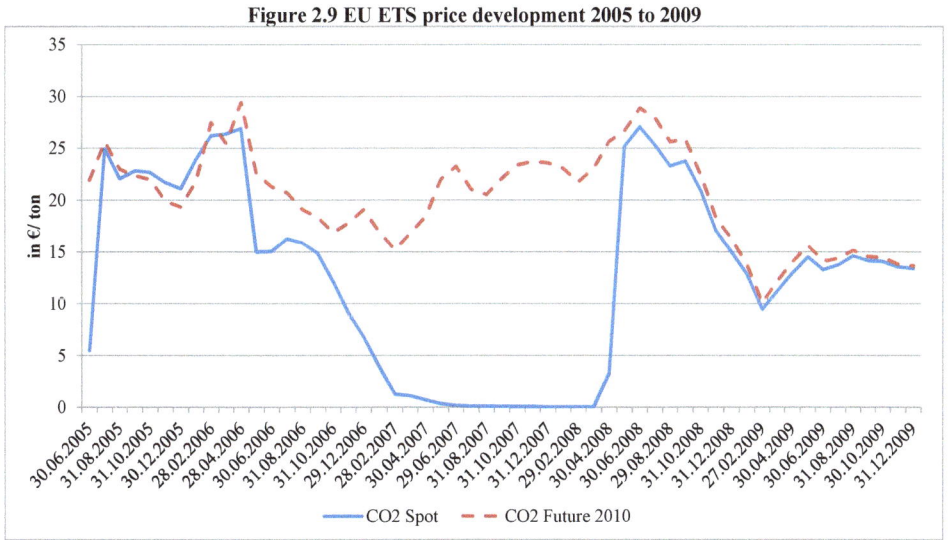

Figure 2.9 EU ETS price development 2005 to 2009

Source: Own graph based on data from BlueNext and ECX.

While the price developments of carbon emission certificates have been irrespective between the two trading periods on spot markets, this seems different for the CO$_2$-

---

[123] See Mansanet-Bataller/ Pardo (2008), p. 4.
[124] See Benz/ Trück (2009), p. 5.
[125] See Benz/ Trück (2009), p. 5.

future prices. In fact, *Phase I* on the one hand and *Phase II* on the other hand are seen as two separate markets. [126]

The price boost of CO_2 certificates between spring and June 2005 on spot markets is threefold:[127] Firstly, oil and gas prices were relatively high compared to coal prices, which caused an increase in carbon prices as power plant operators switched from gas to coal. Secondly, hydro power plants particularly in Southern Europe did not operate on full utilization due to a lack of precipitation. Thirdly, dry temperatures in Europe reduced the amount of cooling water in rivers, which is a prerequisite for the operation of nuclear plants. Consequently, the substitution to fossil generation capacity caused a higher demand for CO_2 emission allowances. Hence, carbon prices on spot markets peaked in July 2005. After a slight decrease, the CO_2 spot price leveled off at around 22 Euros.

The cold winter in 2005/ 2006 caused a renewed increase in carbon prices in March 2006. Two months later CO_2 spot prices suddenly plunged down from around 30 Euros to 11 Euros within one week.[128] The sharp decline in spot price levels refers back to an oversupply of emission certificates, which was made public to the markets in spring 2006.[129]

Additionally, spot prices of natural gas in Europe declined massively in September 2006, so that carbon spot price for emission certificates became almost worthless at the end of the first trading period. In contrast, carbon future prices fluctuate roughly between 15 Euros and 30 Euros in the first trading period. After carbon prices had been recovering within the second trading period, the eruption of global stock markets due to the financial collapse of investment banks in September 2008 caused another drop in carbon markets.

Following *Benz/ Trück* (2009) the drivers on CO_2 emission prices can be classified into: *regulatory and political uncertainty* and *market fundamentals*. The former refers to any decision or announcement of the national regulatory authority which defines total emission budgets and the respective reduction objectives for the industries covered in the ETS within the NAP. Therefore any news might cause price jumps,

---

[126] See Seifert et al. (2008), p. 181.
[127] See Benz/ Trück (2009), p. 12.
[128] See Zachmann/ Hirschhausen (2008), p. 465.
[129] Please refer to section 2.2.3 for further details.

spikes or increase volatility of emission certificate prices.[130] In other words, the CO_2 price pattern is attributed to the information disclosure on the emission market.[131] Compared to prices on financial stock and commodity markets, the influence of regulatory and political uncertainty on prices of CO_2 emission certificates is therefore rather high. Hence, a prediction of the future development of CO_2 emission certificates based on fundamental price data is hardly possible.[132]

However, financial options on emission certificates could be a suitable approach for future emission price projections, as the expectation of market participants is captured in option premiums. The latter depends on the future price development of the respective underlying.[133]

Alongside these institutional uncertainties, market fundamentals have an impact on CO_2 prices. Here, several studies indicate that *fuel prices* of Brent oil, coal and gas influence CO_2 prices.[134] Moreover, the influences of meteorological conditions, technological development as well as operational risks are mentioned:[135]

- *Fuel prices*. Depending on the cost of fuel, power plant operators' switch between coal fired power plants and gas power plants. As long as the gas price exceeds the coal price plus the price of emission certificates, the operator is better off running the coal power plant. Low coal prices on commodity markets, however, boost the demand for emission certificates and the price of emission certificates rises so that it is more economic to run the gas power plant.[136]

- *Weather*. Energy consumption and therefore emissions depend on meteorological conditions. Total sun hours and wind speed determine the operating hours of renewable energies. However, these non-CO_2 power generating sources are usually not available, when in times of low temperatures the demand for power and heat generation increases.[137] In contrast, high

---

[130] See Benz/ Trück (2009), p. 5; Alberola et al. (2009).
[131] See Bonacina/ Cozialpi (2009), p. 3
[132] See Wagner (2007), p. 163
[133] See Bassen/ Rothe (2009a), p. 246.
[134] Mansanet-Bataller et al. (2007); Alberola et al. (2008); Alberola/ Chevallier (2009); Alberola et al. (2009).
[135] See Wagner (2007), pp. 31-32.
[136] See Frondel/ Schmidt (2008), p. 55
[137] See Benz/ Trück (2009), p. 6.

temperatures cause a reduction of nuclear based power generation, which increases operating hours of conventional thermal power plants.

- *Gross domestic product.* Empirically evidenced by *Alberola et al.* (2009), the economic activity of an industry which is obliged to the EU ETS drives carbon prices. In times of a booming economy, production capacity is utilized on a high level, the demand for commodities is soaring and as a consequence emission allowances are requested.[138]

- *Technological development.* The objective of the environmental regulation in terms of emission trading is to promote clean technologies. An investment in state of the art technology pays back earlier as long as the price for emission certificate remains stable on a high level.

- *Technical risk.* Forced or scheduled outages due to technical failures and maintenance, respectively, of nuclear power plants have to be replaced by conventional thermal plants. Since nuclear power plants do not emit CO_2 while in operation, a market situation with an over-demand of emission certificates might occur, in case of nuclear power plant outages.

Keeping the important driving market forces in mind, we now turn the lens on these kinds of fuels which have an impact on carbon prices.

2.3.3 Coal

Hard coal is characterized by a high heating value and consists typically of carbonized vegetal matter. While *thermal coal* is utilized mainly in the generation of damp and process heat in power plants, *coking coal* is a main input factor within the steel production.[139] In contrast, lignite has a lower heating value compared to hard coal and consists mainly of water. As a consequence using lignite for power generation requires

---

[138] In our opinion, the argumentation presented does not necessarily hold in the long run. The EU ETS will lead to a technological change in the production process for goods, in particular for electricity. Ideally, investments in low carbon plants due to environmental regulation will result in a disconnection of GDP and CO_2 prices in future decades of strong economic growth rates. The interaction of GDP growth rates and the demand of energy commodities has shown that there is a coherency as long as the economy is emerging. Industrialized markets, however, characterize an irrespective development of GDP and the demand for commodities.

[139] See Ströbele et al. (2010), p. 87.

a higher amount of input fuel. The quality of coal refers to the carbon, energy, sulphur, and ash content. Consequently, the coal price corresponds with the quality of the coal. For instance, using high quality coal for electricity generation purpose tends to result in more electricity per capture compared to low quality coal.[140]

According to the global primary energy consumption, coal remains the second most important energy resource reaching a share of 30 % in 2008.[141] In comparison to other primary fuels, resources of coal are abundant, as global resources amount to at least 4,000 bn tons of c.e. by a current annual consumption of 5 bn tons of c.e. The burning of coal, however, emits relative to other fuels more carbon which limits the input of coal in industrial processes as well as for power generation.

The literature typically distinguishes between *national* and *international* coal pricing. While the former used to be politically motivated to protect domestic resources, the *Atlantic* and *Pacific markets* determine global coal prices. Unlike the oil and gas markets the coal market is a regional market with different types of coal available depending on the geological characteristics of the specific region.[142] The coal supply in terms of natural reserves is dominated by the United States, Russian Federation, China, India, Australia, Indonesia South Africa, and Kazakhstan.[143]

However, price data is limited compared to other commodities and refers to indices instead of physical goods. Long-term delivery contracts between producers and generators dominate the market. Yet coal trading occurs mainly as OTC trades.[144]

Since transportation cost drives coal prices, any infrastructure problems by the physical settlement cause volatility on the spot markets. The virtue of index markets is the independency of the existing infrastructure.[145] Trading of brown coal, however, is rather scarce and as a consequence the international price formation is in comparison to hard coal non-transparent.[146]

As with other fuels, global thermal coal indices have been continuously increasing in the recent decade peaking in 2007. While meteorological conditions in Australia and

---

[140] See Burger et al. (2007), p.16.
[141] Please refer to Figure 2.6 a).
[142] See Eydeland/ Wolyniec (2003), pp. 13-17.
[143] See BP Statistical Review of World Energy (2009), p. 34.
[144] See Burger et al. (2007), p. 16.
[145] See Ströbele et al. (2010), p. 103.
[146] See Ströbele et al. (2010), p. 99.

Indonesia cause supply pressure in coal markets, the booming iron ore and steel industry cause extra demands for vessels which have a significant impact on freight rates and as a consequence coal market prices. Hence, the ocean freight rates influence the coal price and likewise the competitiveness of coal to oil or gas. The vessels used for international coal trading are also used in the iron ore trade. As long as countries request these commodities for their industry production, the freight rates of the shipping capacity increases which affects the delivery price of coal negatively.[147]

Typically, the coal production is located close to the further processing of the commodity (e.g. as fuel for coal-fired power plants). This is due to the fact that coal has lower energy content than oil and gas, so that transportation for long distances is not economically viable.[148] Consequently, countries with a high coal production like China have high coal consumption for electricity generation as well as steel and iron production.[149]

Soaring coal prices have attracted investments in new mines. Therefore experts do not expect any constraints in the upcoming years, as thermal export capacity should satisfy global demand for the near future.[150]

2.3.4 Oil

Even though oil fired power plants have a small impact on power generation in Europe, the development of oil prices is a crucial factor for power generation. This is due to the fact that natural gas prices in Europe are linked to the Brent crude price.[151]

The main merit of oil is its high energy content making fuel switches very costly in the short and mid run. As a consequence, oil is still the essential energy commodity, particularly for the transportation sector.[152] Within Europe oil accounts for 40% of total primary energy resources.[153] However, oil resources are not abundant. Instead, energy economists estimate global recoverable oil reserves to last 50 years based on today's consumption. Since oil reserves - the amount that can be produced

---

[147] See Rademacher (2008), pp. 68-69.
[148] See Burger et al. (2007), pp. 17-18.
[149] See Burger et al. (2007), p. 17.
[150] See Rademacher (2008), p. 87.
[151] See Kanen (2006), p. 30.
[152] See Ströbele et al. (2010), p. 116.
[153] Please refer to Figure 2.6 b).

economically - are a function of future oil price expectations, a reliable estimate is hardly possible. Yet, the exploration of new oil fields increases oil reserves, which in turn, pushes down oil prices and vice versa. Hence the oil market is inefficient, as it exhibits imperfect information.[154]

In the last decade the price for oil has risen up from 25 US-$ (year 2002) reaching a peak of 150 US-$ in the mid of 2008. While emerging countries like China and India account for extra demand, the supply in terms of refineries are limited to react to material increases in demand. In addition, market participants speculate in further rises in oil prices.[155] The strong Euro against the US-$ at this time, however, has slightly dampened the price increase for European customers.[156] Falling stock markets and decreased economic activity as a result of the financial crisis have caused a decrease in demand for oil pushing down prices on global fuel markets.

The unique oil market structure of suppliers determines the long term future price development. In this respect, the *Organization of Petroleum Exploring Countries* (OPEC) which was founded in 1960 not only produces 40% of the oil consumption but also owns 75% of the global oil reserves. The objective of the OPEC is to stabilize the oil market at a desired price level by regulating production quota. As a consequence the long term price perspective will follow the strategic behavior of OPEC. In contrast to an oligopolistic explanation for an oil price development, the theorem of *Hotelling* (1931) states the time preference of oil producer, which is captured in the discount rate.[157]

However, the strategic behavior regarding production quotas as well political motivation will determine oil price from a supply side. As soon as the world economy has fully recovered, adding China's and India's extra demand, the pressure on oil prices will be restored.

---

[154] See Kanen (2006), p. 32.
[155] See Ströbele et al. (2010), p. 129.
[156] See Kanen (2006), p. 30.
[157] See Ströbele et al. (2010), p. 134.

2.3.5 Gas

Thanks to the flexibility of gas usage, natural gas has recently become the fastest growing energy commodity.[158] Besides, from a physical perspective, the virtues are low emissions and no need for storage compared to other thermal fuels.[159] In 2008, gas consumption in the EU accounted for 25.5% of primary energy sources.[160] Following predictions of energy economists the importance of gas will further rise, in particular for domestic use, as a result of reduced emissions for electricity generation. In addition, proved reserves of natural gas seem to be long-lasting given current consumption in comparison to oil.

Very similar to the case of electricity markets, the EU has opened up gas markets to competition. However, the liberalization process has been slow due to a limited pipeline infrastructure, the oil price link and an oligopolistic supply structure.[161] Nevertheless, gas consumption has been growing quicker than oil consumption. Natural gas serves for electricity generation, transportation and heating.[162] Although gas is difficult to store and to transport, the soaring demand in the world commodity market has increased the price level. Within the last decade, in all EU member states, gas prices have increased sharply.[163] The high price level, however, makes investments in transportation systems profitable.

Even though *liquefied natural gas* (LNG) has been stimulating gas trading, it is limited to the existing pipeline infrastructure. Hence, three regional markets (America, Europe and Asia) exist, as costs of gas transportation are not competitive over large distances compared to oil. As a consequence, in contrast to oil, no global market for natural gas and respective prices exists. The European market mainly consists of gas from Norway, Russia and Algeria.[164]

To finance gas infrastructure projects, gas pricing is historically linked to oil price development. This so-called *netback pricing* is based on the price of gas substitutes namely fuel and gas oil by adjusting the prices accordingly.[165] The market in Central

---

[158] See Geman (2005), p. 227.
[159] See Ströbele et al. (2010), p. 141.
[160] Please refer to Figure 2.6 b).
[161] See Kanen (2006), p. 35.
[162] See Burger et al. (2007), p. 9.
[163] See Kanen (2006), p. 37.
[164] See Geman (2005), pp. 229.
[165] See Kanen (2006), p. 34.

Europe, however, is still dominated by long-term oil prices contracts. In Europe the most important gas trading hubs are the National Balancing Point (NBP) in the UK, Zeebrugge in Belgium and Title Transfer Facility (TTF) in the Netherlands. The largest liquid futures exchange for natural gas in Europe is the ICE in UK.[166]

Since gas competes with coal in European power generation, the pricing formula for European generators takes this into account.[167] The crucial factor, however, in analyzing gas prices if there is any change in the gas infrastructure. This is due to the fact that gas prices neither reflect long distance transport nor the cost of local distribution.[168] For instance, the opening of the *Maghreb-Europe* gas pipeline connecting Algeria to Spain and the Interconnector pipeline between Zeebrugge and the UK pushed down gas prices significantly.[169] However, the recent Ukraine-Russian gas conflict raises fear of security of gas supply and reliable prices.

The physical demand for natural gas fluctuates daily, weekly and seasonally. Although gas has become an important input factor for electricity generation, the heat market still dominates gas usage. Consequently, the demand for gas is linked with meteorological conditions. Therefore, in line with electricity, gas prices exhibit a higher volatility in comparison to price changes on global oil markets.

While gas transport usually depends on a distribution network, new transport mechanisms like LNG (liquefied natural gas) terminals have become particularly important. In comparison to gas which is delivered through pipelines, LNG is generally more expensive and as consequence requires long distance transportation to compete with natural gas. However, a further boost in LNG terminals could connect market areas and diminish European dependency on Russian gas supply thus preventing the likelihood of gas shortage. Since LNG transportation has been established, long distance pipeline networks are not necessary anymore. However, the LNG value chain is very costly, as first of all the natural gas must to be cooled down to transform the gas to liquid. Secondly, after transportation in special LNG vessels regasification is necessary in order to feed the gas in the pipeline for the customer.[170]

---

[166] See Burger et al. (2007), p. 12.
[167] See Geman (2005), p. 235.
[168] See Geman (2005), p. 234.
[169] See Kanen (2006), p. 32.
[170] See Ströbele et al. (2010), pp. 159-161.

The current fundamental change of the European gas industry is mainly threefold: Firstly, the emergence of short-term contracts. Secondly, the increase of gas-based power generation could lead to a break in the link between gas and oil pricing. Thirdly, not only long-term contracts but also agreements regarding production should decrease risks for investors and stimulate the need for further investments in gas infrastructure.[171]

2.3.6 Interactions between energy commodities

Following *Kat/ Oomen* (2006) energy commodity returns in particular are characterized by sudden jumps in their short term price behavior, mainly due to the change of meteorological conditions or supply shocks. In addition, a lack of storage opportunities, which is especially true for electricity, causes a higher volatility of commodity returns.[172] Since oil is quoted on global fuel markets in US-dollar, any currency devaluation or appreciation has an impact on the volatility of the respective commodity price return. Hence, currency risks might drive commodities price volatility. Ultimately, the general economic activity drives the demand for energy commodities. The price volatility, however, turns out to be higher in periods of recessions. The aforementioned reasons for sudden changes of price levels lead on commodity spot markets typically to a positive skewness, whereas the return of commodity futures is hardly skewed.[173]

The price characteristics of energy commodities make extreme short-term price observations more likely. As a consequence energy commodities exhibit, statistically speaking, a kurtosis which is larger than normal.[174] In comparison to ordinary asset classes, energy commodities are autocorrelated meaning that the price increase of one day is correlated to the price development of the next day. Hence, the computation of the annual volatility based on daily data would systematically underestimate the standard deviation of the commodity price return.[175] Ultimately, in comparison to other markets commodities exhibit the so-called Samuelson affect, which means that the volatility of future prices declines by respective maturity.[176]

---

[171] See Geman (2005), p. 236.
[172] This relationship is described first in Kaldor (1939); also Kat/ Oomen (2006), p. 11.
[173] See Kat/ Oomen (2006), pp. 11-12.
[174] See Kat/ Oomen (2006), p. 15.
[175] See Kat/ Oomen (2006), p. 17.
[176] See Bonacina/ Cozialpi (2009), p. 15.

The price behavior of the commodities described in the previous sections indicates mutual dependencies. This interaction drives as a consequence prices of other commodities. However, the issue arises of how these commodities depend on each other to take the interaction for the further analysis into account. Energy commodities can be distinguished in fuels which are either mainly used for power generation or serve even for other purposes, like heating or transportation. The latter is especially true for oil, coal and gas. Since these types of fuels can be easily stored and shipped, they compete on global fuel markets. That is the reason why fuel market development drives electricity prices and not the other way around.[177]

Figure 2.10 illustrates the price development of the crucial kinds of fuels for power generation as well as carbon futures with maturity in 2010. Oil, coal, gas and uranium prices are converted in the dimension €/ MWh and are plotted on the primary y-axis, whereas the future carbon price development is illustrated on the secondary y-axis.

Figure 2.10 Commodity price development 2005 to 2009

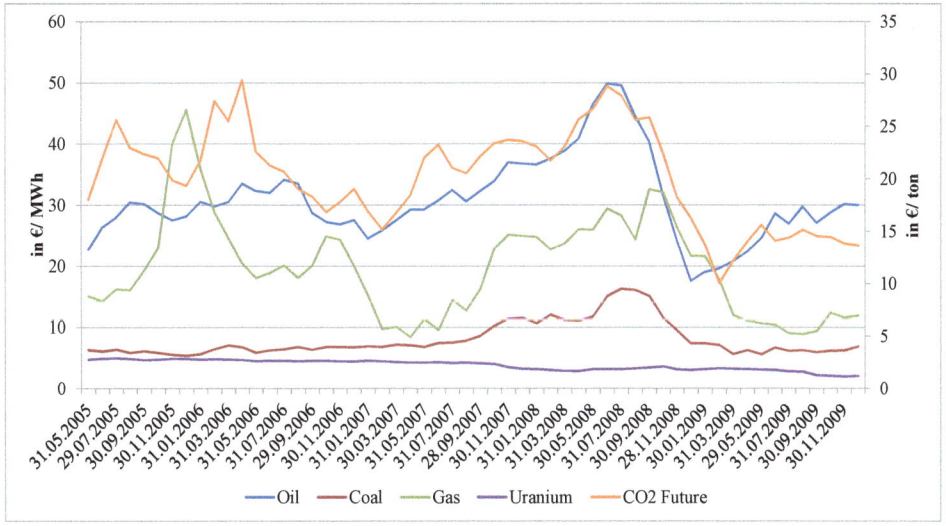

Source: Own figure, data taken from Datastream.

As described in the previous section, the efficiency of power plant technologies differs which is explained by the varying heating value of the respective fuel. Consequently, the heating value of fuel has an impact on the responsiveness of power prices. Therefore a high efficiency rate, e.g. for gas plants, goes along with a stronger reaction

---

[177] See Kanen (2006), p. 45.

of power prices to a change of prices on gas markets. The flexibility of fossil fuels creates an additional demand other than the need for power generation. Besides, the main merit in comparison to electricity is the opportunity to store these commodities. Hence, fuel markets are more liquid compared to power markets.[178]

Since the conversion of thermal fuel in electricity causes emissions, the utility industry accounts for a substantial source of CO_2 emissions. Against this background, the mode of action on electricity markets has changed mainly due to the EU ETS.[179] As pointed out in the previous chapter, the compliance buying of carbon certificates causes a change of the power systems' merit order. Consequently, commodity markets are affected as well. Therefore the causalities between commodity prices and meteorological data on electricity markets are by no means trivial. According to *Keppler/ Mansanet-Bataller* (2009) there are several differences between *Phase I* and *Phase II* of the EU ETS. While their results indicate that gas determines in Phase II base load power prices, coal prices just follow rather than drive commodity prices. However, *Keppler/ Mansanet-Bataller* (2009) empirical analyses refer to electricity prices from *French Powernext*. As the French power market is dominated by Électricité de France (EDF), which mainly relies on nuclear electricity generation, the question arises, if their results hold for electricity markets in Central Europe. The authors consider the influence of meteorological conditions in terms of temperatures, unexpected temperature changes index and total temperature changes index on commodity prices. However, the research of *Keppler/ Mansanet-Bataller* (2009) does not cover wind speed and sun hours to account for power generation of renewable energy plants.

Energy prices are important determinants of carbon prices due to the ability of power generators to switch between their fuel inputs. Hence, these fuel prices also have an impact on CO_2 certificate prices due to the ability of power generators to switch between their fuel inputs.[180] However, the causality is not obvious. For instance, Brent oil prices drive mainly natural gas prices which, in turn, are affected by carbon prices themselves.[181] Soaring carbon prices could also lead to lower coal prices, as power operators tend to switch from coal to gas. As a consequence, the price level of gas might increase on fuel markets.[182]

---

[178] See Kanen (2006), p. 45.
[179] Neuhoff et al. (2006); Weber/ Swider (2006).
[180] See Alberola et al. (2008); Mansanet-Bataller et al .(2007).
[181] Sijm et al. (2006); Zachmann/ van Hirschhausen (2008).
[182] See Kanen (2006), pp. 49-50.

For the foreseeable future it is very likely that thermal fuel prices will stay high, as oil prices still drive other fuel prices including thermal. In addition, emerging countries like China and India are hungry for energy in order to maintain their economic growth. Assuming a phase-out of nuclear energy for power generation, will also lead to an extra demand for thermal fuels, as the respective power plant technologies will have higher utilization rates.

In Central Europe electricity production from wind plants influence the merit order and respective electricity prices significantly.[183] Moreover, a further increase in wind power capacity due to the European climate policy is very likely. Therefore it is necessary to consider the influence of meteorological factors on the level of commodity prices. Indeed, the simulation model aims to implement a proxy for the volume risk of wind and photovoltaic power plants, as power systems indicate an interplay between wind speed and total hours of sun on the one hand and electricity and fuel prices on the other.

In brief, energy price developments are related to each other. In addition, thermal fuel, power and carbon prices might trigger a spiral of reactions, which does not allow for the establishment of clear causalities.

2.4 Summary

This chapter has demonstrated the impact of regulative change towards the utility industry. The liberalization of electricity markets has shifted corresponding risks from the regulator to the utility firm. Now, power generators bear the risks of volatile electricity, fuel and carbon prices in particular. As a consequence, from a utility's perspective, not the so-called *levelized costs* of power generation should be appealed to valuation concepts; instead the economic profitability of a power plant. Against the background of the introduction of the EU ETS, European utilities are exposed to significant carbon risks which mainly materialize as price risks. This is due to the need to buy carbon emission allowances as well as the uncertainty surrounding the implementation of the EU ETS. The tightening emission regulation for the current and post-Kyoto phases may put pressure on carbon prices and as a consequence affect the profitability of thermal conventional power plants. In addition, this section has

---

[183] Bode (2006); Neubarth et al. (2006); Pavlak (2008); Wissen/ Nicolosi (2007).

highlighted the merits of existing power plant technologies which will determine the feasibility set in the upcoming portfolio analysis. Currently, investors rely on building up new gas fired power plant technologies. The virtues of such technologies are lower emission intensity and flexibility in operation in comparison to other conventional thermal power plants.

Finally, the price determinants of energy commodities have been presented and interactions among them analyzed. Oil still influences other energy commodity prices and as a consequence should be captured as a risky variable for the simulation model, even though oil does not play a major role for power generation purpose. In addition, the analysis has shown that meteorological conditions should also be incorporated in the simulation model, as they affect energy prices.

3 Mean-variance valuation approach for power plants

This chapter introduces a theoretical framework to analyze the issues targeted by the thesis. Therefore, first the traditional *discounted free cash flow* (DCF) valuation methodology is presented including a breakdown of the most relevant input parameters. Secondly, we demonstrate how computer simulation experiments are able to take various risk factors into account in order to gain a range of the expected DCF asset value. Thirdly, we introduce the portfolio theory of *Markowitz* (1952) to identify assets which lead to efficient generation portfolios. Fourthly, we present the work of *Roques et al.* (2008) which is taken as a basis to work out our portfolio approach for generation assets. To appraise the performance of generation portfolios we suggest additional ratios to quantify the degree of power plant portfolios' relative efficiency. Lastly, this chapter closes with the development of hypotheses.

3.1 Fundamentals of capital market-based valuation

From a theoretical point of view, it is reasonable to assume that the market price of an asset is the best estimate of its value. Yet, this just holds for *efficient markets*. Efficiency is attributed to markets with perfect and symmetric information.[184] Instead, asset valuation is based upon the perception that markets are inefficient. As a consequence, valuation techniques attempt to discover the so-called *fair asset value*.[185] Besides, a successful investment requires the identification of the asset key value drivers to design the valuation tool accordingly.[186]

Valuation theory distinguishes between three general approaches. While *discounted cash flow techniques* equalize the asset´s fair value to the present value of future cash flows, a *relative valuation* derives the asset value by relying on the comparison of financial ratios, e.g. book value to earnings. Ultimately, option price models serve to determine the asset value which is called *contingent claim valuation*.[187]

---

[184] See Fama (1969), p. 383.
[185] See Damodaran (1996), p. 6.
[186] See Damodaran (1996), p. 1.
[187] See Damodaran (1996), p. 9.

© Springer Fachmedien Wiesbaden GmbH, part of Springer Nature 2011
S. Rothe, *Portfolio Analysis of Power Plant Technologies*, Edition KWV,
https://doi.org/10.1007/978-3-658-24379-1_3

The absence of public trading due to a lack of liquidity for generation assets, however, prevents the use of a relative valuation. As a consequence a comparative valuation for generation assets is not applicable.[188]

Since the operator of a power plant park has the right but not the obligation to run a specific power plant, the operating decision is very similar to an *American call option*. However, the *contingent claim valuation* approach for power generators is particularly suitable on a short-term basis to optimize plant dispatching or to determine the value of operational flexibility.[189]

In order to explore the expected value per MW generation capacity for a power plant portfolio, we rely therefore on a *discounted free cash flow* (DCF) approach which is introduced in the following section.

3.1.1 Discounted free cash flow valuation

3.1.1.1 Methodology

To determine the fair value of a power plant, we rely on principles of capital market theory. In general, the value of goods represents the benefit that the holder of the respective asset is able to enjoy. Therefore, valuation theory derives the fair value of any asset from its future benefit which is associated to the specific asset.[190] Typically, the asset holder pursues solely financial objectives. The latter cause the opportunity of future consumption which goes along with a maximization of utility.[191] As a consequence, the *economic value* of an asset is based on generated future financial surpluses. Hence, any valuation methodology focuses on the expected future profits of an asset. The appraisal is conducted by relying on the determination of the *net present value* of the asset.[192]

---

[188] See Müller (2005), p. 72.
[189] Tseng/ Barz (2002).
[190] See Ross et al. (2005), p. 62.
[191] See Loitz (2000), p. 701.
[192] See Böcking/ Nowak (1998), p. 687.

As stated, the economic value of an asset depends on future earnings. However, instead of discounting earnings, valuation practitioners as well as academics rely on discounting cash flows. In fact, payments instead of earnings bear interest and are therefore discountable according to valuation theory. As a consequence, deriving the so- called *free cash flow* is required to appraise an asset. Since the free cash flow is computed after payments for investments and taxes, it represents the available amount of cash to fulfill the claim of shareholders as well as creditors. In addition, the free cash flow does not directly depend on the capital structure of an investment project. Instead, the capital structure and tax shield are covered by the *weighted average cost of capital* (WACC), the discount rate of the respective investment asset.[193]

The accrual of funds takes place in the future. Therefore, not only the point of time but also the total amount of cash-inflow has to be properly estimated. Besides, the *time value of money* has to be taken into account which is carried out by capitalizing the cash flows.

Valuation theory distinguishes between two traditional approaches considering investment risks. While adjusting asset's cash flows by a certainty equivalent is one method to account for risk, considering a premium for the discount rate is another concept. The application of certainty equivalents requires the knowledge of the characteristic regarding investor's utility function. In contrast, risk premiums are based on objective criteria. The main merit of the reliance on risk premiums within the discount rate is to be independent of investor's preferences. Hence, the formula for computing asset's net present value is equal to:[194]

$$(3.1) \qquad NPV = -I_0 + \sum_{t=1}^{T} \frac{E(FCF_t)}{(1+\mu)^t}$$

where I_0 denotes the initial investment, μ the fair discount rate and $E(FCF_t)$ the expected free cash flow in the specific point of time t.

For estimating assets' free cash flows, valuation theory typically recommends applying a two-phase-model. The first phase covers a detailed planning period, whereas the second phase determines the *terminal value*. The terminal value based on

---

[193] See Damodaran (1996), pp. 62-63.
[194] See Brealey et al. (2010), p. 53.

perpetuity is used, if the prediction of future free cash flows turns out to be impractical and the *going concern principle* of the respective asset owner is assumed.[195]

Hence, today's asset value, V_o, is equal to the present value of the expected free cash flows, $E(FCF_t)$ during the first phase plus the present value of expected free cash flows for the second phase. Or in analytical expression, formula (3.2) reads:

$$(3.2) \qquad V_0 = \sum_{t=1}^{T} \frac{E(FCF_t)}{(1+r_{WACC})^t} + \frac{TV_T}{(1+r_{WACC})^{T-t}}$$

The terminal value, TV_T, is equal to:

$$(3.3) \qquad TV_T = \frac{E(FCF_T)}{(r_{WACC} - g)}$$

whereas g represents the average long-term growth-rate.[196] Since shareholders as well as creditors are eligible for the asset's free cash flow, the discount factor represents the rate of return that the respective asset has to generate in order to satisfy the claims of all investors.[197] For this purpose, the WACC covers the rate of returns for debt, r_{debt}, and equity, r_{equity} based on market values. Assuming the asset is to be financed with debt, D_M, and equity, E_M, *Modigliani and Millers'* (1958) WACC formula reads:[198]

$$(3.4) \qquad r_{WACC} = \frac{D_M}{E_M + D_M} \cdot r_{debt} \cdot (1-\tau) + \frac{E_M}{E_M + D_M} \cdot r_{equity}$$

whereas τ denotes the marginal tax rate. The latter captures the tax advantage, as interest payments to creditors are deductible.

---

[195] See Koller et al. (2005), p. 112.
[196] The growth rate is typically based on the expectation regarding a long-term consumption growth rate for the respective industry as well as an adjustment for inflation. See Koller et al. (2005), p. 279.
[197] See Koller et al. (2005) p. 113.
[198] See Koller et al. (2005) p. 113.

3.1.1.2 Deriving free cash flows

Computing asset's value requires an evaluation scheme to derive respective free cash flows. However, the issue arises regarding what is actually meant by an *asset's free cash flow*. According to *Jensen* (1986) a firm should pay out dividends, if the expected return of a reinvestment is less compared to the return of the best alternative investment beyond the company bearing the same level of risk. Therefore, the difference between the cash flow of a firm and investments that bear an economic advantage should be distributed to shareholders. In general, this difference represents the asset's free cash flow.[199] In fact, accounting theory distinguishes between two methods to derive cash flows. While the indirect method is based on the firm's net income, the direct cash flow takes the respective revenues as a starting point.[200]

Since this thesis evaluates single assets instead of whole firms, we will rely on the following process on the direct method. From a power plant perspective expected revenues are equal to the product of electricity prices and power sold within a specific period. Therefore, Table 3.1 depicts the evaluation scheme of an asset's free cash flow.

Table 3.1 Free cash flow scheme

Revenues
- Operating expenses
= Earnings before interest, taxes, depreciation, and amortization (EBITDA)
- Depreciation and amortization
= Earnings before interest and taxes (EBIT)
- Interest expenses
= Earnings before taxes (EBT)
- Taxes
= Earnings after taxes (EAT)
+ Depreciation and amortization
- Capital expenditures
+/- Working capital change
= Free cash flow

Source: According to Damodaran (1996), p. 100.

---

[199] See Drukarczyk/ Schüler (2009), p. 92.
[200] See Drukarczyk/ Schüler (2009), pp. 98-99.

Assuming a conventional-thermal power plant technology, the operating expenses for this type of generation asset are mainly determined by the cost of fuel and the cost of carbon. Since depreciation and amortization cause a deduction of tax expenses in the income statement, they have to be eliminated to calculate the *earnings before interest and taxes* (EBIT). However, as depreciation and amortization are not cash outflow related, they increase (depreciation) or decrease (amortization) of respective asset's cash flows depending on the netting of both positions.[201]

As stated at the beginning, if an asset investment turns out to be advantageous, cash flow from operations is needed to finance either the creation of replacements or the maintenance. Hence, capital expenditures diminish the asset's operating cash flow. However, the interdependency of depreciation and investments has to be taken into account, when deriving assets' free cash flow as both terms indicate the potential for future growth.[202]

Lastly, the *working capital* affects the asset's free cash flows. In general, working capital equals the difference of current assets and liabilities. In addition, it implies the ability to generate cash over time, so that its change has to be captured to derive free cash flows. While an increase goes along with a cash outflow, a decrease is equal to a cash inflow.[203]

The total amount of working capital, however, depends mainly on the type of industry. In fact, for power generation assets' the working capital is rather low due to the non-storability of electricity. Even though, neglecting the change of working capital will generally cause a slight overestimation of cash flows and as a consequence of the assets' value,[204] we presume in the following a zero-change of working capital for power plant assets.

---

[201] See Damodaran (1996), p. 99.
[202] See Damodaran (1996), p. 99.
[203] See Damodaran (1996), pp. 99-100.
[204] See Damodaran (1996), p. 100.

3.1.1.3 Estimating the cost of capital

According to the WACC formula presented in the previous section, the issue arises of how to determine the cost of equity and debt to complete the required input variables of a DCF-valuation approach. For estimating the cost of equity it is common to rely on the *capital asset pricing model* (CAPM).[205] The CAPM, which initially refers to the work of *Sharpe* (1964), *Lintner* (1965) and *Mossin* (1966), postulates a linear relationship between the expected return on an asset and the asset's beta as a measure of risk:[206]

(3.5) $$r_{equity} = r_i = r_f + (r_M - r_f) \cdot \beta_i$$

whereas r_f and r_M represent the risk-free interest rate and the return of the market portfolio, respectively. The measure of the relative systematic risk, β_i, denotes to:[207]

(3.6) $$\beta_i = \frac{\sigma_{iM}}{\sigma_M^2} = \frac{\sigma_i \cdot \sigma_M \cdot \rho_{iM}}{\sigma_M^2} = \frac{\sigma_i \cdot \rho_{iM}}{\sigma_M}$$

Figure 3.1 depicts the relationship between the asset's return and the respective beta coefficient. Assuming market equilibrium, all assets are located on the security market line (SML). In contrast, the capital market line (CML) demonstrates the relationship of return and risk for efficient assets. Since efficient assets are also part of the SML, the latter can be adapted to the CML for efficient portfolios.[208]

---

[205] See Koller et al. (2005), p. 299. Please note that the CAPM assumes investors to hold efficient portfolios. Thus, the portfolio theory should be introduced before the CAPM model, as it is part of the latter assumptions. For the purpose of the thesis, however, we have decided to change this order so that the chapter turns out to be more reader-friendly.
[206] See Sharpe et al. (1999), p. 235.
[207] See Sharpe et al. (1999), p. 235.
[208] We will rely on the CML for measuring the performance of generation assets in section 3.5.3. For the general relationship between SML and CML, please refer to Sharpe et al. (1999).

Figure 3.1 Security market line of the CAPM

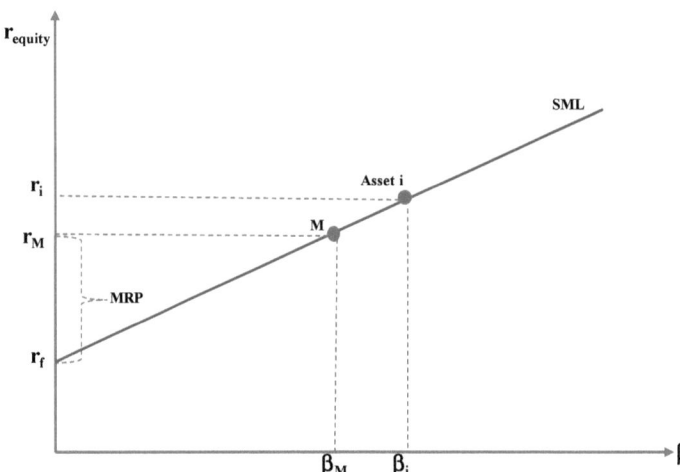

Source: According to Sharpe et al. (1999) p. 235.

Due to the linear relationship the vertical intercept of the straight line in Figure 3.1 is determined by the risk-free interest rate r_f, whereas the positive slope refers to the so-called *market risk premium* (MRP):[209]

(3.7) $$MRP = \frac{(r_M - r_f)}{\beta_M} = (r_M - r_f)$$

According to this equilibrium model, assets with larger betas will have larger expected returns, as they bear more risk relative to the market. In other words; the beta coefficient represents the co-movement of the respective asset to the market portfolio. Therefore the SML depicts the relationship between the covariance of an asset to the market and expected asset return.[210]

The market portfolio is typically approximated by a broad stock market index to determine the equity cost of capital. While the CAPM measures the beta of a stock relative to the market portfolio, the single factor (market) model assumes that the return of an asset depends solely on the return of the market index. The beta coefficient as a measure for the relative systematic risk determines the fair premium for taking the risk of investing in the specific asset. Therefore, the risk premium covers

---

[209] See Sharpe et al. (1999), p. 235.
[210] See Sharpe et al. (1999), p. 235.

the pervasive risk of the respective asset. In contrast, the idiosyncratic risk of an asset is not priced according to capital market theory, as an investor is able to eliminate the risk through diversification.

To sum up, the application of the CAPM for estimating the asset's cost of capital is threefold. Firstly, the risk-free interest rate represents the return of a security which is not correlated to the market portfolio and a zero standard deviation. As a consequence, best rated government bonds indicating no-default risk serve to approximate the risk-free interest rate. Most importantly, the bond chosen should represent the asset's location. In fact, for valuing European assets, it is recommended relying on European bonds with a maturity of 10 years.[211]

Secondly, for the estimation of the market risk premium defined as excess return of the market index and the risk-free interest rate, there is no standard well-accepted approach. Instead, the determination of the market risk premium is controversial in academic literature.[212] However, the estimation of future risk premiums based on measuring and extrapolating historical excess returns seems most common. Thirdly, the beta coefficient which drives asset returns has to be estimated, as the parameter is not directly observable.[213]

Alternatively, multiple factor models have recently emerged for estimating the equity cost of capital. The latter is more powerful than the market model, as it takes various factors as sensitivities of a stock return into account. According to *Fama/ French* (1993), the exposure of a security is related to the excess return of the market, market capitalization and book-to-market-ratios. The theoretical foundation of multiple factor models is the *Arbitrage Pricing Theory* (APT) which states that the reward of the investment risk in a security depends on several macroeconomic factors according to *Ross* (1976). A clear identification of these factors is not given, though.

As stated previously, when valuing an asset the expected return has to be compared to today's best alternative investments. In this respect, the earnings of a comparable investment serve as an indicator to estimate the cost of debt.[214] On the basis of the three variables, namely current interest level, default risk and tax advantage, it is

---

[211] See Koller et al. (2005), p. 302.
[212] See Koller et al. (2005) pp. 303.
[213] For further details of how to estimate an asset beta coefficient, please refer to Koller et al. (2005), pp. 312-321.
[214] See Koller et al. (2005), p. 326.

generally possible to estimate the cost of after-tax debt.[215] Therefore the cost of after-tax debt represents the average return that the asset has to generate in order to repay debts.

3.1.1.4 Critical acclaim

Following the previous section, asset valuation is based on discounting expected future free cash flows using a fair risk premium to account for uncertainty. The traditional DCF valuation approach postulates holding the discount rate constant over time. In fact, the uncertainty of predicting free cash flows properly typically rises over time. The standard valuation approach, however, does not capture any variations of the occurrence from any input parameter (e.g. carbon prices), so that as a consequence the value fluctuates. In fact, assuming uncertain future free cash flows causes that the respective asset's value is determined by a probability distribution, whereas the average of the distribution values represents the expected value. The corresponding dispersion of the expected asset value is denoted as standard deviation.[216]

Hence, to cover as many future scenarios as possible for the development of an asset's free cash flow, it is alternative method required compared to the standard DCF approach.[217] Monte Carlo based simulation models are able to cope with uncertainties and therefore even with this shortcoming of the traditional DCF valuation approach. Thus, we will present the theoretical concept of Monte Carlo simulations to appraise investments under uncertainty in the following section.

---

[215] See Damodaran (1996), pp. 62-63.
[216] See Meyer (2005), p. 57.
[217] See Kulatilaka et al. (1999), p. 191.

3.1.2 Monte Carlo simulation

3.1.2.1 Background

While the application of the Monte Carlo method is used in physics whenever no analytical solution exists, the application in finance is similar.[218] Since existing traditional techniques for capital investment decisions do no not cope with uncertainty properly, *Hertz* (1964) suggested adapting the simulation approach for risk analysis purposes.[219] In comparison to other methods of decision analyses like scenario or sensitivity analysis, the application of a Monte Carlo simulation is more powerful. The latter allows computing outcomes as a function of multiple uncertain variables, whereas the individual risky parameter is expressed as a probability distribution.[220] The virtue of a simulation approach is, therefore, to gain insights in the range of outcomes by varying input parameters.[221] Traditional valuation tools are not able to provide this information.[222]

Compared to traditional mathematical methods, the Monte Carlo simulation relies on random digits to conduct randomized experiments, whereas its outcomes serve for estimating the approximated values.[223] The issue can be described as follows: Assume the following values $v_1, v_2, ..., v_n$ which have to be determined and are attributed to a general problem of ϕ :[224]

$$(3.8) \qquad \phi = \{v_1, v_2, .., v_n\}$$

If (3.8) holds, then the corresponding probability area to equation denotes to (n, σ, p), whereas n, σ, and p represent the number of results, the standard deviation of the occurrences and the probability which refers to n respectively. Defining randomized digits $a_1, a_2, ..., a_n$ to the this probability space ϕ allows an estimation of $v_1, v_2, ..., v_n$.

---

[218] See Benninga (2008), p. 597.
[219] See Hertz (1964), p. 105.
[220] See Spinney/ Watkins (1996), p. 157
[221] See Hertz (1964), p. 105.
[222] See Hertz (1964), p. 105.
[223] See Lehmann (1966), p. 431.
[224] See Lehmann (1966), p. 432.

3.1.2.2 Procedure

Yet, the applicability depends on the ability to detect sensitive project variables and grasp their surrounding uncertainties. As noted, the merit of a Monte Carlo simulation is to study unlimited random scenarios that are in line with the assumptions set regarding the risky variables. Parameters which influence the profitability of the respective asset significantly by even a small variation of the initial value are denoted as risky variables. As a consequence, the selection process should be based on sensitivity analysis to include relevant variables. However, a trade-off exists between accuracy and validity. The increase of total numbers of probability distributions employed in a random scenario goes along with higher risks of results that are biased. This is due to the complexity to assert correlated variables properly. Therefore a good model focuses on relevant parameters and should be able to postulate the relationship between input variables.[225]

In general, a Monte Carlo simulation includes the following steps:[226]

(1) the identification of key uncertain variables that drive the economic advantage of the respective asset;

(2) allocations of proper probability distributions which best explain the uncertain variables;

(3) the examination of the existence of any significant relationships among the uncertain input variables;

(4) simulation runs; and

(5) the depiction of model results by probability distribution.

Thus, the procedure of a Monte Carlo simulation is similar to an experiment, as for each model input parameter random variables are drawn that take the respective risks on the asset appraisal into account. The advantage of Monte Carlo experiments is the ability to analyze risk even for complex interdependencies of uncertain variables, whereas the mathematical expression and solution by hand is limited.[227]

Besides, instead of forecasting the value of an uncertain parameter precisely, the methodology presumes that the real value is part of the associated probability

---

[225] See Savvides (1994), p. 4.
[226] See Spinney/ Watkins (1996), p. 158; Savvides (1994); Hacura et al. (2001).
[227] See Spinney/ Watkins (1996), p. 158.

distribution and its respective limits.[228] After having allocated the probability distribution for each identified uncertain variable, the respective interactions have to be explored before running the computer experiment. Indeed, this is especially true for detecting significant correlations between uncertain variables, whereas uncorrelated variables are simulated separately.[229]

We will keep this in mind for the following, however, the upcoming section shows first of how to implement this procedures for general purposes.

3.1.2.3 Implementation

The key element of this method is to simulate the uncertainty of risky model variables by generating random variables that follows a probability distribution.[230] The latter takes the stochastic behavior of the risky variable into account. This computer-based simulation experiment aligns each risky variable with a specific value depending on the risk profile chosen for the specific risky parameter.[231] In addition, the simulation allows the outcome to be summarized and analyzed to the individual need of the user.[232]

As a consequence the model computes for each run, n, a present value. Hence, the expected value of a simulation $E[V]$ is equal to the mean of the overall runs, or in other words, to all present values. Hence, formula (3.9) reads:

$$(3.9) \qquad E[V] = \mu = \frac{1}{n} \sum_{i=1}^{N} V_i(0)$$

In addition, the simulation allows computing the standard deviation of the expected present value. Hence, the latter represents the risk associated with the expected present asset value and allows generation assets to be located within a μ-σ space.

---

[228] See Savvides (1994), pp. 7-8.
[229] See Savvides (1994), p. 11.
[230] See Meyer (2005), p. 61.
[231] See Meyer (2005), p. 61.
[232] See Hacura et al. (2001), p. 551.

Due to the law of large numbers, the asset value - as shown in the aforementioned formula - is approximated by the simulation-based expected value, whereas the corresponding assets variance, σ_V^2 is equal to:

(3.10) $\qquad \sigma_V^2 = \frac{1}{n} \sum_{i=1}^{N} (V_i - E[V])^2$

In doing so, the term stochastic convergence describes the convergence of sample averages for increasing sample size. Therefore, the random error of the simulation, σ_ε, of the average of n observations amounts to:[233]

(3.11) $\qquad \sigma_\varepsilon = \frac{1}{\sqrt{n}} \cdot \sigma_V$

According to equation (3.11), in order to reduce the random error of the simulation, it is necessary to increase the total runs by n.[234]

3.1.2.4 Critical acclaim

Even though computer simulation experiments seem more powerful relative to other analytical approaches, the application requires accuracy to avoid defective results.[235] Existing literature in this field mainly points out concerns regarding the specification of the probability distribution, interactions of input parameters as well as the complexity. Therefore this section presents critical remarks on the execution of Monte Carlo simulations in the existing literature, but demonstrates also the virtue of this technique particularly for valuing power plant technologies.

Following *Lewellen/ Long* (1972) investment analysis based on simulation technique should solely rely on the risk-free interest rate as a *discount rate*.[236] Otherwise, discounting simulated cash flows by the asset's cost of capital would lead to an overestimation of the respective asset's risks causing an underestimation of the present

---

[233] See Naylor (1971), p. 24.
[234] See Naylor (1971), p. 24.
[235] See Spinney/ Watkins (1996), p. 159.
[236] See Lewellen/ Long (1972), p. 22; also Cox/ Siebert (2006).

value. Besides, they remark that an ordinary investment appraisal by computing assets' present values lead to moderately higher asset values in comparison to simulations.[237]

In fact, the simulation computes for each run a single present value for an expected cash flow. Since simulated variables follow predefined distributions, the probability of each present value computation is equal to the allocated probability distributions. As a consequence the simulation already takes the uncertainty into account, so that the incorporation of a firm- specific discount rate would cause a double count of risk.[238]

In addition, the aforementioned academics point out that the simulation approach does not allow an explicit differentiation between pervasive and non-pervasive risks.[239] Indeed, according to portfolio theory capital markets appraise systematic risk solely by a so-called risk premium, whereas an asset's individual risk can be eliminated through diversification.[240] In our opinion, however, this argument holds for valuing and selecting securities. For this purpose, we question whether the market portfolio is the proper benchmark to quantify the risk premium for assets in general. According to *Chen et al.* (1986) there are other systematic risk factors, like interest rates, inflation and industrial production which drive asset returns beyond the market portfolio.[241] In addition, *Sadorsky* (2001) as well as *Boyer/ Filion* (2007) show that, amongst others, crude oil and natural gas prices are significant sources of risk for energy stocks. Since we look at the electricity business only, systematic risk factors are rather regulative or commodity based like oil price change (*Ferson/ Harvey*, 1994). Hence, the adjusted energy market portfolio has to cover available generation technologies and their respective kinds of fuels. Increasing the amount of analyzed power plant technologies captured in the simulation enables a valid comparison, even though there is a lack of distinction between the kinds of risks.

To avoid a double count of risk, however, the simulation model will rely on a discount rate which is equal to the risk-free interest rate. In fact, many of the concerns mentioned in the literature refer to the 1970s. However, thanks to the technology development the applicability of this method has been improved which means exploring investment risk analysis easier than in the past.[242]

---

[237] See Lewellen/ Long (1972), p. 24.
[238] See Lewellen/ Long (1972), p. 22; Robicheck/ Meyers (1966); Cohen/ Elton (1967); Van Horne (1966).
[239] See Lewellen/ Long (1972), p. 29.
[240] Please refer to the following section for further details.
[241] See Chen et al. (1986), p. 383.
[242] See Spinney/ Watkins (1996), p. 158.

Conducting a Monte Carlo simulation to appraise an asset leads not only to the respective expected value but also to the corresponding standard deviation of the asset's expected value. The resulting risk-return trade-off can be analyzed using portfolio theory concepts. As a consequence, the following section introduces the respective theoretical framework.

3.2 Portfolio theory: Model of Markowitz (1952)

This section deals with the introduction of theories to identify efficient portfolios. First we describe briefly the approach of *Markowitz* (1952), the pioneer in this type of research field, who received the Nobel Prize in 1990. His theory aims to pick securities by optimizing a risk-return trade-off. The approach is not necessarily limited to financial stocks, though. Instead it has become a popular instrument in different business fields like strategic management.[243] However, the application to generation assets will be explained in the following sections. In addition, we introduce the latest alternative developments of asset management and demonstrate that Markowitz's model seems most suitable as a theoretical framework for this thesis.

3.2.1 Assumptions

Markowitz's theory for portfolio selection requires certain assumptions regarding the investment behavior: Firstly, the theory is based on the assumption of *nonsatiation*. Since investors prefer a portfolio with higher expected normal distributed returns compared to an otherwise identical portfolio, they aspire to achieve higher levels of wealth than lower levels of wealth.[244] Therefore investors should "maximize discounted expected returns" (*Markowitz*, 1952, p. 77). Secondly, investors avoid risk or, in other words, are *risk-averse*. While investors aim to grasp for expected returns, the corresponding variance of returns should be treated as non desirable.[245] Thus, an investor confronted with the decision of portfolio choice goes for the one characterized by the lowest standard deviation of the expected return.[246] In addition, risk-aversion describes the attitude to risk of the respective investor and implies he is unwilling to

---

[243] Seitz (1990); Helfat (1988); Herbst (1990).
[244] See Sharpe et al. (1999), p. 141.
[245] See Markowitz (1952), p.77.
[246] See Sharpe et al. (1999), p. 142.

take fair bets. The latter is equal to a game "that has an expected payoff of zero" (*Sharpe et al.*, 1999, p. 142).

Thirdly, in order to identify optimal portfolios a measurement of relative happiness is needed. Therefore, the degree of happiness due to certain activities is geometrically expressed as *utility*. This function is based on the presumption that satisfying activities cause positive utility, whereas dissatisfying activities cause negative utility. Even though people differ in their preferences "they are presumed to be rational and to allocate their resources in order to maximize their own utilities" (*Sharpe et al.*, 1999, p. 142). As a consequence, the portfolio selection process aims to maximize the expected utility which depends on the expected terminal wealth.[247] The relationship is covered by the "investor's utility of wealth function" (*Sharpe et al.*, 1999, p. 142) which depends on the level of wealth and utility. The assumption of *nonsatiation* leads to a positive slope of the function. Yet, the function is concave, though, considering the fact that the utility of the investor declines for an increasing level of wealth.[248]
However, the functional relationship of wealth and utility does not directly assist to identify optimal portfolios. Instead, this functional property has to be transferred to the portfolios risk-return trade-off. Otherwise, the investor's decision does not necessarily lead to holding an optimal portfolio. Hence, a so-called *indifference curve* that plots all risk-return combinations implying the same amount of investor's utility is needed.[249]

Assuming the investor's indifference curves are given and the efficient frontier of the available portfolios is known, the investor's optimal portfolio is clearly determined by the tangent point of the indifference curve and the efficient frontier. The composition of these portfolios leads to holding an efficient portfolio on the one hand and maximizes the investor's utility on the other. Therefore, the portfolio is optimal in comparison to the observable portfolios on the market. [250] Irrespective of the investor's risk attitude, we will show now of how to derive the efficient set of portfolios.

---

[247] See Sharpe et al. (1999), p. 142.
[248] See Sharpe et al. (1999), p. 144.
[249] See Sharpe et al. (1999), p. 144.
[250] See Sharpe et al. (1999), p. 173-174.

3.2.2 Notation

The algebra expected returns and standard deviations become cumbersome, as soon as more than two assets are evaluated. To simplify the computations, this section introduces the analytical notation, as calculations are based on matrix linear algebra. Throughout this chapter we use the following notation: There are N risky assets, whereupon each has an expected return of $E(r_i)$ equally μ_i. The matrix μ_i is the column vector of expected returns of these assets:[251]

$$(3.12) \qquad \mu_i = E(r) = \begin{bmatrix} E(r_1) \\ E(r_2) \\ \vdots \\ E(r_n) \end{bmatrix}$$

In addition, S denotes the $N \times N$ variance-covariance matrix:

$$(3.13) \qquad S = \begin{bmatrix} \sigma_{11} & \sigma_{12} & \cdots & \sigma_{1N} \\ \sigma_{21} & \sigma_{22} & \cdots & \sigma_{2N} \\ \vdots & \vdots & \ddots & \vdots \\ \sigma_{N1} & \sigma_{N2} & \cdots & \sigma_{NN} \end{bmatrix}$$

A portfolio of risky assets is a column vector w_i whose respective weights equal to one:

$$(3.14) \qquad w_i = \begin{bmatrix} w_1 \\ w_2 \\ \vdots \\ w_n \end{bmatrix}, \qquad \sum_{i=1}^{N} w_i = 1$$

Here, each share w_i represents the proportion of the portfolio invested in risky asset i. After having introduced the analytical notation, we will present the portfolio selection process in the upcoming section.

---

[251] See Benninga (2008), pp. 261-262.

3.2.3 Portfolio selection

Assuming an investor has already formed an opinion regarding the future performance of available securities, he is faced with the issue of how to compose the respective portfolio. According to *Markowitz* (1952) the typical investment behavior seeks to maximize returns by avoiding risks. As the objectives are opposed to each other, the investor has to balance this trade-off when making the investment decision.[252] To solve this trade-off, *Markowitz* (1952) advises making use of the so-called *expected return-variance of return (henceforth:* μ_i, σ_i).[253]

The expected return of a portfolio is determined by the weighted sum of the returns of the assets which are part of the respective portfolio. Since the asset returns are uncertain, they represent random variables. From an economic perspective, the asset returns measure "the potential reward associated with any portfolio" , (*Sharpe et al.*, 1999, p. 140). In contrast, the standard deviations of the expected returns represent the level of risk for these portfolios. To compute the variance of the portfolio's expected return, the sum of the product of each assets' variance and square weight plus the co-movement between each pair of assets are taken.[254]

To solve the conflicting objectives of an investor, we will present the analytical computation for the portfolio mean and variance in the general case of N risky assets. The specific proportion of asset i within the portfolio is denoted by w_i. Therefore the expected return of a portfolio, μ_{PF}, is the sum of the weighted average of the expected returns for the individual assets, μ_i :[255]

$$(3.15) \qquad \mu_{PF} = \sum_{i=1}^{N} w_i \cdot \mu_i = w^T \cdot \mu_i$$

whereas w^T represents the transpose of the portfolio weights matrix.

The measure of risk is the standard deviation of the expected return which is the square root of the portfolio variance, σ_{PF}^2 :[256]

---

[252] See Sharpe et al. (1999), p. 139.
[253] See Markowitz (1952), p. 87.
[254] See Markowitz (1952), p. 81.
[255] See Markowitz (1952), p. 81.
[256] See Markowitz (1952), p. 81.

$$(3.16) \qquad \sigma_{PF}^2 = \sum_{i=1}^{N}(w_i)^2\sigma_i^2 + 2\sum_{i=1}^{N}\sum_{\substack{j=1 \\ i\neq j}}^{N} w_i w_j \sigma_{ij}$$

where σ_{ij} denote the covariance between the returns of asset i and asset j. The covariance is a function of the standard deviations and the correlation of the respective asset returns. While the covariance shows how the returns of asset i and asset j relate to each other, the correlation coefficient measures the strength of the linear relation between these assets in the interval of $[-1;+1]$.[257]

In order to make use of nifty matrix notations, we refer to the afore defined variance-covariance S. Therefore, variance equation (3.16) can be transformed to:

$$(3.17) \qquad \sigma_{PF}^2 = w^T \cdot S \cdot w$$

After having estimated the expected return, μ_i, and the corresponding level of risk, σ_i, for each feasible portfolio, an investor's decision should be based on the "relative magnitudes of these two parameters" (*Sharpe et al.* 1999, p.140). As a consequence, the $\mu_i - \sigma_i$ rule leads to choosing portfolios that are efficient and therefore dominate the other available portfolio combinations.[258] In addition, applying the rule "implies diversification for a wide range of μ_i, σ_i" (*Markowitz*, 1952, p. 89). Even though an investment in a single asset might turn out to be better off in terms of higher return and lower risk compared to a diversified portfolio, this will not hold for taking a large number of securities into account. In that case, following a $\mu_i - \sigma_i$ investment strategy will result in efficient and diversified portfolios.[259] An investment in many assets, however, does not necessarily go along with a lower variance of the portfolio return. In fact, in order to realize diversification effects an investor should hold securities from firms operating in different industries. In this case, the covariance between these respective assets is lower than securities belonging to the same industry, as they are typically competing in similar markets. Hence, they are faced with similar economic risks.[260]

---

[257] See Benninga (2008), pp. 242-243. Within this thesis we refer to the correlation coefficient of Pearson.
[258] See Markowitz (1952), p. 82.
[259] See Markowitz (1952), p. 89.
[260] See Markowitz (1952), p. 89.

The issue arises of how an investor should choose a portfolio out of a set of feasible portfolios. The *efficient set theorem* aims to select an efficient portfolio which dominates all obtainable portfolio combinations (μ, σ) on the respective market. Hence, an investor should choose those portfolios with minimum risk in terms of standard deviation for a given level of return. Alternatively, for a portfolio which leads to a maximum expected return for a given level of risk.

Analytically, the general conditions for stochastic dominance of two portfolios i and j are:[261]

(1) $\mu_i \geq \mu_j$

(2) $\sigma_i \leq \sigma_j$

(3) $(\mu_i, \sigma_i) \neq (\mu_j, \sigma_j)$

The third condition postulates that portfolios i and j are not identical.

3.2.4 Analytical determination of the global minimum variance portfolio

To identify the portfolio with the lowest risk under a given universe of assets, the variance equation (3.17) acts as the objective function, whereas the composition of the *global minimum variance portfolio* (GMVP) is determined by the first derivative. Since the GMVP is characterized by the lowest variance among all feasible portfolios, it is located on the *efficient frontier*. If we assume that N assets are available with a variance-covariance matrix S, then the portfolio shares $w_{GMVP} = (w_{GMVP,1}, ..., w_{GMVP,N})$ solve the constrained minimization problem allowing short sales:[262]

(3.18a) $min\ \sigma^2_{GMVP} = w^T_{GMVP} \cdot S \cdot w_{GMVP}$

s.t. $\sum_{i=1}^{N} w_{GMVP} = 1$

Using Lagrange's multipliers, equation (3.18a) can be transformed to:

---

[261] See Markowitz (1952), p. 82; Sharpe et al. (1999), p. 171.
[262] See Merton (1972), p. 1852.

(3.18b) $L\left(w_{GMVP}, \lambda\right) = w_{GMVP}^T \cdot S \cdot w_{GMVP} + \lambda\left(w_{GMVP}^T \cdot 1 - 1\right) = 0$

Then, the first order conditions from the optimization problem can be expressed in matrix notion as:

(3.18c) $\dfrac{\partial L\left(w_{GMVP}, \lambda\right)}{\partial w_{GMVP}} = 2 \cdot S \cdot w_{GMVP} + \lambda \cdot 1 = 0$

(3.18d) $\dfrac{\partial L\left(w_{GMVP}, \lambda\right)}{\partial \lambda} = w_{GMVP}^T \cdot 1 - 1 = 0$

Rearranging equation (3.18c) leads to:

(3.18e) $w_{GMVP} = -\dfrac{1}{2} \cdot \lambda \cdot S^{-1} \cdot 1$

Next, multiplying both sides by 1^T and using (3.18d) to solve for λ:

(3.18f) $1 = w_{GMVP}^T \cdot 1$

(3.18g) $1 = w_{GMVP}^T \cdot 1 = -\dfrac{1}{2} \cdot \lambda \cdot 1^T \cdot S^{-1} \cdot 1$

(3.18h) $\lambda = -2 \cdot \dfrac{1}{1^T \cdot S^{-1} \cdot 1}$

Finally, substituting the value for λ back into (3.18e) to solve for w_{GMVP}:[263]

(3.18i) $w_{GMVP} = -\dfrac{1}{2} \cdot (-2) \cdot \dfrac{1}{1^T \cdot S^{-1} \cdot 1} \cdot S^{-1} \cdot 1 = \dfrac{S^{-1} \cdot 1}{1^T \cdot S^{-1} \cdot 1}$

(3.18j) $w_{GMVP} = \left\{w_{GMVP,1}, w_{GMVP,2}, \ldots, w_{GMVP,N}\right\} = \dfrac{1 \cdot S^{-1}}{1 \cdot S^{-1} \cdot 1^T}$

According to equation (3.18j) the GMVP formula does not require the expected return as input parameter to determine portfolio weights. In other words, the composition of the efficient GMVP can be derived irrespectively of the corresponding asset's yield.

---

[263] See Merton (1972), pp. 1852-1853.

Consequently, the corresponding mean and risk of the minimal variance portfolio are given by the following equations:

(3.19) $\qquad \mu_{GMVP} = w_{GMVP} \cdot E[r]$

(3.20) $\qquad \sigma^2_{GMVP} = w_{GMVP} \cdot S \cdot w^T_{GMVP}$

The optimization leads to the composition of the GMVP with the lowest variance of all observable portfolios on the market. Therefore, among the universe of assets there is no portfolio which dominates the GMVP. Hence, the GMVP is located on the *efficient frontier*. Figure 3.2 depicts the *efficient frontier* which starts from the location of the GMVP. However, another analytical approach is required in order to derive the whole efficient frontier. As a consequence, within the following section we will introduce a method to identify this efficient set of portfolios.

Figure 3.2 Feasible portfolios and the efficient frontier

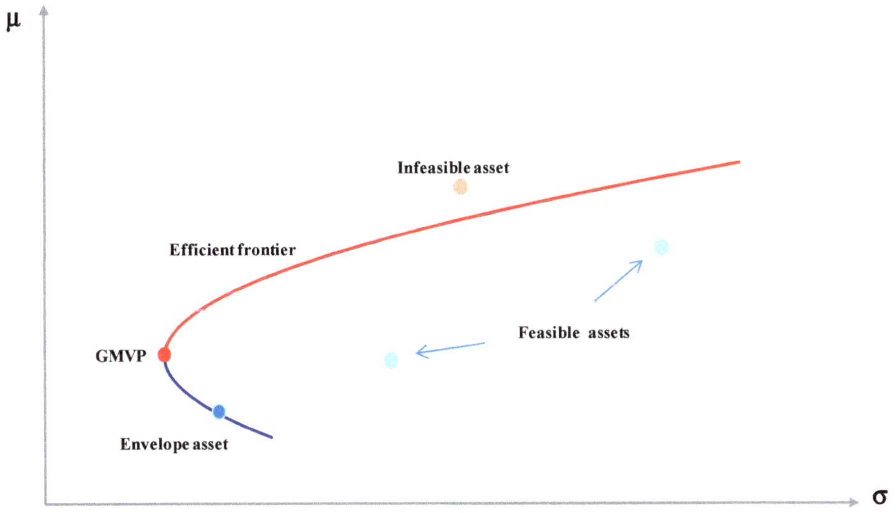

Source: According to Benninga (2008), p. 263.

3.2.5 Analytical determination of the efficient frontier

The identification of efficient portfolios allows spanning a frontier where all efficient assets of the market are located. The latter is required in particular not only to explore the efficient composition of generation portfolios but also to quantify their degree of efficiency. Therefore, in general, the analytical determination of an efficient portfolio for a given level of return is equal to:[264]

(3.21) $$min\,\sigma_{PF}^2 = w^T \cdot S \cdot w$$

s.t.

(3.22) $$\sum_{i=1}^{N} w^T \cdot \mu_i = \overline{\mu}$$

(3.23) $$\sum_{i=1}^{N} w_i = 1$$

whereas $\overline{\mu}$ denotes the fixed rate of return for the respective portfolio.

Following the approach of *Black* (1972), an efficient portfolio can be identified by a weighted combination of two efficient portfolios.[265] Generally speaking, any two efficient portfolios and their corresponding convex combinations denote the efficient frontier.

Hence, if we assume two efficient portfolios, x and y, with their respective portfolio weights of $w_{x,i} = [w_{x,1}, w_{x,2}, ..., w_{x,n}]$ and $w_{y,i} = [w_{y,1}, w_{y,2} ..., w_{y,n}]$ as well as a constant factor a then the portfolio Z turns out to be efficient:[266]

(3.24) $$z = aw_x + (1-a)w_y = \begin{bmatrix} aw_{x,1} + (1-a)w_{y,1} \\ aw_{x,2} + (1-a)w_{y,2} \\ \vdots \\ aw_{x,n} + (1-a)w_{y,n} \end{bmatrix}$$

---

[264] See Black (1972), pp. 447-448.
[265] See Black (1972), p. 447.
[266] See Benninga (2008), pp. 264-265.

This allows determining the whole efficient frontier by varying the constant a in order to gain convex combinations. The mean and the variance of the efficient portfolios x and y are denoted by $\{E(r_x),\sigma_x^2\}$ and $\{E(r_y),\sigma_y^2\}$. If equation (3.24) holds, then the expected return of the portfolio Z is equal to:

(3.25) $E(r_z) = aE(r_x) + (1-a)E(r_y)$

Ultimately, the corresponding variance of the efficient portfolio Z amounts to:

(3.26) $\sigma_z^2 = a^2\sigma_x^2 + (1-a)^2\sigma_y^2 + 2a(1-a)\sigma_{xy}$

3.2.6 Critical acclaim

As explained in the previous section, the approach of *Markowitz* (1952) requires for the optimization of investor's risk-return trade-off, future expectations regarding the returns and the corresponding covariance matrix of all assets which determine the respective opportunity set on the market. Hence, the shares of the optimal portfolio are based on the analytical computation of the risk-return trade-off. The optimization procedure, however, does not include any condition to ensure that the portfolio results are in fact economically intuitive.[267]

Indeed, optimal portfolio shares arc often not in line with the normal behavior of an investor. Instead the optimization might recommend building up extreme investment positions within a specific asset class and moreover results turn out not to be stable. Specifically, the optimal portfolio allocation might suggest holding short positions of specific assets which is not necessarily desired.[268]

Following *Black/ Litterman* (1991) the combination of individual return forecasts and neutral benchmark returns leads to portfolio shares that turn out to be more stable and economic intuitive.[269] In their opinion, the optimization based on historical returns which are used as an indicator of future returns does not result in promising

---

[267] See Drobetz (2002), p. 4.
[268] See Drobetz (2002), pp. 5-6; Michaud (1998); Viebig et al. (2009).
[269] Black/ Litterman (1991); Black/ Litterman (1992).

portfolios.[270] To determine the benchmark returns they suggest relying on a reverse optimization of an equilibrium model. The application of the CAPM, however, presumes a market capitalization of the individual assets. Thus, the *Black/ Litterman* model seems suitable for asset management of securities rather than for power generation technologies. The latter are neither traded on markets nor do market price data exist. Yet, the virtue of the *Black/ Litterman* model is that portfolio shares can be adopted depending on the subjective return forecast in relation to the equilibrium model.

To make use of this idea, the forthcoming portfolio optimization will take constraints into account to gain results, which are stable and not only economically intuitive but also technically feasible. In addition and that is the most important point to rely on the traditional mean-variance approach: The latter turns out to deliver at least relatively good results even when returns are not normally distributed and investor's utility function is not quadratic.[271]

3.3 Model of Roques et al. (2008)

The academic contribution by *Roques, Newbery* and *Nuttall*, which was published in *Energy Economics* in 2008, inspired and motivated us to conduct research in this specific field. As a consequence, the following sections serve to introduce the portfolio approach of the aforementioned academics, which derive optimal generation portfolios for base load technologies in the UK market. After having presented their methodology, we depict the results and discuss the respective economic implications. Finally, we demonstrate in the critical acclaim the need for a comprehensive portfolio analysis. Against this background, we discuss substantial extensions which shed light on the issue to opt for an efficient fuel mix by a cross-national approach.

---

[270] See Viebig et al. (2009), p. 728.
[271] See Elton et al. (2003), p. 232.

3.3.1 Methodology

Roques et al. (2008) study base load technologies to explore optimal power plant portfolios from a *private investor's* perspective in liberalized markets.[272] Since the authors do not explicitly define their understanding of a "private investor", the expression has to be seen against the background of liberalized electricity markets. Formerly state-owned utilities have changed to free business enterprises, which are even traded on stock exchanges.[273] As support for the proper interpretation, the authors use the terminology *private company* as a synonym at the end of their paper.[274]

Therefore, from a theoretical perspective, an investor opts for a rate of return depending on the level of risk which has to be taken. As a consequence, instead of focusing on *power plant costs* to determine an optimal portfolio, they rely on *power plant returns*.[275] This is in line with common investment decisions on competitive markets, like European electricity markets are nowadays, as the respective decisions should in general be based on expected returns. However, the authors do not apply *return* in the classical financial meaning by computing the relation of profit or loss of an investment to the capital employed. In fact, they calculate the *expected net present value* per MW capacity to each technology to measure the returns of an investment in power plants.[276] The discounted cash flow model of *Roques et al.* (2008) comprises of three base load technologies, namely a combined cycle gas turbine (CCGT), a coal and a nuclear power plant which represent state of the art technologies in the UK

On this basis, *Roques et al.* (2008) focus on *market risks* in terms of fluctuating electricity, fuel and emission price levels. While cost and technical parameters are based on UK market data and do not change over time, prices are derived from "UK historical time series of quarter-ahead fuel and power prices from January 2001 to August 2005"(*Roques et al.*, 2008, p. 1836). As a consequence, these risky input parameters are represented by normally distributed random variables. Hence, the Monte Carlo simulation of power plants' free cash flows leads to expected net present values for the specific power plant technology.[277]

---

[272] See Roques et al. (2008), p. 1832.
[273] See Dalebroux (2008), p. 20.
[274] See Roques et al. (2008), p. 1847.
[275] See Roques et al. (2008), p. 1832.
[276] See Roques et al. (2008), p. 1834.
[277] See Roques et al. (2008), p. 1836.

In contrast, the level of risk is determined by the standard deviation of the expected net present value per MW generation capacity. In addition, the correlation between the returns of the sample power plants is constituted between the NPV distributions of the respective power plants.[278]

To analyze the power plant technologies *Roques et al.* (2008) rely on the theoretical framework from *Markowitz* (1952). In this context, the authors not only derive the efficient frontier for the respective generation assets but also for optimal portfolios. The latter depends on the risk attitude of the individual investor. By applying a standard mean-variance utility function, the degree of risk aversion is measured by Lambda.[279] To determine this coefficient for various types of investors, the authors distinguish between low, middle and high risk aversion.

3.3.2 Results and implication

As stated in the previous section the simulation technique serves to analyze base load generation portfolios for private investors. In particular, the methodology allows the determination of the impact of electricity, fuel and carbon prices on the return of coal, gas and nuclear power plants.[280] Therefore, *Roques et al.* (2008) distinguish between three different cases.

The first case abstracts the dependencies between fuel, carbon and electricity prices. As a consequence, the computation assumes uncorrelated risky price parameters. According to the respective results, the efficient frontier comprises only a fuel mix of gas and nuclear base load technologies. However, coal power plants are not an integral part of this portfolio set.[281]

In contrast, the second case takes the correlations between electricity, fuel and carbon prices into account. The degree of the corresponding dependency is empirically derived from UK market data in the period from 2001 to 2005. As it turns out that electricity prices and gas prices are highly correlated in the UK, the standard deviation of the expected net present value from gas diminish rapidly compared to the first case. Furthermore, coal plants are now better off in terms of the riskiness compared to

---

[278] See Roques et al. (2008), p. 1834.
[279] See Roques et al. (2008), p. 1840.
[280] See Roques et al. (2008), p. 1847.
[281] See Roques et al. (2008), p. 1841.

nuclear power plants. This is mainly due to the inverse relation between coal and carbon prices (-0.42).[282]

The last case includes not only the correlation between fuel, electricity and CO_2 prices but also the risk aversion of the investor. The latter could be derived from referring to ex post returns from financial stock market data.[283] According to the findings of the authors, "pure portfolios of CCGT plants" (*Roques et al.*, 2008, p. 1842) turn out to be optimal for risk seeking investors independent of the strength of the correlation between the risky parameters. However, a higher coefficient of risk aversion makes mixed portfolios for investors more attractive. Assuming an average correlation coefficient of 0.5, the investors' optimal portfolio mainly consists of gas, coal and nuclear plants with respective shares of 60%, 20% and 20%.[284] For lower correlation coefficients as the aforementioned, the share of gas and nuclear power increases. Finally, the authors' results imply risk-averse investors should accumulate the share of coal plants in their respective fuel mix.[285]

3.3.3 Critical acclaim

Roques et al. (2008) provide, to the best of our knowledge, the first work that deals with portfolio analysis for power plant technologies taking the perspective of a private investor in liberalized markets. The latter implies a change of perspective from *cost* to *returns* which is appropriate in competitive markets. Even though we approve the work of *Roques et al.* (2008), there are a few things that limit - from our point of view - the explanatory power of their model. Since their discounted cash flow model covers only common base load technologies, the question arises as to whether three different power plant technologies (namely, coal, gas and nuclear) represent the generation mix of a utility firm properly. Obviously, the share of base load generation technologies typically disproportionately characterizes a power plant park due to the large size of the individual generation units. Therefore, the composition of base load technologies should be carefully analyzed. However, the negligence of peak and mid-merit plants leads to a partial portfolio analysis instead of exploring a comprehensive analysis.

---

[282] Roques et al. (2008), p. 1837. Please note, the times series for carbon prices covers the period from November 2004 to August 2005 only.
[283] See Roques et al. (2008), p.1842.
[284] See Roques et al. (2008), p. 1842.
[285] See Roques et al. (2008), p. 1842.

The fuel mix which is analyzed by *Roques et al.* (2008) comprises of coal, nuclear and gas power plants. Since the theoretical framework is based on finance theory, meaning the power plant technologies are regarded as assets, the issue arises of how many assets are required for a diversified portfolio? In addition, what is actually meant by diversification of electricity generation?[286] Obviously, the range of available assets traded on capital markets is not comparable to the technically restricted opportunity set of power plants.[287] The determination of diversification effects is similar, though. However, the exact number of assets needed to achieve a maximum benefit of diversification is controversial discussed in the existing literature. While *Francis* (1986) states that 10 or 15 different financial assets are required for a proper diversification, *Gup* (1983) concludes that about eight or nine assets are needed. In contrast, *Statman* (1987) distinguishes between a borrowing and a lending investor who should include at least 30 and 40 assets, respectively. The contributions in the finance literature underpin the need to include more than three assets like *Roques et al.* (2008) to analyze generation portfolios.

Besides, the model of *Roques et al.* (2008) focuses solely on the British power market which is a well-established liberalized electricity market. Utility firms adapt investors' behaviors in terms of diversifying their generation portfolios internationally.[288] The liberalization process within European electricity markets has enabled utilities to take stakes in foreign generation capacities. While diversification might be one explanation for *mergers and acquisition* (M&A) activities in the power sector, the entry in foreign markets as well as the benefit of a better regulative environment (i.e. the allocation of EU carbon permits in Eastern Europe) is another. Therefore, the generation portfolio analysis should incorporate the opportunity to build up generation capacity abroad, in order to explore how the level of risk and return change for generation portfolios, if utilities are allowed to invest internationally.[289]

In the academic literature different methods are suggested to incorporate the dependency of the risky variables.[290] As a consequence the methodology of how to consider respective dependencies from risky variables is particularly important, as the

---

[286] See Stirling (1994), p. 194.
[287] See Chapter 2.1.4.
[288] However, on capital markets investors tend to hold a disproportionately high amount of national stocks instead of making use of an international diversification (Home bias).
[289] This is related to the research about international diversification of Solnik (1974).
[290] Please refer to Chapter 3 for further details.

generation of random variables is normally linked to the approach chosen. Yet, *Roques et al.* (2008) do not clarify their approach.

Roques et al. (2008) set up a static model which means that the three power plant technologies are valued through their individual life-cycle instead of making use of the *going concern principle* of the respective utility firm. They presume that the feasibility set and therefore the generation assets remain constant. In fact, a utility firm which opts for an efficient fuel mix has to take its existing power plants and their respective age structure as well as new investments due to power plant replacements into account. Thus, the feasibility set consists of the existing generation capacity on the one hand and new generation capacity on the other hand. Since *Roques et al.* (2008) focus on the investor's perspective, they prescind any technical restrictions by deriving optimal portfolios. However, the application of portfolio analysis to generation assets should take technical restrictions into account in order to identify efficient portfolios which are technically feasible.

From an economic point of view, some results of *Roques et al.* (2008) are surprising. Since coal plant operators are faced with the issue of electricity, fuel and carbon price risks, it does not seem attractive for risk-averse investors. In addition, as evidenced by capital market data a power plant park which is dominated by coal plants exhibits a significant carbon price risk which goes along with higher equity costs due to significant carbon price premiums.[291]

In the upcoming sections we will present therefore our own theoretical portfolio approach to analyze generation assets.

3.4 Portfolio approach for power generation assets

This section is devoted to transferring the theoretical framework of *Markowitz* (1952) to generation assets and in addition to refining the model of *Roques et al.* (2008). Against this background, we present first the assumptions and the underlying analytical framework of our theoretical approach. Secondly, this section develops a performance ratio to determine the degree of efficiency for power plant assets. The ratio is meant to capture the *relative efficiency* by quantifying the distance to the efficient frontier for selected power plant technologies. This allows deducing

---

[291] See Bassen et al. (2010), p. 20.

implications to rebalance a power plant portfolio towards the efficient set over a specific period of time. Ultimately, we derive hypotheses which are tested by running simulation experiments.

3.4.1 Assumptions

Since the theoretical framework is based on the mean-variance concept, which was originally developed for selecting financial securities, this section aims to preliminary point out the assumptions and differences from generation assets in comparison to financial securities.[292]

(1) **Normal distribution**

The assumption of normally distributed returns leads to identify solutions which maximize the corresponding utility function of the investor.[293] Therefore, electricity, fuel and carbon prices are presumed to be normally distributed in order to generate normally distributed power plant returns. Indeed, depending on the sample period analyzed commodity prices follow a non-normal distribution.[294]

(2) **Efficient markets**

Classical portfolio theory excludes transaction costs, taxes and subsidies. In addition, market participants benefit from perfect information about all assets, which are traded on capital markets. In comparison to the latter, the market for power plant technologies is inefficient, as power plants are rather illiquid.[295]

(3) **Divisibility**

In the case of financial securities it is reasonable to assume divisibility which allows varying the share of a financial security within the portfolio between 0% and 100%. Yet, capital investments like power plants are typically indivisible due to their unit size.[296] However, the model presumes to build up generation capacity which is not restricted to a certain amount of capacity. Instead to

---

[292] See Berger et al. (2003), p. 83.
[293] See Sharpe et al. (1999), p. 142.
[294] Please refer to Chapter 2 for further details on the price behavior of goods.
[295] See Berger et al. (2003), p. 63.
[296] See Seitz (1990), p. 233

explore target generation portfolios of a utility firm, the model allows building up even small power plant units.

(4) Fungibility

The value of a fungible asset is a function of "amount, timing and certainty of expected cash flows" (*Berger et al.*, 2003, p. 83). In contrast, the location and fuel availability has an impact on the value of generation assets.[297] While renewable energies like wind power plants depend on wind supply and as a consequence are restricted to certain locations, this distinctive feature is not observable on capital markets. Therefore the operation of a wind park close to the coast pledges a higher wind yield in comparison to areas of low wind supply. Thus, the likelihood of generating stable cash flows is a function of the wind supply of the respective area.

(5) Return

Against the background of analyzing generation assets the term *return* diverges from the traditional meaning. Instead of computing the relation of profit (or loss) to capital employed, the literature distinguishes between *levelized costs* (i.e. *Berger et al.* 2003) or value per MW (MWh) to measure the return of a power plant technology. The distinction depends on the perspective of the analysis. While the minimization of generation costs is desirable from a social welfare perspective, the simulation model computes the expected present values per MW generation capacity for each power plant of the sample. This is in line with *Roques et al.* (2008), as it allows analyzing generation portfolios from a utility's perspective operating on liberalized electricity markets.

(6) Volatility

In contrast to the price variability of a commodity which refers to daily and seasonal fluctuations, the model takes solely price risks into account. Following *Roques et al.* (2006) investors are able to anticipate these price changes compared to long-term price trends.[298] Thus, the seasonal impact described in the aforementioned chapter of commodity prices is avoided. Following the efficient set theorem that postulates past prices are the best indicator to predict future price levels, the model input parameter is derived on an annual basis. Since commodities' returns might exhibit autocorrelation due to mean

---

[297] See Berger et al. (2003), p. 83.
[298] See Roques et al. (2006), p. 12.

reversion, the calculation of an annual volatility from daily data leads to underestimating the true price risks.[299]

(7) Technical constraints

Since existing power plants operate until their retirement, and as a consequence represent a specific share of the portfolio, they constrain the composition of generation portfolios to the amount of existing generation capacity. This allows identifying more realistic solutions in comparison to varying the optimization freely. In addition, technical grid restrictions are presumed to balance load in the optimization process. Following *Berger et al.* (2003) we presume, irrespective of the domestic power market, that each power plant is able to feed generated electricity into the network. Besides, the optimization process takes technical limitations in building up generation capacity into account. Specifically, the optimization is subject to an upper limit of wind and photovoltaic power plant capacity of 30% and 15% of total utility's generation capacity, respectively. In addition, at least 10% of generation capacity should refer to coal power plants providing base load.

Having introduced the distinction of the portfolio analysis for generation assets in comparison to financial securities, the following section proposes the analytical approach to identify efficient generation portfolios bearing the lowest standard deviation per MW generation capacity for a given level of return.

3.4.2 Analytical framework

The portfolio approach of *Markowitz* (1952) is used as a starting point. Therefore, we apply the optimization for financial securities to generation assets in terms of portfolio technologies. To identify efficient portfolios we minimize the variance equation of the expected net present value per MW capacity of utility's generation portfolio. Hence, the objective function is:

(3.27) $min \ \sigma_w^2 = w^T \cdot S \cdot w$

---

[299] See Kat/ Oomen (2006), p. 17.

$$\sigma_w^2 = [w_1, w_2, ..., w_N] \cdot \begin{bmatrix} \sigma_1^2 & \sigma_1\sigma_2\rho_{12} & \cdots & \sigma_1\sigma_N\rho_{1N} \\ \sigma_2\sigma_1\rho_{21} & \sigma_2^2 & \cdots & \sigma_2\sigma_N\rho_{2N} \\ \vdots & \vdots & \ddots & \vdots \\ \sigma_N\sigma_1\rho_{N1} & \cdots & \cdots & \sigma_N^2 \end{bmatrix} \cdot \begin{bmatrix} w_1 \\ w_2 \\ \cdots \\ w_N \end{bmatrix}$$

s.t.

(3.28) $$\sum_{i=1}^{N} w_i = c$$

(3.29) $$\sum_{i=1}^{N} w_i \mu_i = \overline{\mu}$$

(3.30) $$\sum_{i=1}^{N} w_i = 1 - c$$

(3.31) $$w_i \geq 0$$

The constraint (3.28) considers the fact that a utility firm already operates a power plant park so that the optimization is limited to the power plants, which have to be either replaced or additionally required to reach planned generation capacity in the target year. As a consequence the model distinguishes new generation capacity by replacements or investments. Existing power plants operate until the economic life of the respective power plant expires. Therefore c represents a column vector of the generation capacity from initial power plants operating beyond the target year.

Contrary to an optimization of risky financial assets, we exclude the opportunity of short sales (3.31). The assumption refers to the fact that power plants are rather illiquid compared to financial assets.[300] Hence, we exclude the opportunity of disinvestments. Therefore the relative share of a power plant for the portfolio is computed by dividing the capacity of the respective plant by total generation capacity in MW. The latter has to be positive and add up to one (3.30).

By varying the required return of the power generation park, the efficient path which minimizes the total risk can be identified. Thus, the optimization of equation (3.27) is subjected to the constraint of (3.29). Alternatively, as demonstrated in the previous section, the linear combination of two efficient generation portfolios span up the

---

[300] See Müller (2005), p. 71.

efficient frontier.[301] In fact, we rely on the latter approach to generate the efficient frontier within the model.

Depending on the risk attitude of a utility firm the optimal generation portfolio can be selected based on the results provided by the portfolio generation analysis.

3.4.3 Discount rates for power plant technologies

As stated in the previous section, power plants' cash flows should be discounted using the risk-free interest rate, if the valuation is based on a simulation technique.[302] This is due to the fact that the project risk is already captured within the simulation. Even though the empirical estimation of power plant technologies discount rates is beyond the objective of this thesis as well as inconsistent with the valuation technique chosen, this section briefly presents approaches discussed in the academic literature to derive power plants specific discount rates.

Following the original *Markowitz* model, each assets discount rate should reflect its systematic risks. As power plant technologies differ in their risk profiles, it is crucial for the investment appraisal to assess the respective risk.[303] Alongside, capital theory based discount rates should capture a fair market premium in order to take the systematic risks of the specific power plant technology into account.[304] Thus, the discount rate reflects the uncertainty of expected future cash flows of the power plant.[305] In contrast to the exposure of financial securities, however, the issue arises which risk factors of power plant investments are attributed as systematic. The pervasive risk of an asset is the amount of risk which cannot be diversified on the market. Hence, these sources of risk affect all generation technologies independent of their technical and operating characteristics. In general, the main risks which face generation capacity investments are threefold:[306]Against this background, the national economic activity which drives demand for electricity is one source. As a consequence, competitive power markets cause a price and volume risk for power plant operators. Secondly, any regulative change of the energy policy can affect the

---

[301] Please refer to section 3.2.5 for further details of a general approach to derive efficient portfolios.
[302] Please refer to section 3.1.2.4 for further details.
[303] See Awerbuch (1993), p. 24.
[304] See Awerbuch (1995), p. 52; also Qin (2007), p. 4.
[305] See Dimson (1989), p. 175.
[306] See IEA (2007), p. 24.

profitability of a power plant (i.e. EU ETS). Ultimately, energy sector investments are faced with jurisdictional risks. As stated in the theoretical part of the thesis, the *beta coefficient,* expressed as the sensitivity of a power plant returns in relation to the variance of the expected market returns, should be taken as risk measure.

The exposure of utility stocks has become a popular research field. While *Bower et al.* (1984) favor the Arbitrage Pricing Theory (APT) to estimate expected returns of utility stocks, other researchers base their theoretical considerations on the Capital Asset Pricing Model (CAPM). For instance, *Litzenberger et al.* (1980) estimate the cost of equity for a public utility company using the CAPM. *Riddick* (1992) shows that regulation reduces the systematic risk for a utility causing lower cost of equity capital. In contrast, *Dietrich/ Heckerman* (1983) find that regulatory treatment has only a small impact on systematic utility risk. Instead, sales, cost structures and growth expectations of the utility firm are attributed to be a systematic kind of risk. While the determination of risk factors for utility stocks has spurred extensive research particularly within the regulative area before liberalization, the estimation of power plant specific discount rates operating on competitive markets in the literature is rather scarce. Nevertheless, due to the capital intensity and irreversibility of a power plant, this investment seems riskier compared to an investment in a single utility stock.[307]

Following *Cahyadi et al.* (2003), the beta coefficient is a ratio between the covariance of the power plants' expected return with the average return of the market portfolio and the respective variance of the expected return. The results indicate that wind power plants are the most risky compared to alternative coal and gas power plant investment projects. This is due to the authors' linkage of commodity growth rates to the development of economic growth rates. According to their empirical results, irrespective of the economic scenario the coal price turns out to grow slower than the electricity price growth. This leads to positive yet small beta coefficient for coal power plants. Their study, however, does not include any affects from the emission regulation. Therefore the validity of the model is somehow limited. In contrast, the beta coefficient for gas power plant investment is negative, as gas prices are more sensitive to any change of the economic growth activity in comparison to electricity prices. This finding is in line with a study conducted by *Qin* (2007), which takes four major risk factors, namely carbon, oil, global and national economic activity into account to estimate a discount rate for a gas and wind power plant in Norway. In

---

[307] See Dimson (1989), p. 176.

addition, *Dimson* (1989) suggests a discount rate for nuclear power investments of at least 11% making coal power plants more attractive due to a lower cost of capital.

To sum up, the estimation of a fair discount rate for power plant technologies operating on competitive markets should capture the main systematic risks. In detail, the systematic risk of a power plant should be decomposed by referring to its operating cash flows through the plant's life cycle and reflect this against the change of the market return.

3.4.4 Relative efficiency of power plant portfolios

In order to shed light on efficient generation portfolios, it is necessary to define a performance ratio. To evaluate the performance of investment funds capital market theory distinguishes between three traditional approaches. All of them are based CAPM and evaluate the performance, *ex post*, to either the SML or the CML.

First the *Treynor's ratio ("reward-to-volatility")* makes use of the SML by computing the average excess return relative to the systematic risk factor of the specific asset.[308] This risk factor is a measure of sensitivity and indicates the risk of an asset relative to the market risk. Second, *Jensen's alpha* refers to the ex post SML as benchmark to measure vertical distance as performance ratio.[309] While *Jensen's alpha* and *Treynor's ratio* both rely on the systematic risk factor of the CAPM, *Sharpe's* measure covers the total risk of an investment, where total risk is the standard deviation of portfolio returns.[310] The *Sharpe's ratio ("reward-to-variability-ratio")* is a measure to appraise the excess return of a fund relative to the standard deviation of the expected return.[311]

---

[308] Treynor (1965).
[309] Jensen (1968).
[310] See Sharpe et al. (1999), p. 844.
[311] See Sharpe (1966), pp. 121-122.

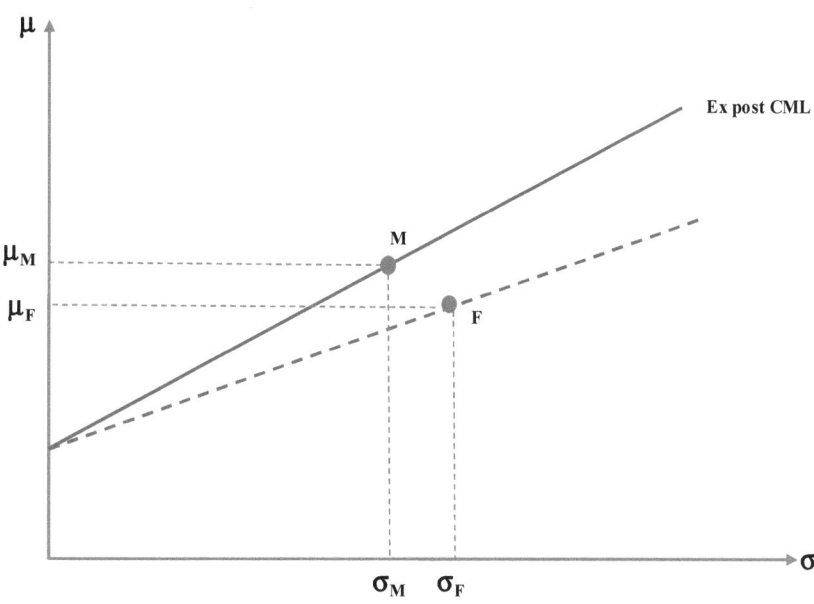

Figure 3.3 The Sharpe performance ratio

Source: According to Sharpe et al. (1999), p. 845.

The Sharpe ratio, which can be used to evaluate the performance of any type of asset, is designed to measure the expected return per unit of risk for a zero investment strategy. The difference between the returns on two investment assets represents the results of such a strategy.[312] However, this ratio requires identifying the location of the ex-post CML first as Figure 3.3 illustrates. *Sharpe's* ex post measure is defined as: [313]

$$(3.32) \qquad Sh(F) = \frac{\overline{r}_F - \overline{r}_f}{\sigma_F}$$

where $\overline{r}_F$, $\overline{r}_f$, σ_F denote the average realized yield over n prior periods, the return of the risk-free investment and the standard deviation of realized return, respectively. If it turns out that the Sharpe ratio of equation (3.32) is larger than the Sharpe ratio of the market then the fund bears a comparative advantage. Even though this kind of ratio requires elements like risk-free rate, the CML seems more suitable to estimate the degree of efficiency for generation portfolios than *Jensen's alpha* and *Treynor's ratio*.

---

[312] See Sharpe (1994), p. 53.
[313] See Sharpe et al. (1999), p. 844.

The reasons are threefold: Unlike, the other aforementioned performance ratio, the *Sharpe ratio* does not require knowledge regarding the systematic risk factor of a power plant asset relative to the market. Instead, the Sharpe ratio enables the evaluation of the reward of return for each unit of an asset's total risk. As a consequence, the ratio allows a comparison of the performance for generating assets competing on liberalized electricity markets.

Bar-Lev/ Katz (1976) rely on an adjusted *Sharpe ratio* to compare utilities fuel mix in different regions of the US based on the level of "costs burned" instead of returns. As stated in the previous chapter utilities used to pass through cost to customers in regulated markets. However, we need a ratio which is suitable for competitive electricity markets. Hence, instead of referring to operational cost we compute generations' net asset values per MW capacity. To compare the degree of relative efficiency between feasible generation portfolios we adjust the suggestion of *Bar-Lev/ Katz* (1976) performance ratio in order to account for competitive markets. Consequently the performance of power plant portfolios is measured by:[314]

$$(3.33) \qquad Z_i = \frac{\mu_i}{\sigma_i}$$

In comparison to the *Sharpe ratio* we do not take the risk-free interest rate $\bar{r}_f$ into account, as all plant technologies which are analyzed bear either price or volume risks. In the following we compare the degree of efficiency between different compositions of power plant technologies, namely fuel mix A, B and C. Then for each of these portfolios we need a vertical point on the efficient frontier above point A, B and C respectively. To determine the horizontal difference we refer to an efficient point which is far west located to the aforementioned points. Figure 3.4 presents the measurement of relative efficiency to the efficient frontier for generation portfolios where return and risk are measured, respectively, on the vertical and horizontal-axis.

---

[314] See Bar-Lev/ Katz (1976), p. 941.

Figure 3.4 Measuring the degree of efficiency

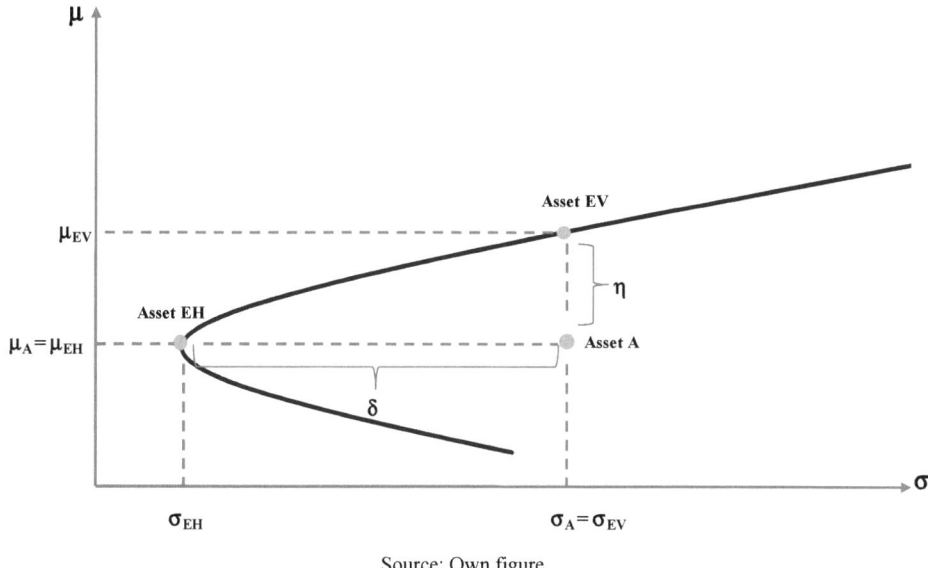

Source: Own figure.

Based on the Z_i values for three portfolios indicating a different composition of power plant technologies, we introduce two ratios, η and δ, which depend on the value of Z_i to specify the level of return and risk, respectively. The ratio η determines the highest return in terms of expected present value per MW capacity for the same level of risk. Consequently, the standard deviation of the expected return from a portfolio A equalizes a portfolio EV which is vertically located in relation to A on the efficient frontier. As both portfolios bear the same amount of risk, it is $\sigma_A = \sigma_{EV}$, we define η as:

$$(3.34) \qquad \eta = \frac{Z_A}{Z_{EV}} = \frac{\mu_A}{\sigma_A} \cdot \frac{\sigma_{EV}}{\mu_{EV}} = \frac{\mu_A}{\mu_{EV}} \qquad for\ 0 \leq \eta \leq 1$$

Hence, it is possible to identify these portfolio technologies and their corresponding share to increase the value of the asset base by a given amount of risk. Consequently, a higher ratio of η goes along with a higher performance in terms of larger expected asset values.

The counterpart is denoted by δ and measures the relative horizontal distance between two portfolios. In other words, δ represents the possible amount of risk that can be reduced, whereas the level of return remains constant.

$$(3.35) \qquad \delta = \frac{Z_A}{Z_{EH}} = \frac{\mu_A}{\sigma_A} \cdot \frac{\sigma_{EH}}{\mu_{EH}} = \frac{\sigma_{EH}}{\sigma_A} \qquad for\ 0 \leq \delta \leq 1$$

In equation (3.35) EH describes a portfolio which is efficient and horizontally located to portfolio A. Therefore both portfolios bear the same level of return by different risk levels. Very similar to η, assuming a rational utility firm prefers a higher ratio compared to a lower level of δ, as it indicates less risk for the same amount of return. If δ is equal to one, the analyzed generation portfolio is located on the efficient frontier.

We will use these performance ratios in the empirical part of the paper to determine the degree of relative efficiency for generation portfolios. According to the results, the ratios are able to classify the different analyzed fuel mixes and derive recommendations for balancing generation portfolios towards efficiency. In addition, the ratios serve as an indicator to test hypotheses, which are derived in the following section.

3.4.5 Development of hypotheses

The application of portfolio concepts to power plant technologies has spurred extensive research and is still subject to much controversy in academic literature.[315] The reasons are threefold: Firstly, the development of renewable technologies (e.g. wind, solar and geothermal) causes – against the background of portfolio theory – an enlargement of the feasibility set of generation portfolios. Secondly, liberalizing electricity markets has forced utilities to change their business concept.[316] Lastly, the establishment of the European Trading Scheme (EU ETS) has entailed an additional source of risks that has to be integrated in portfolio planning concepts. The latter mainly materializes as price risks resulting from the company's need to buy carbon

---

[315] For a literature overview, please refer to Chapter 1.
[316] See Dyner/ Larsen (2001), p. 1145; Felder (1996).

emission allowances as well as uncertainty surrounding the implementation of the EU ETS.[317] While most of the prior research concentrates on a fuel mix from a country perspective leading to a social welfare optimum, others change the perspective towards a utility firm competing on liberalized markets.

Even though European power plant parks are aging, which gives rise to the need for replacements in the near future, dynamic concepts of portfolio analyses towards time are rather scant. Instead, static analyses which have been explored so far concentrate on certain types of plant technologies (i.e. base load plants, *Roques et al.*, 2008; renewable energies, *Awerbuch et al.*, 2003). Therefore, the aim of this paper is to fill that gap and conduct further research on a power plant level. Thus, to the very best of our knowledge, the analysis of a dynamic power plant which covers existing power plant technologies towards the merit order to balance generation portfolios has been neglected so far. As a consequence, we have distinguished between base, mid-merit and peak load power plants to cover the whole merit order. In addition, the age structure of plants has to be taken into account to allow replacements in order to explore the impact to respective portfolio return and risk.

According to *Markowitz* (1952) a portfolio is *efficient* if the respective portfolio is not dominated by any other feasible portfolio. We expect inefficiency, even though we believe utilities are able to realize their investment strategy in terms of the replacement of old plants on the one hand and the increase in total generation capacity on the other hand. However, the thesis explores the relative efficiency of generation portfolios. As a consequence, we compute the relative degree of efficiency by evaluating the identified target generation portfolio to the efficient frontier. This expands existing research, as the degree of efficiency – to our knowledge – is measured the first time for generation portfolios competing on liberalized markets.

---

[317] See Neuhoff (2007), p. 2.

In the foregoing theoretical section selecting efficient portfolios is emphasized. This means from a utility's firm perspective to opt for a plant technology combination that is based on an efficient fuel mix. Since we are not only interested in the efficiency of existing generation portfolios but also in the efficiency target generation mix communicated by the respective utility firm, the underlying hypothesis of the thesis posits:

Hypothesis (1):   *Utility's target generation portfolios are not efficient.*

Furthermore, if hypothesis (1) holds, we explore how to rebalance respective portfolios from a base year to a target year. This is especially interesting since little is known about the dynamic process of power plant parks towards time. In addition, the analysis is conducted for individual power plants instead of an aggregated data set. Therefore the underlying model is set up to be able to establish precisely which power plant investments are necessary to minimize the distance from the efficient frontier.

Nowadays, utilities do not operate solely in domestic generation markets. Instead, they have widened their business activities beyond national borders due to the liberalization of European electricity markets. In this respect, we have gone beyond existing research by testing the consequence of holding generation assets in different European electricity markets. Therefore, we have conducted a cross-national analysis enlarging the feasibility set towards the UK, the Netherlands and Spain. As a consequence, the simulation model is able to explore the virtue of international diversification. Accordingly, utilities should invest in generation capacities towards liberalized markets to make use of diversification effects. As a consequence, the subordinated hypothesis reads:

Hypothesis (2.1)   *International diversified electricity generation portfolios are relatively more efficient than purely domestic portfolios.*

Contrary to *Roques et al.* (2008), who state the attractiveness of pure gas power portfolios compared to diversified portfolios due to the correlation of electricity, gas and carbon, we believe this is not necessarily true for Central European electricity markets. Instead we expect that diversified generation portfolios dominate pure portfolios of a single type of fuel.

From the main hypothesis (1) the following subordinated hypotheses are derived:

Hypothesis (2.2)   *Diversified generation portfolios dominate pure portfolios of a single type of fuel.*

The analysis particularly sheds light on the question related to how the change of the emission regulation in EU ETS of Phase II affects the composition of generation portfolios. The EU ETS favors electricity generation based on renewable energies, since fossil power plants have to comply with allowances for their emissions. Thus, operating low-emitting power plantparks based on non-fossil technologies should be better off compared to a generation portfolio of high-emitting plant technologies in terms of expected value per MW generation capacity and risk as respective standard deviation of the expected value.

Technically speaking we think that a generation system based on pure renewable energy requires geographic and climate prerequisites, which are not fulfilled for most Central European countries in terms of wind supply and total sun shining hours. Economically speaking cash flows of green power plants are riskier due to volatile wind or sun supply compared to ordinary plants. Hence, we expect that generation portfolios solely based on renewable energies are not efficient. However, we agree with *Awerbuch* (2004) that renewable energies cause diversification of generation portfolios. Consequently, we expect renewable energies to be part of efficient portfolios.

Hypothesis (2.3)   *Generation portfolios solely based on renewable energies are not efficient.*

The hypotheses posited in the foregoing, will be tested by a computer simulation experiment and either amplified or discarded. In the following chapter we present the model as well as the application of the Monte Carlo simulation towards generation portfolios.

3.5 Summary

Having introduced the technique to appraise the value of an investment asset by relying on a DCF valuation methodology, we have demonstrated in particular the merit of a simulation approach to take various uncertain parameters into account. The Monte Carlo simulation allows not only discovery of the expected value but also the corresponding standard deviation as a measure of risk. In addition, we have presented the theoretical framework based on the portfolio selection process of *Markowitz* (1952) to identify efficient portfolios in general. Before transferring the portfolio optimization for financial securities to generation assets, we have discussed the model developed by *Roques et al.* (2008). The latter has served as a starting point to expand their static approach covering three different kinds of base load technologies to a comprehensive portfolio analysis from a utility's perspective. Against this background, we have demonstrated the need for substantial extensions which not only shed light on the issue to opt for an efficient fuel mix by taking a cross-national approach but also to test the efficiency target generation portfolios. To explore the degree of efficiency, we have suggested a measure based on the adjusted Sharpe performance ratio. Finally, we have derived hypotheses which will be tested by a simulation model which will be introduced in the upcoming chapter.

4 Simulation based model for analyzing generation portfolios

This chapter deals with the simulation procedure of the valuation model. For this purpose, we will first introduce the risky variables and corresponding probability distributions. In addition, we will show a methodology to cope with dependencies among the risky model input variables. Secondly, we will define technical, cost and price assumptions. The projected commodities price development will be derived based on a model capturing annual and long-term price risks for commodities. In contrast, we will present the fixed remuneration for generated electricity from renewable energies over time. Thirdly, we will describe the simulation procedure and the valuation methodology of generation assets. Starting in 2010 and taking the age structure of plants into account as well as the investment plants, the model enables evaluating generation target portfolios. Furthermore, the dynamics of the model allow rebalancing utility's energy mix from a base year to a target year. At last, we will introduce the portfolio optimization procedure and distinguish with this respect between economic and technical efficiency.

4.1 Defining model requirements

Referring to the research questions and hypotheses, the model not only explores the composition of efficient generation portfolios but also determines the degree of efficiency. In particular, the model aims to shed light on the issue of how to rebalance generation portfolios for utilities. Therefore the computer simulation should be able to fulfill the following requirements:[318]

Most importantly, the model is set up in line with the **research goals** in order to avoid any redundancy. Hence, we focus particularly on the supply side which means including different generation technologies to quantify economic and technical efficiency. The latter describes a portfolio which is feasible and consistent with the *merit order*. Moreover we take the opportunity to build generation capacity abroad into account. Since we are interested in the target energy mix communicated by the individual utility, the model should be able to capture the dynamics of the power plant park over time. Therefore, the model substitutes plants which exceed their technical

---

[318] The requirements are based on Lutz/ Kalina (2010), pp.75-77; also Naylor (1971).

© Springer Fachmedien Wiesbaden GmbH, part of Springer Nature 2011
S. Rothe, *Portfolio Analysis of Power Plant Technologies*, Edition KWV,
https://doi.org/10.1007/978-3-658-24379-1_4

life time by a replacement strategy in order to build up the target power plant park. While aging power plants require developing a proper methodology for replacements, the incensement of total generation capacity is captured by additional investments in generation capacity. The latter equals the total generation capacity defined as target.

Secondly, the model should handle the trade-off between **simplicity** and **complexity** in line with the defined research goals. For instance, power plants are characterized by different technical characteristics like heat rate, start-up time etc. Against the background of the thesis, no short-term valuation in terms of the daily value of a power plant is conducted.[319] As a consequence, the model captures the main technical characteristics (efficiency, net capacity, merit order) in order to estimate the annual power production properly. However, the fuel prices drive the virtue of the individual plant. From a portfolio theory perspective, the price variables in particular determine the correlation between power plants. Power prices, on base and peak load, are drawn from Germany, the United Kingdom, the Netherlands and Spain, as the power plant sample operates in these markets. Moreover, the model considers fuel prices (coal, lignite, gas, and uranium), carbon prices as well as weather data (total sun hours and wind speed) in order to capture interactions. Yet, the characteristics of the individual technologies should not be neglected as modern coal plants are more efficient than elderly power plants.

Thirdly, the model aims to be **flexible** in order to allow not only adjustments of replacement strategies but also technical and economic characteristics of the plants as well as dependencies of the risky price variables. Even though the model will be applied to analyze a specific utility firm running a heterogeneous power plant park, it is irrespective and flexible in order to evaluate any other generation portfolio of a utility firm by changing input power plant data. Most importantly, the modeling proceedings are **consistent** throughout the whole model.

Lastly, the model structure allows an interaction between input data, corresponding calculations and the output. In other words, the power plant data are automatically processed through the model so that the results of the portfolio analysis can be directly used for defining a target energy mix which is efficient and feasible. Furthermore the model enables to conduct **robustness** tests for the validation of the results.

---

[319] Tseng/ Barz (2002); Abadie/ Chamorro (2008).

4.2 Risk analysis process

Compared to a traditional DCF valuation, the Monte Carlo simulation enables to incorporate uncertainty by computing unlimited scenarios. Moreover, it allows taking different sources of risk and their corresponding dependencies into account. While the application focuses on price risks, it may consider any other sources, e.g. operational risks. Therefore, we will identify first the risky variables which have an impact on the profitability of a power plant. Secondly, we describe the generation of random numbers with respect to choosing a proper probability distribution for the risky variables. Since commodity prices and meteorological data might turn out to be correlated, we introduce at last a methodology to incorporate mutual dependencies among these risky input variables within the simulation model.

4.2.1 Risk variables

Generally, before running a simulation to value a project in terms of profitability it is necessary to identify the variables which influence the net present value most.[320] In other words, in order to set up a reliable model all relevant variables and particularly the proper mutual dependencies have to be considered.[321]

The profitability of a regular fossil-driven power plant mainly depends on the electricity price, cost of fuel and the cost of carbon. In order to stabilize plants' cash flows, trading with spread options has become popular. The difference between the price of electricity and the price of its primary fuel is termed as *spark spread*.[322] However, the emission regulation requires holding emission certificates at the end of the trading period due to the EU ETS. Therefore, these costs have to be incorporated in the operational decision of a power plant. *Clean spread* options serve as a hedging instrument for power plant operators as the cost of carbon, as well as the cost of fuel, are deducted from the electricity price. Consequently, these variables are assumed to be risky within the simulation. Since the model should capture the opportunity to invest in different European electricity markets, we take country specific price data to analyze diversification effects by international investments.

---

[320] See Hacura et al. (2001), p. 551; Savvides (1994), p. 5.
[321] See Savvides (1994), p. 5.
[322] See Eydeland/ Wolyniec (2003), p. 49. See also Chapter 3 for further details regarding this issue.

In detail we distinguish between base and peak load prices of the *EEX, APX UK, APX NL* and Spanish *OMEL*. Moreover, we consider oil, lignite, coal, gas and uranium as risky fuel prices. Lastly, we take prices for emission certificates as risky variables into account.

Power plant parks do not just consist of conventional thermal power plants. In contrast, utilities have started to invest considerably in power plants which are based on renewable energies. In order to evaluate the power plant park from a portfolio perspective we have to identify the main sources of risk for these power plant technologies as well. Otherwise renewable energies will always be better off compared to regular plants. The risk level is based on *volume* rather than on prices for renewable energies. Currently, "green" power plants benefit from financial support by national fixed tariffs compared to volatile power prices on energy exchanges. Therefore, we take a measure of wind speed as proxy for the likelihood of wind power production as risky variable into account. Moreover, we use the total hours of sun to simulate the power generation of photovoltaic power plants. Wind speed as well as total hours of sun are then transferred to a plant specific utilization rate. In contrast, we assume that all water power plants sell the electricity on the market instead of relying on fixed price levels. In other words we transfer the volume risk to a price risk for water power plants.

In the following section, we will describe the evolution of random numbers for the model input variables and their corresponding probability distribution.

4.2.2 Probability distributions

Taking just the most sensitive project variables into account, namely price and volume risk variables, is mainly due to the issue of "…the setting and monitoring relationships for correlated variables" (*Savvides*, 1994, p. 5). Moreover, if the costs of defining accurate probability distributions for parameter exceed the impact on the net present value, they should be eliminated.[323] To generate random numbers, we rely on computer based so-called *pseudo random numbers*. Even though they are not real random numbers, as "arithmetical methods of producing random digits is, of course, in a state of sin" (*Neumann*, 1951, p. 36), they serve as a proxy. In other words,

---

[323] See Savvides (1994), p. 5.

computers are not able to draw a number randomly. Indeed, the total number of available random figures is limited and therefore the system will repeat these after a while. Yet, the implications of rebalancing portfolios should not be biased. The merit of programming in spreadsheets is that *Excel* transfers uniformly distributed random digits directly to the inverse of the normal distribution. This is in line with the assumptions of portfolio theory.

Before analyzing time series data of the risky variables in the following chapter, we refer to the assumptions of the theoretical foundation. Since we conduct the portfolio analysis using the theoretical framework of *Markowitz (1952)*, the returns of the generation assets should be normally distributed. As the returns of the different power plant technologies depend mainly on the kind of fuel and the allocated place in the merit order, fuel prices as well as electricity prices should follow a normally distributed process as well. Therefore we rely on simulating normally distributed random variables for the commodity prices by taking their empirical mean and standard deviation into account. From a short-term perspective, i.e. daily data, this assumption does not hold for electricity prices in particular.[324] Yet, by focusing on monthly data we minimize volatility caused by price jumps during weekdays and weekends.

In contrast to the commodity price behavior, which is explained by normally distributed random variables, we rely on the triangular distribution to describe the meteorological data (wind speed and total sun hours). A random variable, y, which is characterized by the following density function, is generally called triangularly distributed: [325]

$$(4.1) \qquad f(y) = \begin{cases} \dfrac{2(y-a)}{(b-a)(m-a)} & \text{for } a < y \leq m \\[2mm] \dfrac{2(y-b)}{(b-a)(m-b)} & \text{for } m < y \leq b \\[2mm] 0 & \text{otherwise} \end{cases}$$

---

[324] Please refer to section 2.3.5 for further details.
[325] See Rosenkranz/ Missler-Behr (2005), pp. 226-227.

In equation (4.1) the parameters a, b and m represent the minimum, maximum and most frequently, respectively. If we transfer a random variable z which is equally distributed in the interval [0, 1] by applying formula (4.2), then y is characterized by a triangular distribution.[326]

$$(4.2) \qquad f(y) = \begin{cases} a + [z(b-a)(m-a)]^{\frac{1}{2}} & \text{for } z \leq \dfrac{(m-a)}{(b-a)} \\ b - [(1-z)(b-m)(b-a)]^{\frac{1}{2}} & \text{for } z > \dfrac{(m-a)}{(b-a)} \end{cases}$$

First, we generate random figures between [0, 1] for the level of wind speed and the amount of total sun hours, respectively. Second, we define a range between a minimum and a maximum value in terms of utilization hours for photovoltaic and wind power plants, to make sure that generated values lie within the margin of fluctuation. Moreover, the specification of the most frequently value, m, ensures that random variables remain close to this value. Lastly, we transfer the results to compute the utilization ratio of the power plant by dividing the random figure of utilization hours by the operational hours per annum 8,760.[327]

The following section deals with the transformation of these independent generated random variables to correlated variables.

4.2.3 Correlated variables

After having identified the variables which drive the profitability of a power plant most and their corresponding distributions, the following section deals with different methodologies to implement the relation between the risky variables properly. Therefore, the issue of how to consider correlations between risky variables arises. In other words, which are the opportunities to make sure that the empirically observed correlation equals the correlation of risky variables? If the simulation neglects dependencies of variables, the likelihood of a biased risk profile increases.[328] One opportunity is to conduct a regression analysis of electricity prices on fuel prices and

---

[326] See Rosenkranz/ Missler-Behr (2005), p. 233.
[327] We assume that a year consists of 365 days. Therefore the total amount of hours within a year equals 24 (hours per day) times 365 which is equal to 8,760.
[328] See Dannenberg (2009), p. 63.

other explanatory variables. However, this specific statistical approach requires that the causalities between the variables incorporated in the simulation model are correctly identified which facilitate an accurate establishment of the dependent and independent variables.[329]

To sum up, we refrain from conducting a regression analysis to determine electricity prices for three reasons: Firstly, the interplay between the risky variables is not clear. Secondly, very similar to the results of *Keppler/ Mansanet-Battaler* (2010) it seems likely that causalities will change due to a shift in energy generation and carbon regulation. Lastly, most of the commodity prices which are indicated as risky model input parameters do not fulfill the requirements to rely on ordinary least squares (OLS) analyses. Hence, we rely on a correlation analysis for the risky variables captured in the simulation model. A correlation coefficient measures the strength between two variables without making any predication on the causality. The approach is based on the following relationship between two correlated variables x and y :[330]

We simulate these prices by generating a random variable, z :

(4.3) $z = x + y$

Since x and y are correlated, the variance of random variable z is determined by equation (4.4) where ρ_{xy}, σ_x and σ_y denote the correlation coefficient between x and y, the standard deviation of x and y, respectively.[331]

(4.4) $\sigma_z^2 = \sigma_x^2 + \sigma_y^2 + 2\sigma_{xy}$

                          $= \sigma_x^2 + \sigma_y^2 + 2 \times \rho_{xy}\sigma_x\sigma_y$

If we assume that values of x are generated by a normally distributed random variable z_1, then the generated random variable y depends on the normally distributed random variables z_1 and z_2.

(4.5) $y = \rho_{xy} \times z_1 + z_2 \sqrt{(1-\rho_{xy}^2)}$

---

[329] See Dannenberg (2009), p. 64.
[330] See Rosenkranz/ Missler-Behr (2005), p. 234.
[331] See Rosenkranz/ Missler-Behr (2005), pp. 234.

Depending on the strength of, ρ_{xy}, a positive or negative relationship in the interval of $[-1;+1]$ between x and y will be generated.

As noted in the previous section, however, we take various variables into account which have an impact on the profitability of a power plant. Therefore, we consider k risk factors which are independently simulated in a first step according to their predefined distributions. However, we aim to achieve that corresponding correlations of these k simulated risk factors are equal to the empirical correlations A of these risk factors. For instance, an increase of fuel prices should go along with an increase of power prices within the model. Since we incorporate multiple correlated variables, we are faced with the issue for solving symmetric indefinite systems of linear equations. *Bunch/ Parlett* (1971) provide an overview of different methods for solving symmetric indefinite systems of linear equations.[332]

Technically speaking, we generate a correlation matrix following the approach of *Cholesky*,[333] which is applicable to normally distributed random variables. In general, any regular matrix $A \in \Re^{n \times n}$ of the form:

(4.6) $$A = LL^T$$

which has a lower triangular matrix $L \in \Re^{n \times n}$ is called a *Cholesky decomposition* or *Cholesky matrix*.[334] This algorithm is commonly used to decompose a symmetric and positive definite matrix into a lower and upper triangular matrix.[335]

(4.7)
$$
\begin{bmatrix}
a_{11} & a_{12} & \cdots & a_{1n} \\
a_{21} & a_{22} & \cdots & a_{2n} \\
\cdots & \cdots & \vdots & \cdots \\
a_{n1} & a_{n2} & \cdots & a_{nn}
\end{bmatrix}
$$

---

[332] Other illustration are presented in Jorion (2003), pp. 97-98; Schnabel/ Eskow (1990), pp. 1136-1158; Rosenkranz/ Missler-Behr (2005), pp. 234-235; McLeish (2004), pp. 201-202; Zangari (1996), pp. 253-254.
[333] André-Louis Cholesky (1875-1918).
[334] See Wang/ Liu (2006), p. 343.
[335] See Wang/ Liu (2006), p. 344.

$$= \begin{bmatrix} l_{11} & 0 & \cdots & 0 \\ l_{21} & l_{22} & \cdots & 0 \\ \cdots & \cdots & \vdots & \cdots \\ l_{n1} & l_{n2} & \cdots & l_{nn} \end{bmatrix} \cdot \begin{bmatrix} l_{11} & l_{12} & \cdots & l_{1n} \\ 0 & l_{22} & \cdots & l_{n2} \\ \cdots & \cdots & \vdots & \cdots \\ 0 & 0 & \cdots & l_{nn} \end{bmatrix}$$

Basically the correlation matrix based on empirical data represents the starting point, or in other words the initial matrix A. The *Cholesky* decomposition aims to identify a triangular-matrix L , which multiplied with its transpose matrix, L^T, equals to the initial matrix A. To complete the decomposition, matrix A has to be positive definite. In other words, all eigenvalues of the matrix A have to be positive. [336] The method and triangular factorization are fast in terms of necessary computations $(1/6)n^3$, stable and preserve symmetry.[337] As long as A is symmetric and positive definite, the expression under the square root is also positive and therefore all elements in L are real. The elements of the triangular matrix L are computed using equation (4.8), where i and j represent the row and column index, respectively.[338]

(4.8)
$$l_{ij} = \begin{cases} 0 & \text{for } i < j \\ \sqrt{1 - \sum_{k=1}^{i-1} l_{ik}^2} & \text{for } i = j \\ \dfrac{1}{l_{ii}}\left(a_{ij} - \sum_{k=1}^{j-1} l_{ik} \times l_{jk} \right) & \text{otherwise} \end{cases}$$

Within the formula, a_{ij} denotes the element of the starting matrix A. The matrix of the k independently generated risky random variables is then multiplied by the *Cholesky* matrix L so that the matrix B consists of transformed risky variables.

(4.9) $B = L \cdot k$

The product of the *Cholesky*'s lower triangular matrix and the matrix of the risky variables result in transformed risky variables, the cross correlation of which tends to be close to the empirical observed correlation.

---

[336] See Wang/ Liu (2006), p. 344.
[337] See Bunch/ Parlett (1971), p. 639.
[338] See Dannenberg (2009), p. 67.

As an illustration, Figure 4.1 depicts the procedure to gain variables which follow predefined probability distributions by taking the correlations between these risky variables into account to value power plant technologies. Before presenting the empirical correlation as well as the simulation results for the risky variables as part of Chapter 5, we will introduce the underlying technical assumptions and commodity price patterns in the upcoming sections.

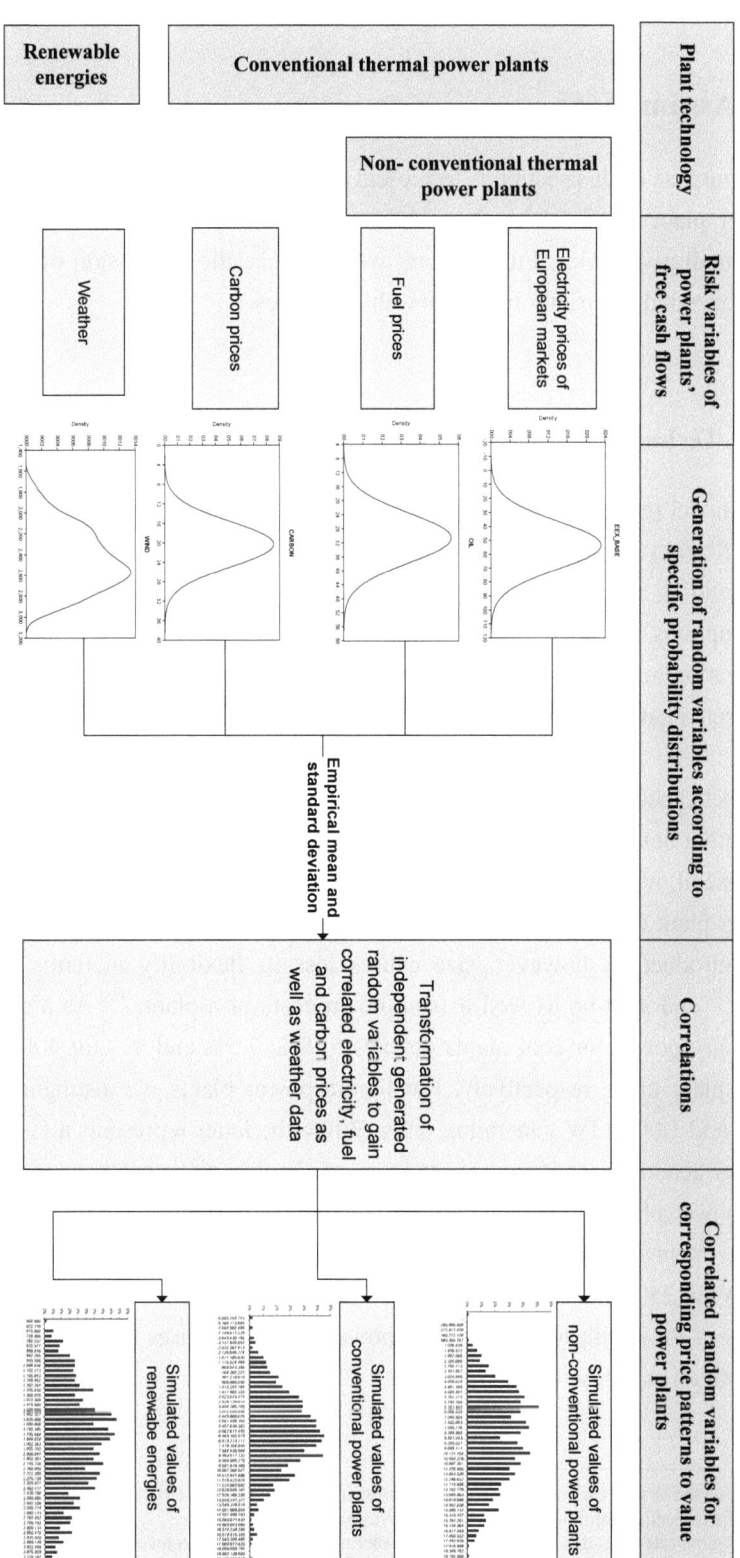

Figure 4.1 Risk analysis process

Source: Own figure.

4.3 Assumptions

The purpose of this section is to present technical and cost assumptions for the specific power plant technologies. In addition, we develop future price trajectories for the commodity variables. Furthermore, we introduce the degression of the remuneration for generated electricity from renewable energies.

4.3.1 Technical and cost assumptions

The model rebalances power plant portfolios from a base year to a target year in terms of efficiency. Thus the base year of the model is defined to be 2010 and the target portfolio is reached by 2020.[339] In the following we present technical and cost assumptions for power plant technologies, which currently dominate the electricity generation in Europe. The assumptions regarding the technical and cost parameters for different plant technologies are summarized in Table 4.1:

The net capacity of a plant is the difference between the gross capacity in MW and the operating hours needed to generate electricity for own consumption (auxiliary power). In general, net capacity varies depending on the size of the power plant unit. A larger power plant unit enables the operator to realize *economies of scale*. As pointed out in the introduction, however, size causes loss in flexibility in terms of higher ramp rates[340] and start-up as well as shut-down costs of a plant.[341] As a consequence, the auxiliary power for coal plants denotes to 8%, 7.5% and 4% for 400, 600 and 1,000 MW plant units, respectively. For lignite power plants we distinguish between 600 MW and 1,000 MW generating units. While the latter represents a factor of 4.5%, the former generating unit assumes to have a need for auxiliary power of 5.5%. Typically, gas power plants are smaller in terms of gross capacity per unit compared to lignite power plants. Therefore, the factor of gas power plants is 2.5%, 2.2% and 1.5% for 150 MW, 250 MW and 400 MW plant units, respectively. For larger power plant units the need for auxiliary power of gas power plants increases by 0.5% for each 200 MW generation capacity.

---

[339] We set the target year equal to 2020, as the efficiency test of utility's target generation portfolios is restricted to the respective communicated long-term investment strategy.
[340] The ramp rate measures the time needed in order to change generation level in MW per minute.
[341] See Eydeland/ Wolyniec (2003), p 14.

Table 4.1 Technical and cost parameters for power plant technologies

Parameters	Unit	CHP	Coal	Gas	Lignite	Nuclear	Oil	Water	Wind	PV	Other
Technical parameters											
Net capacity	%	99	92–96	97.5–99.5	94.5–95.5	95.5	99	100	99.8	98	99
Efficiency	%	80	46	58	43	35	35	85	45	35	35
Adjustment rate of efficiency	%	0.1	0.25	0.1	0.25	0.2	0.1	0	0.05	0.1	0.1
Plant lifetime	Year	25	45	40	45	40	35	100	20	20	25
Cost parameters											
Old plants											
Variable O&M	€/MWh	3.5	2.8	3.7	1.7	8.3	1.2	0.0	0.0	0.0	1.2
Fixed O&M	€/MW	61,600	22,000	16,500	27,500	77,000	16,500	66,000	49,500	33,000	16,500
New plants											
CO_2 intensity	t CO_2/MWh	0.35	0.73	0.35	0.93	0.00	0.40	0.00	0.00	0.00	0.40
Variable O&M	€/MWh	2.1	1.7	2.2	1.0	5.0	0.7	0.0	0.0	0.0	0.7
Fixed O&M	€/MW	56,000	20,000	15,000	25,000	70,000	15,000	60,000	45,000	30,000	15,000
Investment costs	€/kW	800	1,150	600	1,250	2,250	600	3,000	1,200	3,500	1,000

Source: EWI/ EEFA (2008), p. 20; Erdmann/ Zweifel (2008), p. 300;
Konstantin (2007), pp. 234-235; own assumptions.

Following Table 4.1 the renewable energy capacities are characterized by a net capacity factor which is higher than the corresponding factors for conventional thermal power plants. This is due to the presumption that the need for auxiliary power amounts to 0.2% and 2% for wind and photovoltaic (PV) power plants, respectively. In contrast, for water power plants, combined heat and power (CHP)[342] plants and other plants we assume a net capacity factor of 100%, 99% and 99%, respectively.

The efficiency rates mentioned in Table 4.1 refer to state of the art power plant technologies. Since the thesis takes also existing and therefore old power plants of a sample utility firm into account, the efficiency is adjusted for elderly power plants. Typically, the efficiency increases due to technological improvement. Hence, the efficiency of a plant which is built before the base year is estimated by a function of plant age. The adjustment rate is estimated by a gradual decline of efficiency subjected to the individual plant age. Since the model captures a period of ten years in total we neglect for simplicity further technological developments in terms of improvements in efficiency rates.[343]

Irrespective of plant technology we presume a maintenance rate of 10% of the defined operating hours of the specific plant. The operating hours of a plant depend on the position in the merit order. Since the model analyzes the supply side we assume a simple merit order and neglect any change of demand. Consequently, base, mid-merit and peak load denote to 8,760, 6,000 and 1,000 total operating hours, respectively.[344]

For the plant technologies considered in the model, we assume a certain lifetime. Usually, the technological lifetime of a power plant is longer than the economic lifetime. Therefore the assumption regarding the operational life of a plant lies above the theoretical economic lifetime of power plants.

Recent studies on levelized costs serve to derive capital investment costs, variable and fixed costs for operation and maintenance (O&M) for different plant technologies.[345] Nuclear variable cost for O&M include 3 €/ MWh for nuclear waste disposal. Since coal market prices do not capture cost for domestic transport, we presume transportation cost of 0.7 €/ MWh which is added to the variable cost of O&M for coal

---

[342] In the following we use CHP and cogen as synonyms for combined heat and power plants.
[343] The simplification does not affect the economic intuitions, which are derived within this thesis.
[344] Base load plants run the whole year irrespectively of the load level. A year is represented by 360 days. Hence, the 8,760 total operating hours are equal to 360 days times 24 hours.
[345] We exclude cost of decommissioning for simplicity.

plants. Alongside we take a transportation fee of 1.5 €/ MWh for natural gas into account.

Since the sample covers old and new power plants we distinguish between cost parameters for both categories. Based on the assumptions for new power plants we derive cost parameters for old power plants. The latter is derived by multiplying variable cost parameters of new power plants by a factor of 1.67. As a consequence, average variable costs of an old power plant lay 67% above the respective cost of a state of the art power plant. This reflects a learning effect so that technology development over time lowers variable operating costs of a power plant. In addition, we presume that fixed costs per plant technology are 10% higher for old generation technologies in comparison to new power plants.[346] Ultimately, we adjust investment costs for the individual power plant technologies by an annual growth rate. The latter indicate the inflation rate which is assumed to be 2% per year.

4.3.2 Projected commodity price development

In addition to the technical and cost parameters, we gather essential commodity price assumptions from recent studies conducted by *EWI/ EEFA* (2008). In this respect, the authors distinguish between different energy and climate scenarios of the EU policy which have an impact on the price development of commodities. From our point of view, the policy scenario with full auctioning of emission certificates from 2012 and a European 2020 emission reduction target of 30%, reflects recent EU policy developments best and serves therefore as a proxy for future price projections. While a low price scenario is based on low crude oil prices and, therefore, also on low prices for natural gas due to the oil price peg, the high price trajectories represent the corresponding opposed scenario.[347]

Table 4.2 summarizes the price assumptions for commodity prices today, P_0, which is equal to the base year (2010) and the next two decades, P_{10} (2020) and P_{20} (2030), respectively. Since the EEX is the leading power exchange in Europe[348], we take the

---

[346] See Konstantin (2007), p. 234.
[347] It is common to derive commodity price trajectories from future oil price presumptions. While the energy report from IEA (2008a) predicts an oil price which is higher than the price forecast of EWI/ EEFA (2008), the latest energy report from Hundt et al. (2009) presumes commodity prices which slightly lie above the price assumptions presented.
[348] See Burger et al. (2007), p. 35.

EEX price forecast as best proxy to derive growth assumptions for the other remaining European electricity markets. Specifically, we assume that the rise for base and peak load prices from the UK, the Netherlands and Spain is equal to the absolutely average increase of high and low EEX electricity prices, whereas the individual historical mean represents the equilibrium price in P_0 for the European power prices.

Table 4.2 Commodity price assumptions

Commodity parameter	Unit	P_0	P_{10}	P_{20}
Revenue parameter				
EEX-Base				
High price	€/MWh	52.20	67.90	89.30
Low price	€/MWh	38.10	51.90	72.70
EEX-Peak	€/MWh	75.00	90.00	111.00
Cost paramter				
Oil				
High price	€/MWh	31.39	36.12	41.05
Low price	€/MWh	20.92	24.08	27.37
Gas				
High price	€/MWh	24.17	27.76	30.18
Low price	€/MWh	16.48	19.31	20.52
CO_2				
High price	€/ tCO_2	20.87	37.42	43.46
Low price	€/ tCO_2	16.48	22.93	32.59
Coal	€/MWh	7.96	9.19	9.79
Lignite	€/MWh	4.72	5.19	5.19
Uranium	€/MWh	3.80	4.00	4.50

Source: See EWI/ EEFA (2008), p. 11, own assumptions.

These price scenarios presented, however, are presumed to be uncertain. In other words, instead of assuming a constant annual growth rate for the aforementioned commodities, we presume that commodity prices follow a non-linear price trajectory over time. As a consequence, we derive random price trajectories for all risky model input commodity variables (German, Dutch, British, and Spanish base and peak load prices, gas, oil, coal, lignite, uranium and CO_2 prices) by drawing a series of Monte Carlo simulations. Thus, we determine a lower and upper price bound based on the data mentioned in the table above as well as an expected price forecasts for the commodity prices.

For the price modeling, we lean on the methodology presented by *Roques et al.* (2006). The virtue of their price model is that it captures annual and long-term price risks for commodities. The latter is derived by referring to an exponential price formula which predicts the expected price level for P_{10} (2020) and P_{20} (2030):[349]

(4.10) $P(t) = P_{20} - \alpha \cdot e^{-\beta \cdot t}$

whereas α measures the difference between the projected price in P_{20} (2030) and P_{10} (2020),

(4.11) $\alpha = P_{20} - P_{10}$

and β indicates the average compounded return over the two decades.

(4.12) $\beta = -\dfrac{1}{10} \cdot \ln\left(\dfrac{P_{20} - P_{10}}{P_{10} - P_{0}}\right)$

The expected price trajectory is computed by taking the historical mean of the specific commodity as initial price level for the base year and the expected growth is then calculated as average increase of the low and high price scenario between the two decades. Besides, the short-run risk is represented by the annual volatility in respect to the individual commodity price. Due to the high annual volatility of commodities we rely on the respective variation coefficient[350], which is a measure for commodities relative standard deviation, to limit the divergence from the mean over the specific period of time.[351] Commodities relative price standard deviation and the corresponding annual volatility based on continuous compounded monthly returns are shown in Table 4.3. In addition, the table covers the mean of the risky variables, which represent the starting point for deriving the individual simulated price pattern by referring to the formula presented above.

---

[349] See Roques et al. (2006), p. 13.
[350] In the following we use variation coefficient and relative standard deviation as synonyms.
[351] A high volatility does not necessarily go along with a high variation coefficient. The latter shows the divergence from the corresponding mean of a commodity price, whereas the former indicates the price change.

Table 4.3 Historical mean and standard deviation of risky parameters

Commodity parameters	Unit	Mean	Std. Dev.	σ*	σannual
Base load price					
APX-NL base	€/MWh	57.94	19.05	26%	134%
APX-UK base	€/MWh	59.24	23.49	33%	101%
EEX base	€/MWh	53.59	17.22	23%	175%
OMEL base	€/MWh	50.57	13.74	25%	80%
Peak load price					
APX-NL peak	€/MWh	113.70	62.97	43%	209%
APX-UK peak	€/MWh	71.50	30.03	34%	130%
EEX peak	€/MWh	67.47	23.57	24%	198%
OMEL peak	€/MWh	56.98	16.12	28%	153%
Fuel and carbon price					
Oil	€/MWh	30.81	6.84	20%	39%
Gas	€/MWh	19.81	8.28	34%	78%
CO_2	€/ tCO_2	20.16	4.63	23%	48%
Coal	€/MWh	8.02	2.84	29%	61%
Lignite**	€/MWh	4.32	2.00	29%	61%
Uranium	€/MWh	3.84	0.85	23%	18%

Source: Own calculation based on monthly data from May 2005 to December 2009.
*The variation coefficient is the quotient of commodities' standard deviation and corresponding mean. This ratio is computed after eliminating data points with at least four times standard deviation above or below the mean of the EEX base load prices.
** Due to a lack of trading for lignite, we take the variation coefficient of coal as proxy to develop the respective price trajectory.

Technically speaking, we multiply the expected price level for each year by a uniformly distributed random variable, whereas commodities relative price standard deviations determine the upper and lower bound of the simulated commodity price pattern.[352] This is in line with the theoretical price behavior described in Chapter 2, as commodity prices do not increase continuously over time. In contrast, commodity prices revert back to an equilibrium price level that is represented by the expected price pattern.

Figure 4.2 depicts the historical and projected price development of German EEX base load prices. Historical power prices computed as annual average for the years 2005 until 2009 are represented by a continuous line. In 2010, however, the curve changes to a dotted line which shows the simulated power price path. The divergence to the expected price pattern refers to the variation coefficient of the commodity. For the first decade (2010 until 2020), the expected average annual growth rate amounts to 2.5% for German base load prices.

---

[352] See Roques et al. (2006), p. 14.

Figure 4.2 Expected and simulated EEX base load price development

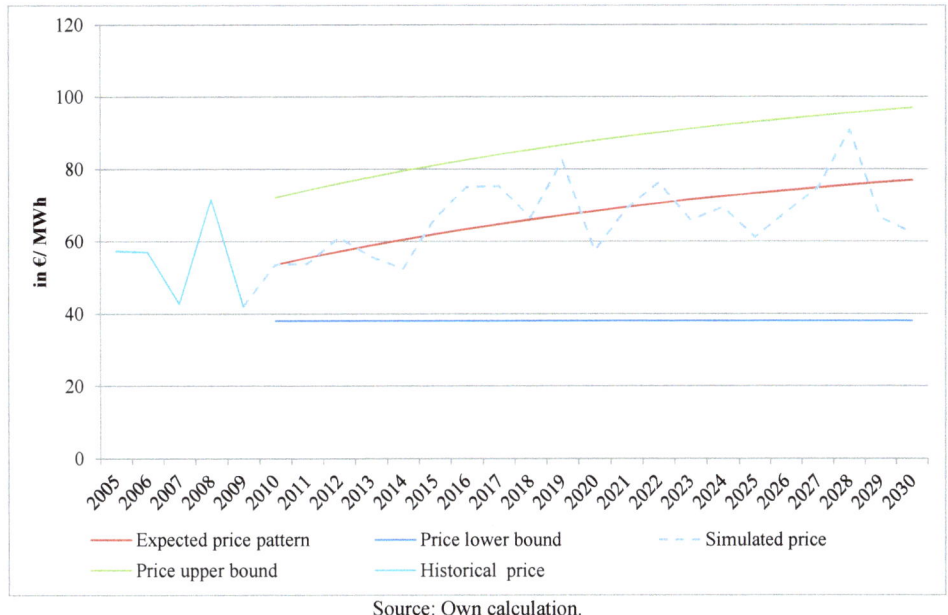

Source: Own calculation.

In addition, Figure 4.3 depicts the price development of EUAs based on the same methodology.

Figure 4.3 Expected and simulated CO$_2$ price development

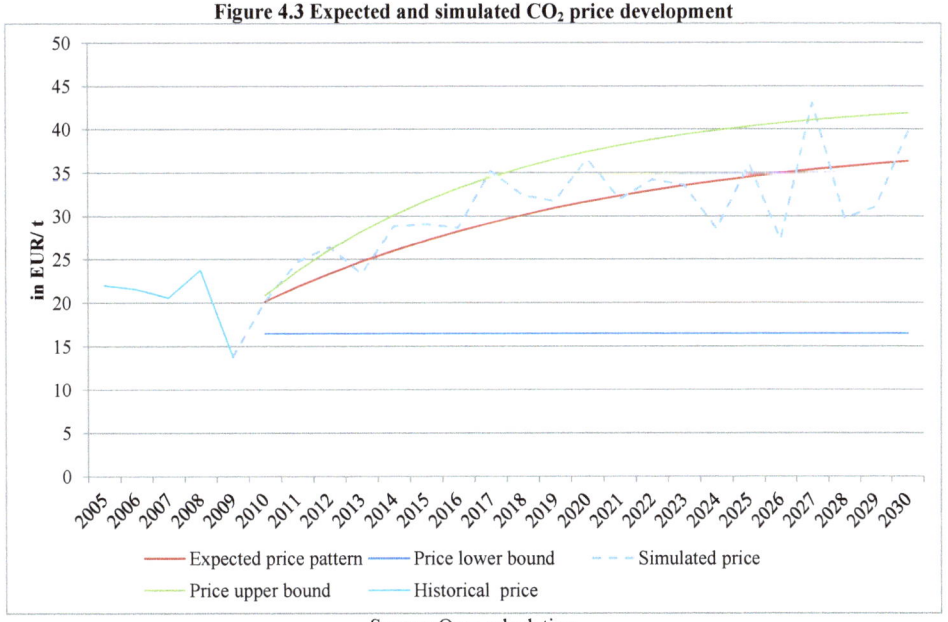

Source: Own calculation.

As demonstrated by the simulated price path of CO_2 emission certificates shown in the graph above, the price modeling procedure takes the regulative change of the EU ETS into account. Due to the full auctioning of emission certificates starting in 2012, the model expects a strong price increase within the first decade with an average annual growth rate of 4.6%, whereas the growth in the second decade is rather smooth (1.3%). Compared to the expected growth of EUA prices, the annual expected growth rate of the oil price is moderate (1.21%) as shown in Figure 4.4

Figure 4.4 Expected and simulated oil price development

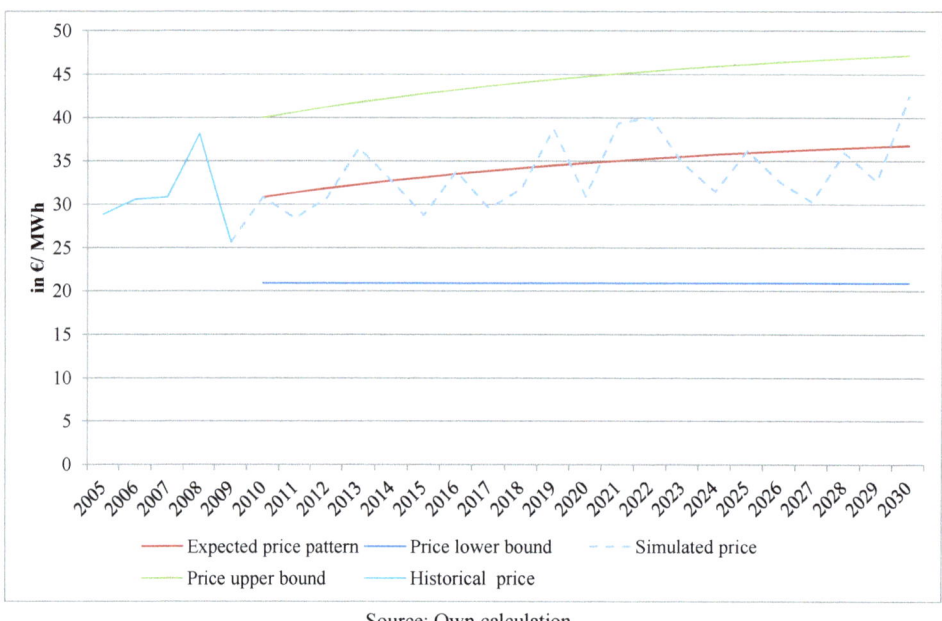

Source: Own calculation.

Since the annual price volatility of oil is lower than the annual volatility of EUAs, the divergence of the simulated oil price path tends to be closer to the expected oil price pattern. Even though power generation based on oil is limited, oil prices drive gas prices and, therefore, it has impact on power generators fuel mix.[353] As a consequence, Figure 4.5 depicts the projected gas price trajectory. As explained in Chapter 2, the importance of gas will rise due the flexibility of usage and reduced emissions for electricity generation.

---

[353] Please refer to Chapter 2 for further details.

Therefore the expected annual growth rate of gas prices based on the assumptions defined above amounts to 1.5% for the first decade. Alongside high volatility as observed on gas markets cause jumps over time.

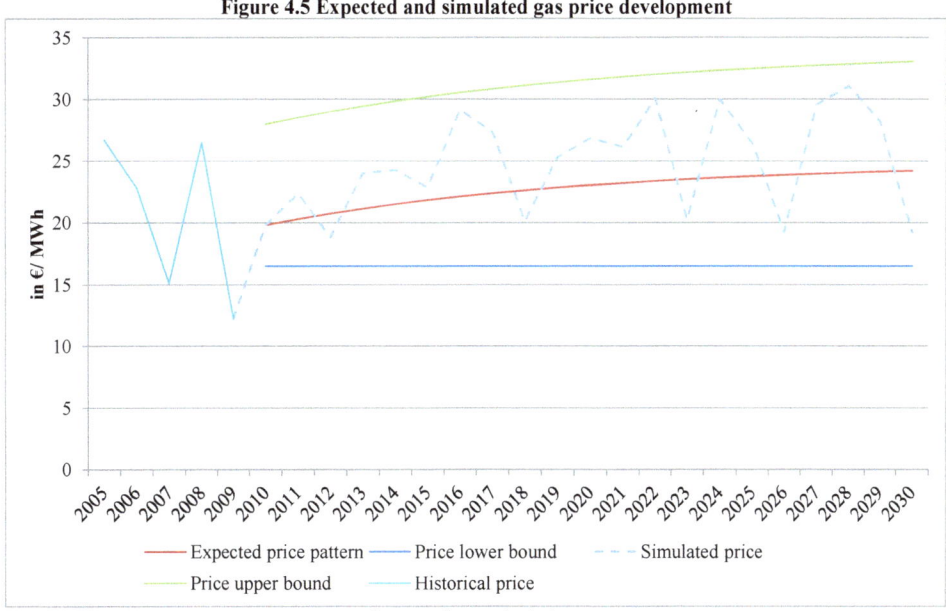

Figure 4.5 Expected and simulated gas price development

Source: Own calculation.

Ultimately, the simulated coal price path is depicted in Figure 4.6. Since coal reserves are abundant in comparison to other energy commodities and price shocks as seen in 2007 seem less likely, the price trajectory indicate a slow growth rate (0.7%) within the two decades.

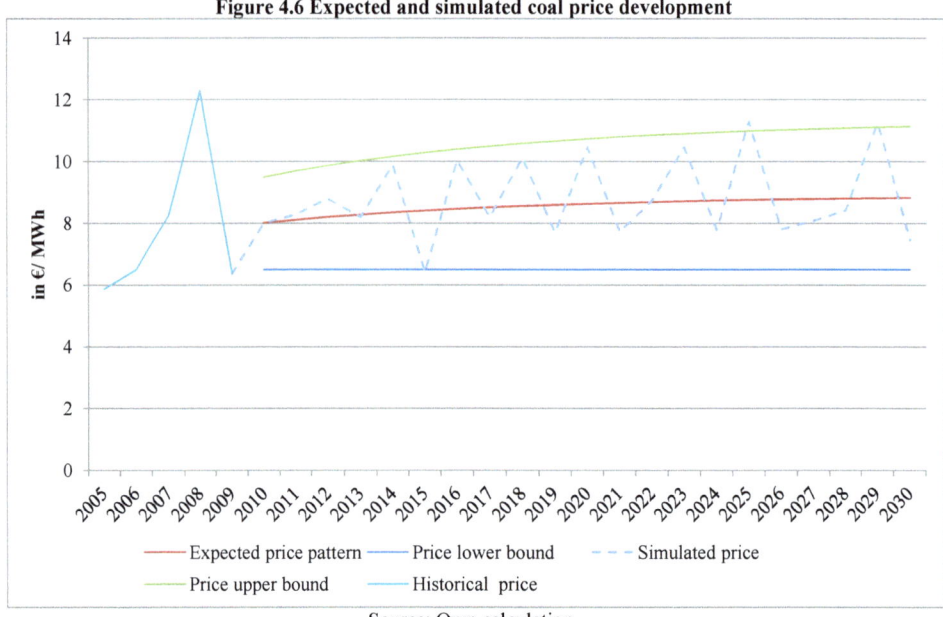

Figure 4.6 Expected and simulated coal price development

Source: Own calculation.

We model similar price trajectories for the *EEX peak load*, *British*, *Dutch* and *Spanish base* and *peak load prices*, lignite and uranium. The average expected annual growth rate, however, differs as the price assumptions in Table 4.3 indicate.

While lignite and uranium prices are expected to grow by 0.5% and 0.6%, respectively, on an annual average, the corresponding growth of European power prices is presumed to be stronger. As explained above, the European power prices are linked to the absolute increase of German base load prices.[354] Consequently, the average annual growth rate tends to be close to the *EEX base load price* trajectory. Since the historical mean of power prices which serves as initial price differ in these markets (see Table 4.3), the modeling of the individual price pattern leads to different average growth rates for the European power prices. In detail we presume an average annual growth rate for the first decade of 2%, 2.2%, 2.8%, 2.2%, 1.8%, 2.5% and 3.4% for *EEX peak*, *UK base*, *UK peak*, *NL base*, *NL peak*, *Spanish base* and *peak prices*, respectively.

Here, the simulation is based on 1,000 runs for each price path, whereas the initial price in 2010 is set equal to a normal distributed random variable with historical mean

---

[354] This linkage is due to the fact that the EEX is the largest power exchange in Europe and therefore we take its power price development as a proxy for the price growth of the other European power markets.

and relative standard deviation of the specific commodity. In addition, these variables take the correlation which is empirically observed on commodity markets for the base year into account.

4.3.3 Renewable energies

In order to reach climate policy goals defined by the European Council in March 2007, the EU aims to expand renewable generation capacities.[355] Against this background, member states are obligated to promote investments in renewable energies. While the majority of countries rely on fixed feed-in tariffs (e.g. Germany, Netherlands, Spain), a few others (e.g. United Kingdom) apply an opposed system based on quotas and tradable green certificates.[356]

As a consequence, the average remuneration level of wind and photovoltaic power plants differs between the European countries.[357] The UK, Ireland and the area around the North and Baltic Sea seem favorable in terms of low wind generation costs; in fact Germany and Spain, however, dominate European wind generation capacity. In addition, the virtue of Southern Europe for using photovoltaic power is the guarantee of higher operating hours in comparison to Central Europe. The strongest increase in photovoltaic power generation capacity refers to Germany, though.[358]

Renewable energies do currently not compete with conventional power plant technologies on spot markets, as operators of renewable energy capacities do not bear price risks. Instead, from a risk perspective, the operator is faced with the uncertainty of the *annual energy yield* of a plant, due to the dependency of meteorological conditions. In contrast, we assume that hydro power plants already compete with conventional thermal power plants and, therefore, these plants are faced with price risks. Since hydro power plants are base load plants, respective base load prices act as risk variables.

As the modeling of country-specific conditions in terms of meteorological and regulative remuneration for individual renewable power plants, would go beyond the

---

[355] Please note that the forthcoming assumptions regarding renewable energies are based on the EU policy status of March 2007.
[356] See EWI/ EEFA (2008), pp. 128-129.
[357] See IEA (2008b), p. 106 and p. 126.
[358] See EWI/ EEFA (2008), p. 131; see also IEA (2008b), p. 121.

focus of the thesis, we define input parameter which are valid irrespectively of the location of the renewable plant within the model.

In line with our assumptions regarding the commodity price development, we rely on the forecast of the development of renewable energy capacities from *EWI/ EEFA* (2008). Here, we assume that a scenario of 25% and 35% of total power generation is attributed to renewable energies is very likely in Germany in 2020 and 2030, respectively. As a consequence, we adjust annually average remuneration for generated power out of wind or photovoltaic energy by the following degression, presented in Table 4.4.

Table 4.4 Expected degression of the remuneration of renewable energies

Renewable	2005	2010	2020	2030	Average annual degression 2010-2015	Average annual degression 2015-2020
Wind	100%	88%	79%	77%	*1.4%*	*0.4%*
Photovoltaic	100%	75%	49%	34%	*3.2%*	*2.0%*

Source: Own graph according to EWI/ EEFA (2008), p. 18.

In comparison to the *German Renewable Energy Act* (EEG), this scenario assumes lower degression quotas to force additional investments to build up new renewable energy generation capacity, as Figure 4.7 demonstrates:

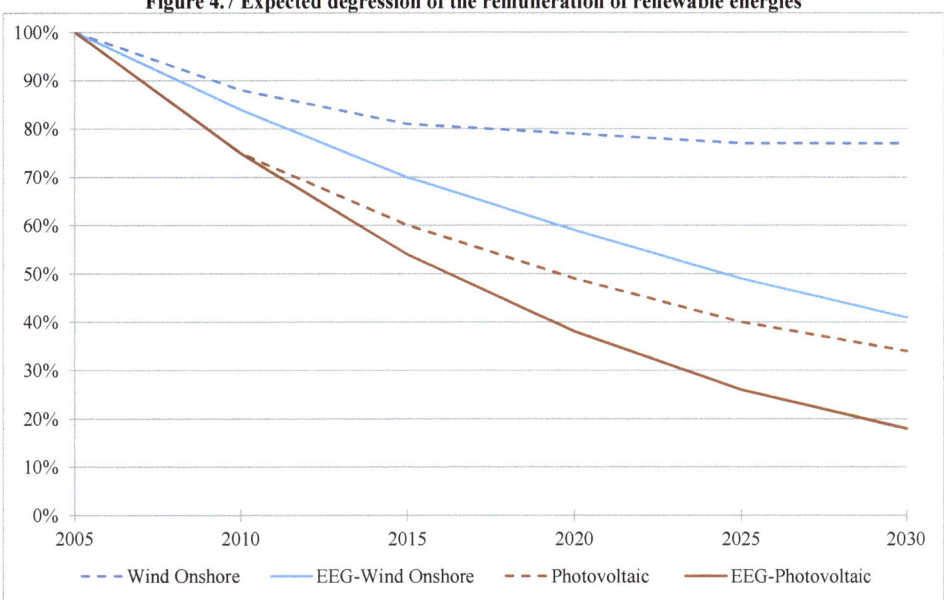

Figure 4.7 Expected degression of the remuneration of renewable energies

Source: Own graph according to EWI/ EEFA (2008), p. 18.

Therefore the dashed lines represent the assumption of a homogenous remuneration of renewable energy generation, which is consistent with the objective of the EU and acts also as proxy for European renewable energy generating capacities.[359] Table 4.5 summarizes the annual average remuneration for wind and photovoltaic power plants for the period between 2010 and 2020, whereas prices are computed by taking the aforementioned degression quotas into account.

---

[359] The European Union aims to pass a homogenous remuneration scheme for renewable energies starting in 2014. See EWI/ EEFA (2008), p. 135.

Table 4.5 Operating hours and remuneration of renewable energies

Parameter	Wind	PV
Operating annual hours		
Min	1,650	860
Max	3,050	1,750
Mode	2,650	1,250
Remuneration in €/ MWh		
2010	80.76	420.86
2011	79.63	408.23
2012	78.51	395.98
2014	76.33	372.58
2016	74.96	350.56
2017	74.66	340.04
2018	74.36	329.84
2019	74.06	319.95
2020	73.77	310.35

Source: Kaltschmitt et al. (2006), p. 243 and 260; EWI/ EEFA (2008), p. 133; own assumptions.

According to the previous section, we model wind and photovoltaic power plants as risky variables, which follow a triangular distribution.[360] As a consequence, we distinguish between minimum, maximum and mode of wind and photovoltaic power plants. In this respect, the model simulation captures the risk of the annual energy yield by varying annual operating hours of the respective power plants.

Following *Kaltschmitt et al.* (2006) a photovoltaic power plant unit of 1 MW typically reaches 860h operating hours.[361] Due to technology development and the fact that bigger units increase respective load factor, we define 1,250 hours as mode for the average annual operating hours of photovoltaic power plants. In addition, we assume a capacity factor of 20%, representing 1,752 full operating hours as a maximum for photovoltaic power plants.

---

[360] Please, refer to the previous section for further details. A triangular distribution is often used for approximation purpose and its merit is the implementation within a simulation model. See Rosenkranz/ Missler-Behr (2005), p. 226.

[361] See Kaltschmitt et al. (2006), p. 260.

In comparison to conventional thermal power plants, the gross generation capacity of wind power plant does not indicate the economic value properly.[362] Instead, the energy yield and, therefore, the economic value, depend on the technical characteristics in terms of rotor and plants size as well as the respective level of wind supply. Against this background, energy yield of a wind plant increases with the third power of average wind speed.[363] Hence, operating hours and therefore average wind speed determine the economic profitability of a wind power plant most.[364]

As a consequence, we assume annual operating full load hours in respect of different levels of wind speed. Assuming a 2.5 MW reference wind plant unit and an average wind speed of 5.5 m/s goes along with 1,650 hours or a capacity factor of 18.8%. This represents the minimum of plants' average annual operating hours. Alongside, the maximum is defined to 3,050 full load hours (34.8%) which is equal to an average annual wind speed of 7.5 m/s. Ultimately, the mode of full operating hours amount to 2,650 or a capacity factor of 30.3%.[365]

Simulated operating hours are then transferred to compute annual average capacity factor of the respective renewable power plant to determine the energy yield. Solar radiation strictly follows a seasonal trend with a maximum sun supply in the summer and a minimum sun supply in the winter. The temporal availability of wind supply, however, is inversely related to the solar radiation. Figure 4.8 demonstrates the relationship between monthly maximum wind speeds and average monthly temperature for the period 2005 until the end of 2009 observed for German weather stations.

---

[362] See Hau (2008), p. 539.
[363] See Kaltschmitt et al. (2006), p. 313.
[364] See Kaltschmitt et al. (2006), p. 330.
[365] See Kaltschmitt et al. (2008), p. 243.

Figure 4.8 Average monthly wind speed and total sun hours (May 31st, 2005 to December 31st, 2009)

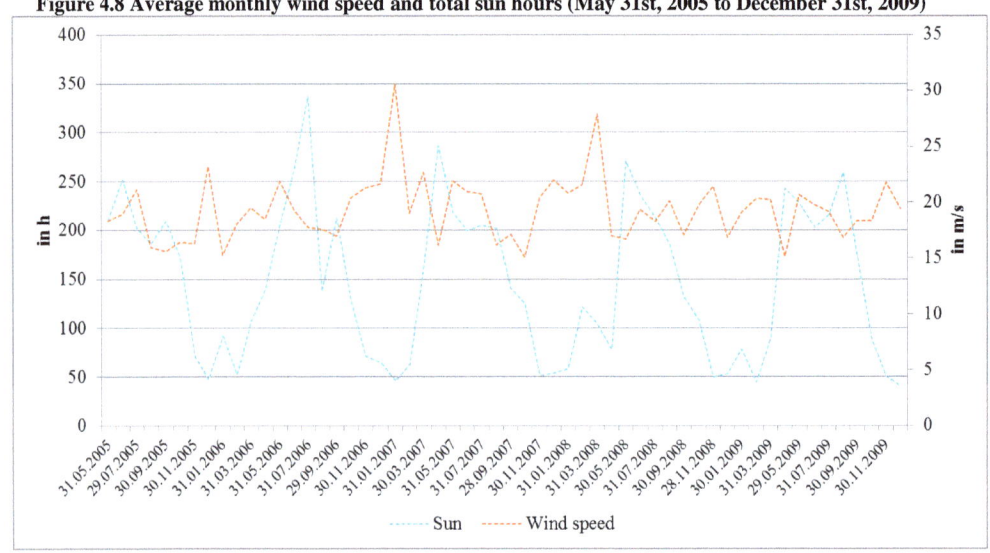

Source: Own graph based on data from DWD.

Hence, we take the empirical correlation into account of maximum wind speed and total sun hours for the simulation. We introduce the procedure of the model simulation in the upcoming section.

4.4 Modeling procedure

In order to identify investment strategies, which rebalance generation portfolios of European utilities towards an efficient generation mix, the model is based on *Excel*. The model distinguishes between three main parts, data input, simulation and results, respectively. Figure 4.9 depicts the modeling procedure. The spreadsheet "Assumptions" enables the user to define assumptions regarding the replacement strategy for each type of plant, the lifecycle of plants, the mean and standard deviation of the power, fuel and carbon prices, and interactions of risky variables as well as the allocation of emission certificates of the EU. In addition, it is possible to determine a base and target year with corresponding capacities in MW. By defining the total amount of generation capacity in a specific year, i.e. 2020, the model automatically builds up the generation capacity with respect to the target fuel mix within the modeling period. Hence, the model is not restricted to the specific years, instead it guarantees flexibility. The emission data for each power plant is taken from the

Community Independent Transaction Log (CITL) and stored in the spreadsheet called "CO$_2$ Data". Furthermore, the spreadsheet allows importing carbon emission data from the Carbon Monitoring for Action (CARMA) database, which is an open database of worldwide operating power plants and their corresponding emission data.[366] However, we have recognized differences between CITL data and CARMA data. Therefore, the analysis relies on the data provided by the CITL of the EU as they should be more reliable.

The power plant data for the utility are obtained by the energy data provider *Platts*. For editing the *Platts* data a separate model is built first. This separate model, or what we call assistant tool, summarizes the units of each power plant with corresponding gross capacity, fuel type, commissioning and country for operating, currently under construction and planned power plants. To continue processing the power plant data the spreadsheet "Power Plant Data" is expanded by details regarding the merit order, efficiency, net capacity, maintenance hours and carbon emission factor for each power plant.[367] Hence, the spreadsheet calculates automatically the total electricity generated within one year, the total amount of fuel needed as well as the corresponding carbon emissions.

As already pointed out in previous sections, utilities are faced with an aging power plant park, which necessitates investments in generation capacity in the near future. Therefore in the next step, the need for replacements and additional capacity will be quantified for each year of the simulation period within the spreadsheet "Investment Planning". For instance, if a coal plant has to be decommissioned in a specific year, the spreadsheet "Replacements" ensures that the plant is replaced in the model. For this purpose, the spreadsheet refers to the defined replacement strategies in the assumptions of the model in order to consider a proper substitute like gas for coal plants.

Over the entire model period generation capacity is replaced by new power plants. Moreover, the model takes the growth of the generation capacity into account by additional investments in order to reach the target capacity. Therefore the model distinguishes between three groups of power plants. While the first group comprises of the existing plants as well as plants under construction which operate beyond the target

---

[366] The database CARMA means Carbon Monitoring for Action and discloses the carbon emissions of more than 50,000 power plants and 4,000 power companies in every country on earth.

[367] For details regarding the assumption, please refer to section 4.2.1.

year (henceforth: *old power plants*), the second group covers the replacements of generation capacity (henceforth: *new power plants*). Finally, we consider power plants which are actually planned according to *Platts* as well as additional investments in power plants to build up the target fuel mix (henceforth: *target power plant*s). For new as well as target power plants a calculation is conducted to determine total electricity generated within one year, the total amount of fuel needed as well as the corresponding carbon emissions. Therefore, these plants are allocated to the merit order, which defines total operating hours.

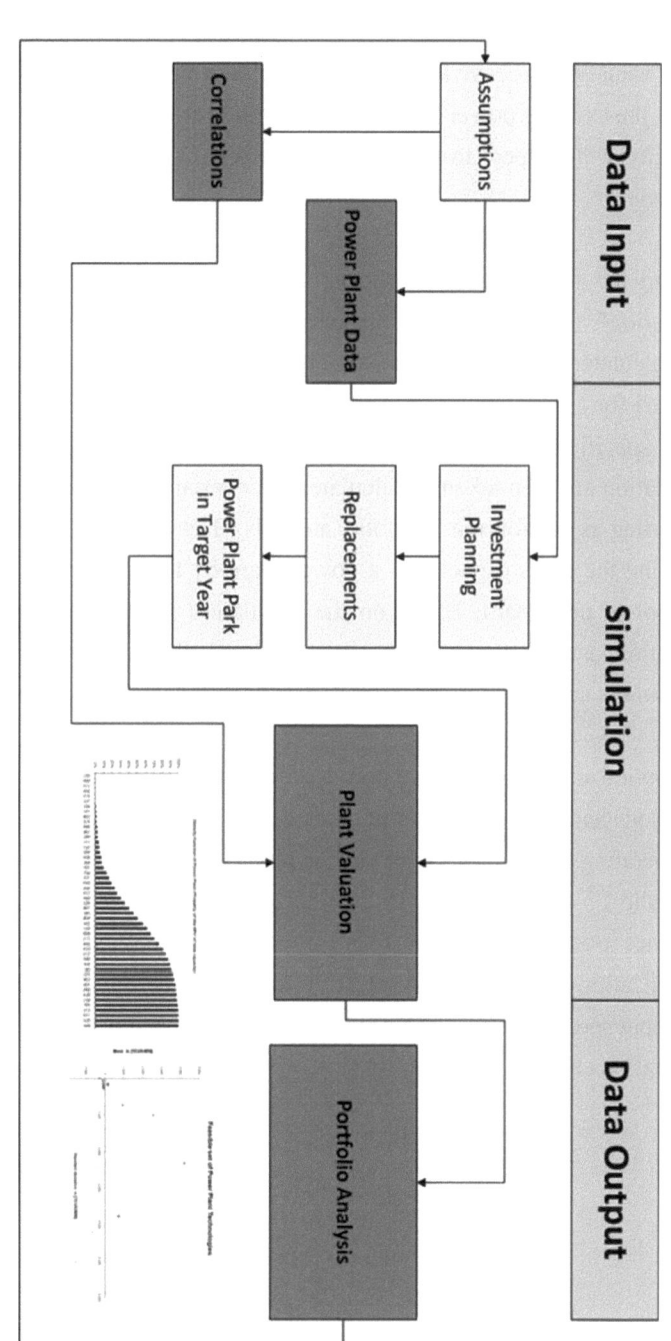

Figure 4.9 Loop diagram of the portfolio valuation model

Source: Own figure.

Additionally, the spreadsheet takes the efficiency, net capacity, maintenance hours and carbon emission factors of the new and target plants into account. Before starting the DCF valuation process for each power plant, the model provides an overview sheet about the existing power plants in the target year. This allows verification whether the capacity with respect to the target fuel mix is reached and if the model has worked properly.

Within the following spreadsheets, which are summarized in Figure 4.9 as "Plant Valuation", the expected net present value and the corresponding standard deviation are calculated for each plant separately. Moreover the empirical distribution function is derived for risk analysis. The valuation refers to the previous spreadsheets, where the plant specific generation, technical and economic data are given. The results of the simulation are then taken to calculate the covariance matrix of the generation assets as a starting point for the portfolio analysis. The portfolio weights are computed by dividing the gross capacity of a power plant by the total gross generation capacity of the power plant park. Based on the simulation the portfolio value and the standard deviation as measure of risk are calculated. This specific portfolio refers to the investment strategy, communicated by the individual utility firm.

For optimization purpose, we derive the efficient frontier assuming that the investment decisions had not been taken. In other words, we take the power plants, which will still be operating beyond the target year as given and identify the global minimum variance portfolio.[368] Consequently, if the utility firm aims to realize the global minimum variance portfolio, the investment strategy has to be changed. The results of the optimization including the portfolio weights per fuel type are then transferred back to the input spreadsheets in order to define the optimized investment strategy for new generation capacity of the utility firm.

---

[368] For further details, please refer to section 3.5.2.

4.4.1 Power generation

Using *Platts* plant data base for Europe (December 2008) as a data source for the utility's power plants in operation, the corresponding gross capacity in MW and the location enables to set up a calculation spreadsheet for the estimated annual generated electricity. In the first step we subtract according to the individual plant assumptions plant capacity which is needed for own operation from the *gross plant capacity* resulting as *net plant capacity*.

After having assigned the location of each plant in the *merit order* and considering time for maintenance, the amount of electricity generated per year is computed (see Table 4.6). Moreover, the spreadsheet calculates the efficiency, which is the reciprocal of the *heat rate* for every single plant as gradual function of age. The plants' free cash flow calculation refers to the efficiency in order to estimate fuel needed. To capture carbon risk the data sheet "Plants Operation" refers to a spreadsheet which contains total emissions. If emission data are not available for a specific plant, emissions are estimated by the carbon intensity of the specific fuel type. This particularly applies to plants which are replaced or built additionally to increase total capacity.

Moreover, the spreadsheet brings together all other parameters which are necessary for the valuation by referring to the assumptions; variable and fixed costs, technical lifetime and investment costs. The latter is needed to determine annual depreciation for each plant which is later on used in the free cash flow calculation. According to the requirements defined in the previous chapters, the same logical data processing is used for the different subsidies of the sample utility.

Table 4.6 Preparation of operating power plants

Power plant	Gross capacity (MW)	Efficiency	Net capacity (MW)	Merit order	Load factor	Maintenance	Power generation (in MWh)	Emissions (tCO$_2$/year)	CO$_2$ efficiency	Commissioned	Country
UR											
1975OLD UR1	2,525	28.2%	2,411	Base Load	8,760	876	19,011,281	0	0	1975	GER
UR TOTAL	**2,525**		**2,411**				**19,011,281**	**0**	**0**		
COGEN											
2001OLD COGEN1	60	79.2%	59	Base Load	8,760	876	468,310	208,058	444	2001	GER
1987OLD COGEN2	43	77.8%	43	Base Load	8,760	876	339,368	150,772	444	1987	GER
COGEN TOTAL	**103**		**102**				**807,678**	**358,830**	**444**		
LIGNITE											
1963OLD LIGNITE1	2,100	31.6%	1,872	Base Load	8,760	876	14,758,848	18,550,352	1,257	1963	GER
1991OLD LIGNITE2	171	38.5%	150	Base Load	8,760	876	1,186,384	1,541,638	1,299	1991	GER
1988OLD LIGNITE3	90	37.8%	77	Base Load	8,760	876	610,222	770,819	1,263	1988	GER
1974OLD LIGNITE4	2,100	34.2%	1,980	Base Load	8,760	876	15,610,320	17,950,484	1,150	1974	GER
1972OLD LIGNITE5	3,826	33.8%	3,598	Base Load	8,760	876	28,365,371	24,866,476	877	1972	GER
1966OLD LIGNITE6	2,100	32.3%	1,968	Base Load	8,760	876	15,515,712	21,440,879	1,382	1966	GER
LIGNITE TOTAL	**10,387**		**9,646**				**76,046,856**	**85,120,648**	**1,119**		
COAL											
1985OLD COAL4	752	40.0%	722	Middle Load	6,000	600	3,898,368	4,335,320	1,112	1985	GER
1984OLD COAL5	670	39.8%	643	Middle Load	6,000	600	3,473,280	2,298,778	662	1984	GER
2011OLD COAL8	1,600	46.0%	1,600	Base Load	8,760	876	12,614,400	2,958,417	235	2011	GER
2011OLD COAL9	2,200	46.0%	2,200	Base Load	8,760	876	17,344,800	2,958,417	171	2011	GER
1971OLD COAL10	310	36.5%	285	Middle Load	6,000	600	1,540,080	1,054,825	685	1971	GER
1969OLD COAL11	320	36.0%	294	Middle Load	6,000	600	1,589,760	2,958,417	1,861	1969	GER
COAL TOTAL	**5,852**		**1,945**				**10,501,488**	**10,647,340**	**1,014**		

Power plant	Gross capacity (MW)	Efficiency	Net capacity (MW)	Merit order	Load factor	Maintenance	Power generation (in MWh)	Emissions (tCO$_2$/year)	CO$_2$ efficiency	Commissioned	Country
GAS											
1957OLD GAS1	28	52.8%	27	Peak Load	1,000	100	24,570	110,976	4,517	1957	GER
1975OLD GAS2	854	54.6%	840	Middle Load	6,000	600	4,535,730	870,094	192	1975	GER
1973OLD GAS3	842	54.4%	828	Middle Load	6,000	600	4,472,550	332,928	74	1973	GER
1980OLD GAS4	255	57.4%	251	Middle Load	6,000	600	1,356,345	1,654,636	1,220	1980	GER
1959OLD GAS5	284	53.0%	277	Middle Load	6,000	600	1,495,260	665,856	445	1959	GER
1975OLD GAS6	614	54.6%	608	Middle Load	6,000	600	3,282,444	562,123	171	1975	GER
2000OLD GAS10	580	57.1%	567	Middle Load	6,000	600	3,063,096	551,545	180	2000	GER
2004OLD GAS11	10	57.5%	9	Peak Load	1,000	100	8,424	7,120	845	2004	GER
1996OLD GAS12	325	56.7%	317	Middle Load	6,000	600	1,711,125	414,693	242	1996	GER
2007OLD GAS13	380	57.8%	372	Middle Load	6,000	600	2,006,856	414,693	207	2007	GER
1984OLD GAS14	112	55.5%	109	Middle Load	6,000	600	589,680	332,928	565	1984	GER
2009OLD GAS40	530	52.0%	522	Middle Load	6,000	600	2,819,070	665,856	236	2009	GER
GAS TOTAL	**5,134**		**4,728**				**25,365,150**	**6,583,448**	**260**		
WATER											
2000OLD WATER41	205	85.0%	205	Base Load	8,760	876	1,619,484	0	0	2000	GER
WATER TOTAL	**205**		**205**				**1,619,484**	**0**	**0**		
WIND											
2001OLD WIND46	9	44.7%	9	Base Load	8,760	876	73,211	0	0	2001	GER
WIND TOTAL	**9**		**9**				**73,211**	**0**	**0**		
PV											
2000OLD PV1	1	35.0%	1	Base Load	8,760	876	7,930	0	0	2000	GER
PV TOTAL	**1**		**1**				**7,930**	**0**	**0**		
TOTAL	**24,217**		**19,048**				**133,433,078**	**102,559,494**	**769**		

Source: Own table.

4.4.2 Replacements

Usually, the national regulator has to approve the request of a utility firm before the latter is allowed to invest in new generation capacities. Therefore the commissioning of new plants is a rigid process, which typically takes up to four years. In addition to the regulatory uncertainty other sources of risk come into play which might prolong the planning process (e.g. public acceptance).

However, we assume that the sample utility firm is able to realize its investments and as a consequence reach its respective target generation capacity. Since the German government has passed a law to define the phase out for nuclear power plants, we assume that new nuclear energy capacity can be built solely abroad. Moreover, we do not consider the time lag between investment plan and commissioning.[369]

The technical application within the *Excel* model distinguishes between four spreadsheets in total. While the spreadsheet "Replacement Planning" is needed in order to identify aging power plants and the corresponding replacements over time (see Table 4.7 and Table 4.8), the objective of two more assistant spreadsheets serve to automate the data flow for the replacement process within the model. Lastly, the spreadsheet "Replacement Overview" computes electricity generation and other parameters which are relevant for deriving specific plant cash flows.[370]

We operationalize the identification of aging plants and the corresponding replacements over time by inserting a column defining the specific year of replacement for each plant. By referring to this specific replacement year column, the spreadsheet tests whether the generation capacity exits in every year. This enables to sum up the capacity, which has to be substituted for each type of power plant technology. The model highlights the capacity which has to be replaced, the following spreadsheet supplants power plants according to the assumptions defined. The other assistant spreadsheet serves to assign the replacements to the corresponding power plant technology.

---

[369] We consider time lags of construction in the robustness test.
[370] Please refer to section 4.3.2 for further details.

Table 4.7 Identifying the need for replacements

Power plant	Gross capacity (MW)	Commissioned	Replacement	2010 Capacity	Replacement	2011 Capacity	Replacement	2019 Capacity	Replacement	2020 Capacity	Replacement	Country
UR												
1975OLD UR1	2,525	1975	2015	2,525	0	2,525	0	2,525	0	2,525	0	GER
UR TOTAL	**2,525**			**2,525**	**0**	**2,525**	**0**	**2,525**	**0**	**2,525**	**0**	
COGEN												
2001OLD COGEN1	60	2001	2026	60	0	60	0	60	0	60	0	GER
1987OLD COGEN2	43	1987	2012	43	0	43	0	43	0	43	0	GER
COGEN TOTAL	**103**			**103**	**0**	**103**	**0**	**103**	**0**	**103**	**0**	
LIGNITE												
1963OLD LIGNITE1	2,100	1963	2008	0	2,100	2,100	0	2,100	0	2,100	0	GER
1991OLD LIGNITE2	171	1991	2036	171	0	171	0	171	0	171	0	GER
1988OLD LIGNITE3	2,100	1974	2019	2,100	0	2,100	0	0	2,100	2,100	0	GER
1974OLD LIGNITE4	3,826	1972	2017	3,826	0	3,826	0	3,826	0	3,826	0	GER
1972OLD LIGNITE5	90	1988	2033	90	0	90	0	90	0	90	0	GER
1966OLD LIGNITE6	2,100	1966	2011	2,100	0	0	2,100	2,100	0	2,100	0	GER
LIGNITE TOTAL	**10,387**			**8,287**	**2,100**	**8,287**	**2,100**	**8,287**	**2,100**	**10,387**	**0**	
COAL												
1971OLD COAL10	310	1971	2016	310	0	310	0	310	0	310	0	GER
1985OLD COAL4	752	1985	2030	752	0	752	0	752	0	752	0	GER
1984OLD COAL5	670	1984	2029	670	0	670	0	670	0	670	0	GER
1969OLD COAL11	320	1969	2014	320	0	320	0	320	0	320	0	GER
1976OLD COAL6	1,500	1976	2021	1,500	0	1,500	0	1,500	0	1,500	0	UK
1973OLD COAL3	1,920	1973	2018	1,920	0	1,920	0	1,920	0	1,920	0	UK
1971OLD COAL2	1,050	1971	2016	1,050	0	1,050	0	1,050	0	1,050	0	UK
1987OLD COAL7	1,245	1987	2032	1,245	0	1,245	0	1,245	0	1,245	0	NL
2011OLD COAL8	2,200	2011	2056	0	0	2,200	0	2,200	0	2,200	0	GER
2011OLD COAL9	1,600	2011	2056	0	0	1,600	0	1,600	0	1,600	0	GER
COAL TOTAL	**11,567**			**7,767**	**0**	**11,567**	**0**	**11,567**	**0**	**11,567**	**0**	

GAS

Power plant	Gross capacity (MW)	Commissioned	Replacement	2010 Capacity	2010 Replacement	2011 Capacity	2011 Replacement	2019 Capacity	2019 Replacement	2020 Capacity	2020 Replacement	Country
1957OLD GAS1	28	1957	1997	0	28	28	0	28	0	28	0	GER
2000OLD GAS10	580	2000	2040	580	0	580	0	580	0	580	0	GER
2004OLD GAS11	10	2004	2044	10	0	10	0	10	0	10	0	GER
1975OLD GAS2	854	1975	2015	854	0	854	0	854	0	854	0	GER
1973OLD GAS3	842	1973	2013	842	0	842	0	842	0	842	0	GER
1980OLD GAS4	255	1980	2020	255	0	255	0	255	0	0	255	GER
1959OLD GAS5	284	1959	1999	0	284	284	0	284	0	284	0	GER
1975OLD GAS6	614	1975	2015	614	0	614	0	614	0	614	0	GER
1996OLD GAS12	325	1996	2036	325	0	325	0	325	0	325	0	GER
2007OLD GAS13	380	2007	2047	380	0	380	0	380	0	380	0	GER
1984OLD GAS14	112	1984	2024	112	0	112	0	112	0	112	0	GER
1967OLD GAS7	900	1967	2007	0	900	900	0	900	0	900	0	UK
1933OLD GAS8	420	1933	1973	0	420	420	0	420	0	420	0	UK
1994OLD GAS15	441	1994	2034	441	0	441	0	441	0	441	0	UK
1974OLD GAS9	60	1974	2014	60	0	60	0	60	0	60	0	NL
1995OLD GAS16	24	1995	2035	24	0	24	0	24	0	24	0	NL
1992OLD GAS17	0	1992	2032	0	0	0	0	0	0	0	0	NL
1977OLD GAS41	1,278	1977	2017	1,278	0	1,278	0	1,278	0	1,278	0	NL
1994OLD GAS18	34	1994	2034	34	0	34	0	34	0	34	0	NL
1975OLD GAS42	76	1975	2015	76	0	76	0	76	0	76	0	NL
1995OLD GAS19	42	1995	2035	42	0	42	0	42	0	42	0	NL
1991OLD GAS20	43	1991	2031	43	0	43	0	43	0	43	0	NL
1994OLD GAS21	24	1994	2034	24	0	24	0	24	0	24	0	NL
1993OLD GAS22	4	1993	2033	4	0	4	0	4	0	4	0	NL
1988OLD GAS23	1	1988	2028	1	0	1	0	1	0	1	0	NL
1995OLD GAS24	178	1995	2035	178	0	178	0	178	0	178	0	NL
1993OLD GAS25	1	1993	2033	1	0	1	0	1	0	1	0	NL
1999OLD GAS26	156	1999	2039	156	0	156	0	156	0	156	0	NL
1993OLD GAS27	2	1993	2033	2	0	2	0	2	0	2	0	NL
1999OLD GAS28	7	1999	2039	7	0	7	0	7	0	7	0	GER

Table 4.8 Identifying the need for replacements contd.

Power plant	Gross capacity (MW)	Commissioned	Replacement	2010 Capacity	2010 Replacement	2011 Capacity	2011 Replacement	2019 Capacity	2019 Replacement	2020 Capacity	2020 Replacement	Country
GAS												
1998OLD GAS29	96	1998	2038	96	0	96	0	96	0	96	0	GER
2000OLD GAS30	40	2000	2040	40	0	40	0	40	0	40	0	GER
1994OLD GAS31	5	1994	2034	5	0	5	0	5	0	5	0	GER
2002OLD GAS32	52	2002	2042	52	0	52	0	52	0	52	0	GER
1999OLD GAS33	12	1999	2039	12	0	12	0	12	0	12	0	GER
1999OLD GAS34	135	1999	2039	135	0	135	0	135	0	135	0	GER
2001OLD GAS35	13	2001	2041	13	0	13	0	13	0	13	0	GER
1993OLD GAS36	3	1993	2033	3	0	3	0	3	0	3	0	GER
1996OLD GAS37	38	1996	2036	38	0	38	0	38	0	38	0	GER
2010OLD GAS38	1,700	2010	2050	1,700	0	1,700	0	1,700	0	1,700	0	GER
2011OLD GAS39	864	2011	2051	0	0	864	0	864	0	864	0	UK
2009OLD GAS40	530	2009	2049	530	0	530	0	530	0	530	0	GER
GAS TOTAL	11,462			8,965	1,633	11,462	0	11,462	0	11,207	255	
WATER												
2000OLD WATER41	205	2000	2100	205	0	205	0	205	0	205	0	GER
1970OLD WATER42	6	1970	2070	6	0	6	0	6	0	6	0	UK
2010OLD WATER43	304	2000	2100	304	0	304	0	304	0	304	0	GER
1967OLD WATER44	6	1967	2067	6	0	6	0	6	0	6	0	ESP
1989OLD WATER45	13	1989	2089	13	0	13	0	13	0	13	0	NL
WATER TOTAL	533			533	0	533	0	533	0	533	0	
WIND												
2001OLD WIND46	9	2001	2021	9	0	9	0	9	0	9	0	GER
2001OLD WIND47	468	2001	2021	468	0	468	0	468	0	468	0	UK
2002OLD WIND48	384	2002	2022	384	0	384	0	384	0	384	0	GER
1994OLD WIND45	177	1994	2014	177	0	177	0	177	0	177	0	NL
2009OLD WIND49	90	2009	2029	90	0	90	0	90	0	90	0	UK
2009OLD WIND50	207	2009	2029	207	0	207	0	207	0	207	0	NL
WIND TOTAL	1,336			1,336	0	1,336	0	1,336	0	1,336	0	

Power plant	Gross capacity (MW)	Commissioned	Replacement	2010 Capacity	2010 Replacement	2011 Capacity	2011 Replacement	2019 Capacity	2019 Replacement	2020 Capacity	2020 Replacement	Country
PV												
2000OLD PV1	1	2000	2020	1.016	0	1.016	0	1.016	0	0	1	GER
PV TOTAL	**1**			**1.016**	**0**	**1.016**	**0**	**1.016**	**0**	**0**	**1.016**	
OIL												
1967OLD OIL1	35	1967	1987	0	35	35	0	35	0	35	0	UK
1982OLD OIL2	160	1982	2002	0	160	160	0	160	0	160	0	UK
1969OLD OIL3	100	1969	1989	0	100	100	0	100	0	100	0	UK
1970OLD OIL4	1,035	1970	1990	0	1035	1,035	0	1,035	0	1,035	0	UK
1981OLD OIL5	730	1981	2001	0	730	730	0	730	0	730	0	UK
1965OLD OIL6	18	1965	1985	0	18	18	0	18	0	18	0	UK
OIL TOTAL	**2,078**			**0**	**2,078**	**2,078**	**0**	**2,078**	**0**	**2,078**	**0**	
OTHER												
1997OLD OTHER1	472	1997	2017	472	0	472	0	472	0	472	0	UK
1996OLD OTHER2	250	1996	2016	250	0	250	0	250	0	250	0	UK
1998OLD OTHER3	102	1998	2018	102	0	102	0	102	0	102	0	NL
1995OLD OTHER4	10	1995	2015	10	0	10	0	10	0	10	0	NL
1976OLD OTHER5	42	1976	1996	0	42	42	0	42	0	42	0	NL
1986OLD OTHER6	7	1986	2006	0	7	7	0	7	0	7	0	NL
1994OLD OTHER7	10	1994	2014	10	0	10	0	10	0	10	0	NL
1997OLD OTHER8	180	1997	2017	180	0	180	0	180	0	180	0	NL
1999OLD OTHER9	90	1999	2019	90	0	90	0	0	90	90	0	NL
OTHER TOTAL	**1,164**			**1,115**	**49**	**1,164**	**0**	**1,074**	**90**	**1,164**	**0**	
TOTAL in 2010	**36,491**			**30,631**	**5,859**	**39,055**	**2,100**	**38,965**	**2,190**	**40,899**	**256**	

Source: Own table

Regarding the replacements of power plants we generally prescind regulatory uncertainty by rejecting investment plants by the national regulator.

4.4.3 Investments in generation capacity

In addition to the issue of considering replacements over time to dynamize the power plant park, the model allows, depending on the target capacity of the utility, to build up additional capacity. In order to match the target energy mix with the capacity development over time we choose to implement an iterative process. Table 4.9 illustrates this part of the model. On the left hand side power plants serve as placeholders for each technology. This is due to the fact, that the model should compute the effect of building up additional capacity automatically. Since the target energy capacity is flexible, the placeholders are necessary to balance the power plant park. In a first step, the spreadsheet sums up the additional investments by plant technology over time (see Table 4.9). Then the spreadsheet takes the result of the table on the right hand side above of Table 4.9 and adds these to the replacements which are already conducted on the previous spreadsheet. Lastly, the capacity of the initial power plant park of the year 2010, which still exists in the target year, is added. Additional investments are varied as long as the proportion of the individual power plant technology equals the target capacity by type of fuel.

Table 4.9 Investment planning

Power plant	Gross capacity (MW)	Efficiency	Net capacity	Merit order	Load factor	Maintenance	Power generation (in MWh)	Emissions (tCO₂/year)	CO₂ efficiency	Commissioned	Replacement	Country
UR												
UR TARGET PLANT 1	1,000	35%	995	Base Load	8,760	876	7,844,580	0	0	2013	2060	UK
UR TARGET PLANT 2	1,000	35%	995	Base Load	8,760	876	7,844,580	0	0	2017	2060	UK
UR TARGET PLANT 3	1,000	35%	995	Base Load	8,760	876	7,844,580	0	0	2020	2060	UK
UR TARGET PLANT 4	1,127	35%	1,121	Base Load	8,760	876	8,839,351	0	0	2020	2060	UK
UR TARGET PLANT 5	0	35%	0	Base Load	8,760	876			0	2020	2060	UK
UR TOTAL	**4,127**	35%	**4,106**				**32,373,091**	**0**	**0**			
COGEN												
COGEN TARGET PLANT 1	250	80%	245	Base Load	8,760	876	1,927,638	676,601	351	2013	2060	GER
COGEN TARGET PLANT 2	250	80%	245	Base Load	8,760	876	1,927,638	676,601	351	2017	2060	GER
COGEN TARGET PLANT 3	250	80%	245	Base Load	8,760	876	1,927,638	676,601	351	2018	2060	GER
COGEN TARGET PLANT 4	250	80%	245	Base Load	8,760	876	1,927,638	676,601	351	2019	2060	GER
COGEN TARGET PLANT 5	106	80%	104	Base Load	8,760	876	817,692	287,010	351	2020	2060	GER
COGEN TOTAL	**1,106**		**1,082**				**8,528,244**	**2,993,414**	**351**			
COAL												
COAL TARGET PLANNED 1	2,400	46%	2,388	Base Load	8,760	876	18,826,992	13,800,185	733	2012	2057	UK
COAL TARGET PLANNED 2	411	46%	405	Base Load	8,760	876	3,193,428	2,340,782	733	2014	2059	UK
COAL TOTAL	**2,811**		**2,793**				**22,020,420**	**16,140,968**	**1,364**			
GAS												
GAS TARGET PLANNED 1	2,000	58%	1,990	Middle Load	6,000	600	10,746,000	3,771,846	351	2011	2051	UK
GAS TARGET PLANNED 2	469	58%	462	Middle Load	6,000	600	2,494,611	875,608	351	2010	2050	NL
GAS TARGET PLANNED 3	250	58%	245	Middle Load	6,000	600	1,320,300	463,425	351	2018	2058	NL
GAS TARGET PLANNED 4	50	58%	49	Peak Load	1,000	100	43,875	15,400	351	2018	2058	NL
GAS TARGET PLANNED 5	426	58%	420	Middle Load	6,000	600	2,265,894	795,329	351	2011	2051	NL
GAS TARGET PLANNED 6	65	58%	63	Peak Load	1,000	100	57,038	20,020	351	2018	2058	GER
GAS TARGET PLANT 1	500	58%	493	Middle Load	6,000	600	2,659,500	933,485	351	2013	2060	GER
GAS TARGET PLANT 2	500	58%	493	Middle Load	6,000	600	2,659,500	933,485	351	2016	2060	GER
GAS TARGET PLANT 3	342	58%	334	Middle Load	6,000	600	1,805,674	633,792	351	2020	2060	GER
GAS TOTAL	**4,602**		**4,548**				**24,052,391**	**8,442,389**	**351**			

Power plant	Gross capacity (MW)	Efficiency	Net capacity	Merit order	Load factor	Maintenance	Power generation (in MWh)	Emissions (tCO₂/year)	CO₂ efficiency	Commissioned	Replacement	Country
WATER												
WATER TARGET PLANNED 1	10	85%	10	Base Load	8,760	876	79,944	0	0	2015	2115	UK
WATER TARGET PLANNED 2	7	85%	7	Base Load	8,760	876	53,040	0	0	2015	2115	UK
WATER TARGET PLANT 1	200	85%	195	Base Load	8,760	876	1,537,380	0	0	2014	2114	GER
WATER TARGET PLANT 2	200	85%	195	Base Load	8,760	876	1,537,380	0	0	2015	2115	GER
WATER TARGET PLANT 3	200	85%	195	Base Load	8,760	876	1,537,380	0	0	2016	2116	GER
WATER TARGET PLANT 4	59	85%	58	Base Load	8,760	876	454,842	0	0	2020	2120	GER
WATER TOTAL	**617**		**660**				**4,745,123**	**0**	**0**			
WIND												
WIND TARGET PLANNED 1	90	45%	88	Base Load	8,760	876	691,821	0	0	2008	2060	ESP
WIND TARGET PLANNED 2	3,391	45%	3,374	Base Load	8,760	876	26,604,109	0	0	2010	2060	UK
WIND TARGET PLANNED 3	652	45%	645	Base Load	8,760	876	5,085,062	0	0	2018	2060	UK
WIND TARGET PLANT 1	305	45%	298	Base Load	8,760	876	2,347,979	0	0	2014	2060	GER
WIND TOTAL	**4,437**		**4,405**				**34,728,970**	**0**	**0**			
PV												
PV TARGET PLANT 1	500	35%	493	Base Load	8,760	876	3,882,870	0	0	2014	2034	ESP
PV TARGET PLANT 2	500	35%	493	Base Load	8,760	876	3,882,870	0	0	2015	2035	ESP
PV TARGET PLANT 3	208	35%	203	Base Load	8,760	876	1,601,981	0	0	2016	2036	ESP
PV TOTAL	**1,208**		**1,188**				**9,367,721**	**0**	**0**			
OTHER												
OTHER TARGET PLANNED 1	65	35%	63	Peak Load	1,000	100	57,038	22,815	400	2018	2038	UK
OTHER TARGET PLANNED 2	45	35%	44	Peak Load	1,000	100	39,488	15,795	400	2018	2038	UK
OTHER TARGET PLANT 1	200	35%	195	Base Load	8,760	876	1,537,380	614,952	400	2020	2060	GER
OTHER TARGET PLANT 2	38	35%	37	Peak Load	1,000	100	33,472	13,389	400	2020	2060	GER
OTHER TOTAL	**348**		**339**				**1,667,377**	**666,951**	**400**			

Source: Own table.

4.5 Monte Carlo based valuation of generation portfolios

This section describes the idea of the valuation methodology based on a Monte Carlo simulation. In particular, the VBA-code structure will be presented, which is the crucial element within the power plant valuation model.

4.5.1 Expected value and risk

A power plant is a real asset and therefore the asset allocation process is very similar to financial assets. However, instead of relying on returns the valuation approach is based on a DCF model. In this section we distinguish between conventional thermal power plants and renewable energies free cash flows.[371] Analytically, we compute the EBIT of fossil fuel plants as follows:[372]

$$(4.13) \quad EBIT_t = \tilde{P}_t^E\left(\frac{\text{€}}{MWh}\right) \cdot Q_t^E(MWh) - E^{-1}(\%) \cdot \tilde{P}_t^F\left(\frac{\text{€}}{MWh}\right) \cdot Q_t^F(MWh) - \tilde{P}_t^C\left(\frac{\text{€}}{t}\right) \cdot Q_t^C(t) - c_{O\&M}\left(\frac{\text{€}}{MWh}\right) - c_{Fix}\left(\frac{\text{€}}{MW}\right) - D_t$$

In equation (4.13) $\tilde{P}_t^E$, $\tilde{P}_t^F$ and $\tilde{P}_t^C$ denote the prices of electricity, fuel and carbon in the specific year t, respectively. The quantities of generated electricity, used fuel and the amount of emission allowances are denoted by Q_t^E, Q_t^F and Q_t^C, respectively. In order to calculate the cost of fuel, the technical efficiency, E, is divided by the price and quantity of fuel. While $c_{O\&M}$ represent the cost of operation and maintenance, c_{Fix} denotes the fixed costs. Lastly, we subtract the annual depreciation, D. In order to derive annual free cash flows of power plants, we deduct taxes, τ, from power plants' EBIT, add annual depreciation, D, and eliminate investment costs IC:

$$(4.14) \quad FCF_t = EBIT_t \cdot (1-\tau) + D_t - IC_t$$

The free cash flow is forecasted over a period of 10 years. The uncertainty of future cash flows is mainly driven by the electricity price, cost of fuel and the price of carbon. The other variables are not stochastic. Instead they remain constant between periods.

---

[371] We take different fuel technologies of power plants into account. Namely, lignite, coal, nuclear, gas, oil and cogen. Moreover, we distinguish between wind, water, photovoltaic and other power plants.
[372] For simplicity we neglect the change of net working capital.

Compared to the forecast of the free cash flow of regular fossil fuel based plants, the calculation for renewable generation capacity differs. Due to the governmental subsidies in terms of guaranteed fixed prices for generated green energy, the electricity price is not stochastic from the perspective of the owner from a renewable capacity. Instead, the uncertainty occurs due to the volatile meteorological conditions of wind and photovoltaic capacity during the year. Hence, the model considers the uncertainty rather in terms of generated electricity as volume risk instead of price risk. Moreover, renewable energies do not emit carbon. Therefore these kinds of generation technologies possess a comparative carbon cost advantage to fossil plants based on lignite or coal. The characteristics of renewable energies are included in the analytical computation of the free cash flow. In general, the EBIT of renewable generation capacity is calculated by equation (4.15):

$$ (4.15) \qquad EBIT_t = \overline{P}_t^E \left(\frac{\text{\euro}}{MWh} \right) \cdot \tilde{Q}_t^E (MWh) - c_{O\&M} \left(\frac{\text{\euro}}{MWh} \right) - c_{Fix} \left(\frac{\text{\euro}}{MW} \right) - D_t $$

whereas $\overline{P}_t^E$ denotes the fixed electricity price for generated green energy defined by the national regulator. The stochastic volume of generated electricity is captured by the random variable $\tilde{Q}_t^E$. Renewable energies' free cash flows are computed, as stated in formula (4.14).

The DCF methodology to determine the value of a power plant is applied irrespectively of the kind of plant technology. Hence, equation (4.16) is capable to determine the value of thermal power plants as well as renewable energies. Today's DCF value, V_i, of a power plant is calculated therefore as follows:[373]

$$ (4.16) \qquad V_i(0) = \sum_{t=1}^{T} \frac{FCF_t}{(1+r_{WACC})^t} + \frac{FCF_T}{(r_{WACC}-g)} \cdot \frac{1}{(1+r_{WACC})^{T-t}} $$

whereas $r_{WACC} = r_f$.[374] Here, we rely on a 10-year European government bond rate of 4.5% to approximate the risk-free interest rate.

---

[373] The discount rate of the terminal value in 2020 is adjusted by a long term growth-rate, g, of 0.5%.
[374] Please refer to Chapter 3.1.2.4 for further details.

The expected DCF value per MW power plant capacity is equal to the mean average of the overall simulation runs:

$$(4.17) \qquad E[V] = \mu = \frac{1}{n} \sum_{i=1}^{N} V_i(0)$$

For the further analysis, we define the standard deviation of the expected DCF value per MW plant capacity. Therefore, the variance of the expected plant value is computed as:

$$(4.18) \qquad \sigma_V^2 = \frac{1}{n} \sum_{i=1}^{N} (V_i - E[V])^2$$

Taking the square root of equation (4.18) equals the standard deviation of the expected power plant value:

$$(4.19) \qquad \sigma_V = \sqrt{\sigma_V^2}$$

By defining the expected value of plant per MW capacity and the corresponding standard deviation of the expected plant value, the Markowitz approach can be applied in order to analyze generation portfolios.[375]

---

[375] For details regarding the portfolio theory of Markowitz (1952), please refer to Chapter 3.

4.5.2 Loop programming

As stated in the previous section the model distinguishes the uncertain variables of electricity (base, peak), fuel (coal, lignite, gas oil, and uranium), carbon prices as well as meteorological data in terms of total hours of sun and wind supply. In order to identify the power plant technology to be valued by the Monte Carlo simulation, we use the following code structure summarized in Table 4.10.

Table 4.10 Classification for VBA-Macro

Characteristics	**Power price**	**Type of fuel**	**CO₂**	**Country**
Base	1	-	-	-
Peak	2	-	-	-
Coal	-	1	-	-
Lignite	-	2	-	-
Gas	-	3	-	-
Cogen	-	3	-	-
Oil	-	4	-	-
Nuclear	-	5	-	-
Wind	-	6	-	-
PV	-	7	-	-
Water	-	8	-	-
Other	-	9	-	-
CO₂-Yes	-	-	1	-
CO₂ -No	-	-	2	-
Germany	-	-	-	1
United Kingdom	-	-	-	2
The Netherlands	-	-	-	3
Spain	-	-	-	4

Source: Own table.

For instance, base and peak load plants are classified as "1" and "2", respectively. In order to encompass the range of plant technologies, the model sets numbers in a range from "1" to "9" for identification. However, as we assume that cogen plants run solely on gas, this kind of plant technology is marked like a regular gas power plant. Note that the codification is necessary for classification of the simulated prices to the specific power technology. Depending on the power plant fuel type, the model tests if the plant emits carbon ("1") or does not bear any carbon price risk ("2"). The latter is particularly true for nuclear, wind, photovoltaic and water power plants. Lastly, for country identification the model classification runs from "1", "2", "3" and "4" for Germany, United Kingdom, the Netherlands and Spain, respectively. Taking the country distinction into account allows on the hand to describe the sample properly, and to explore international diversification effects for generation portfolios on the other hand. The country code determines the power exchange on which electricity is sold. Therefore the model refers to base and peak load prices from the *European Energy Exchange, APX UK, APX NL* and *OMEL* for Germany, United Kingdom, the Netherlands and Spain, respectively. In brief, the classification allows studying the impact of 48 different types of power plants on generation portfolios.[376]

After having defined a classification for electricity, fuel, carbon prices and countries we are able to make use of a loop program written in *Visual Basic for Application* (VBA).[377] In the process of the VBA program every power plant is tested as long as the code of column E3, G3, I3 and K3 representing the classification of the electricity price, fuel type, carbon risk and location, respectively, matches with the codification defined in the table above. Then the simulation runs by plugging the simulated risky variables in the cells C16, C21 and C26 and computing 1,000 times the free cash flow of each plant (see Figure 4.10). In contrast, for the valuation of renewable power plants, cell G6 serves as a placeholder to consider volume risk. This cell is the reference cell for the determination of the generated electricity in MWh for each year in row 17.

The calculated net present value of the specific plant is stored for every single run (1,000 runs for each plant), in order to calculate the mean for the whole simulation and the corresponding standard deviation (see Figure 4.11). Moreover, the model divides the plant value by the total gross plant capacity for comparability.

For every single plant the present value of a MW capacity as well as the standard deviation of the net present value of the MW capacity are then transferred to the portfolio element of the model for further analyses. Moreover, for each power plant the valuation tool provides a summary of statistics including the skewness, kurtosis, minimum, maximum, range and confidence interval of power plants' net present values.

---

[376] We distinguish between 10 different kind of power plant fuels and 4 countries. Additionally, gas and oil are supposed to run during peak loads in these markets. Hence, 40 plus 8 amounts to 48 different options.

[377] Please refer to the appendix of the thesis for further details on the VBA-code.

Figure 4.10 Spreadsheet plant valuation

2011NEW COAL15 2011		Base Load	1	COAL	1	CO₂	1	GER	1

Plant Valuation

Total Capacity:	2,100
Tax rate	30%

Volume Risk

in €	2010	2011	2012	2013	2014	2015	2016	2017	2018	2019	2020
Sales											
Power price	36.55	35.49	32.87	51.47	38.30	44.02	52.42	43.45	41.43	55.25	43.66
Volume MWh	16,473,618	16,473,618	16,473,618	16,473,618	16,473,618	16,473,618	16,473,618	16,473,618	16,473,618	16,473,618	16,473,618
Total Sales	0	584,652,462	541,548,689	847,871,901	630,952,931	725,145,494	863,576,517	715,794,440	682,455,014	910,114,831	719,238,767
Cost of fuel											
Fuel price	7.82	10.04	7.02	6.05	6.40	6.82	10.54	6.26	8.03	8.92	9.16
Volume	35,812,213	35,812,213	35,812,213	35,812,213	35,812,213	35,812,213	35,812,213	35,812,213	35,812,213	35,812,213	35,812,213
Total cost of fuel	0	359,546,366	251,420,114	216,600,899	229,314,445	244,064,293	377,500,088	224,052,599	287,591,317	319,600,782	328,102,197
Cost of carbon											
CO₂ price	24.27	24.49	29.64	34.38	36.91	24.88	37.25	28.91	40.28	40.72	33.25
Volume	4,830,065	4,830,065	4,830,065	12,075,162	12,075,162	12,075,162	12,075,162	12,075,162	12,075,162	12,075,162	12,075,162
Total cost of carbon	0	118,267,935	143,154,479	415,178,868	445,680,112	300,410,316	449,801,271	349,094,780	486,412,648	491,706,946	401,445,957
Other											
O & M	0	28,565,254	28,565,254	28,565,254	28,565,254	28,565,254	28,565,254	28,565,254	28,565,254	28,565,254	28,565,254
Fix	0	42,840,000	42,840,000	42,840,000	42,840,000	42,840,000	42,840,000	42,840,000	42,840,000	42,840,000	42,840,000
Total other costs	0	71,405,254	71,405,254	71,405,254	71,405,254	71,405,254	71,405,254	71,405,254	71,405,254	71,405,254	71,405,254
EBITDA	0	35,433,908	75,568,842	144,686,879	-118,446,879	109,265,632	-35,130,095	71,241,807	-162,954,205	27,401,850	-81,714,641
Depreciation	0	-98,532,000	-98,532,000	-98,532,000	-98,532,000	-98,532,000	-98,532,000	-98,532,000	-98,532,000	-98,532,000	-98,532,000
EBIT	0	-63,099,092	-22,963,158	46,154,879	-213,978,879	10,733,632	-133,662,095	-27,290,193	-261,486,205	-71,130,160	-180,246,641
Tax	0	0	0	13,846,464	0	3,220,090	0	0	0	0	0
EAT	0	-63,099,092	-22,963,158	32,308,416	-213,978,879	7,513,542	-133,662,095	-27,290,193	-261,486,205	-71,130,160	-180,246,641
Depreciation	0	98,532,000	98,532,000	98,532,000	98,532,000	98,532,000	98,532,000	98,532,000	98,532,000	98,532,000	98,532,000
Investments	2,463,300,000	0	0	0	0	0	0	0	0	0	0
Free cash flow	-2,463,300,000	35,432,908	75,568,842	130,840,416	-115,446,879	106,045,542	-35,130,095	71,241,807	-162,954,205	27,401,850	-81,714,641

Source: Own figure.

Figure 4.11 Spreadsheet plant valuation contd.

43	**WACC**	4.5%		**Growth**	0.5%							
44												
45	**Discount rate**	0.9569	0.9157	0.8763	0.8386	0.8025	0.7679	0.7348	0.7032	0.6729	0.6439	16.0982
46												
47	**Present value**	-2,357,224,880	32,446,975	66,220,720	109,717,715	-92,640,469	81,431,920	-25,814,594	50,096,179	-109,652,606	17,644,809	-1,315,457,985
48												
49	**2011NEW COAL15**	**-3,543,232,216**										
50												
51	Mean total	3,875,302,565										
52	Std total	5,679,498,800										
53	Skew	-0.1218										
54	Kurt	0.0832										
55	Runs	1,000										
57	Min	-13,720,878,567										
58	Max	22,432,809,077										
59	Range	36,153,687,644										
60												
61	MEAN/ rel	1,845,382										
62	STD rel	2,704,523										
63												

Source: Own figure.

And lastly, the spreadsheet represents graphically the probability function and corresponding density function for power plants' net present value per MW capacity which offers a comparability between power plant technologies (see Figure 4.12).

Figure 4.12 a) Frequency distribution and b) density function of power plants net present value

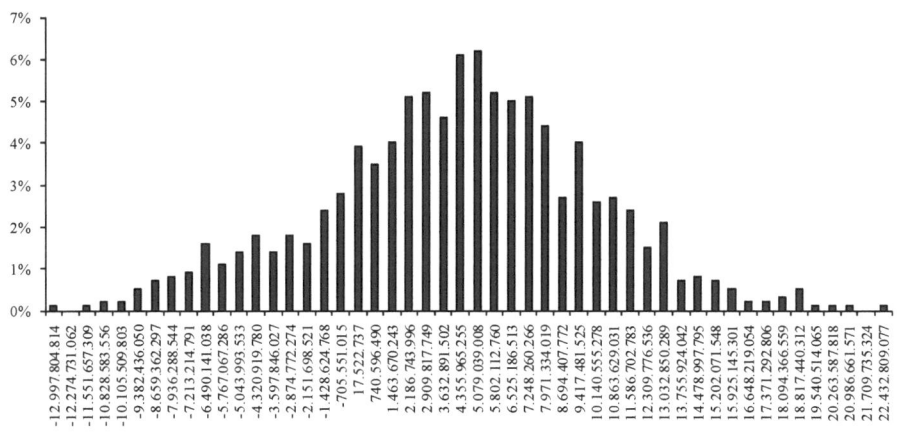

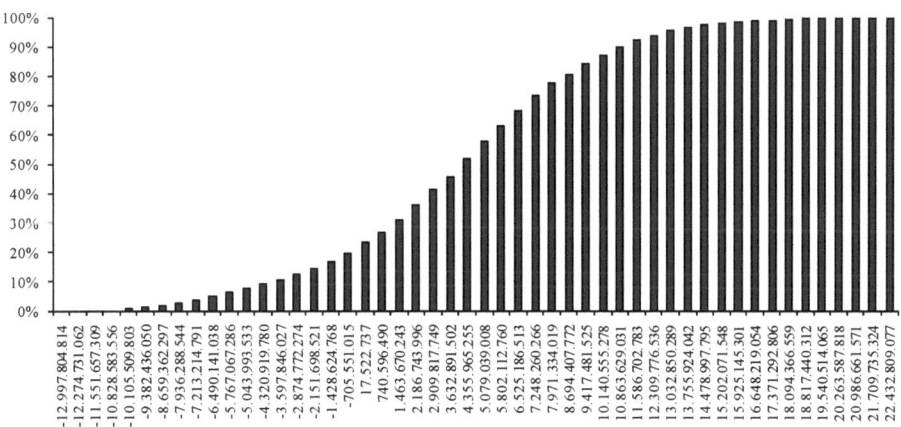

Source: Own calculation and graph.

The following section introduces the portfolio analysis for power plant technologies within the simulation model. After having discussed the general optimization procedure, we are clarifying the distinction of economical vs. technical efficiency.

4.5.3 Optimization

The simulation results of the power plant valuation are transferred to the module *"Portfolio Analysis"*. This element serves to compute the correlation matrix for the existing plants in the generation portfolio of the target year, as well as the corresponding covariance matrix. The correlation between two power plants is calculated by referring to the valuation results of the individual power plant which is stored in the respective spreadsheet. Please note that the analysis is based on plant technology rather than type of fuel. Assuming a perfect correlation would cause a bias of the results of the portfolio analysis, and perfect correlation will not be the case as plants differ in e.g. their efficiency levels. The analysis of the power plant park in detail rather than on a fuel basis sheds light on the issue of future investments in generation capacity, as independencies are included in depth even technically.

To determine the covariance matrix of the power plant park, we make use of a cell reference to the correlation matrix, as well as to the corresponding power plants' standard deviation of the expected net present value per MW generation capacity. As presented in the theoretical section of the thesis, the covariance matrix allows to compute the standard deviation of the expected value in €/ MW for the generation portfolio. However, the calculation requires determining the weight of the specific asset. Very similar to stocks, the portfolio weight of a power plant is equal to the gross capacity divided by the capacity of the power plant park in total.

Taking the gross capacities of each plant as portfolio weight allows easily identifying the mean in €/ MW and the standard deviation of the expected value in €/ MW for the power plant park. The implementation in Excel is based on array-functions. This allows appraising the target portfolio within the risk-return framework. We conduct the optimization by using *Solver* which is an add-in for solving linear optimization problems. Consequently, Solver conducts the calculation relying on an iterative process as long as the objective function, here portfolios variance function, is minimized subject to the restrictions defined.[378] In order to set the restrictions for the optimization properly, it is necessary to distinguish between economical and technical efficiency in the portfolio optimization. The following two sections deal with this difference.

---

[378] Please refer to Chapter 3 for further details.

4.5.4 Economic efficiency

In our simulation model we use the expression *economic efficiency* to describe a generation portfolio which – based on our assumption – leads to a maximum return by a given level of risk and vice versa. Very similar to *Markowitz*, we allow investing in all types of generation assets. Hence, we assume that neither geographic conditions nor regulatory authorities are restricting investments in certain type of power plant technologies. As a consequence, nuclear power plants are part of the feasible set of utilities' generation assets. In addition, there are no limitations regarding the technical feasibility of the electricity grid. Furthermore, we assume that all other stakeholders (government, habitants etc.) do not prevent any kind of investment in power plants, e.g. coal plants. This allows varying replacement and investment strategies independently of the strategy communicated by the individual utility firm in order to identify efficient portfolios from a strictly economical point of view. Hence, we test whether alternative strategies lead to portfolios which are not dominated by other portfolios.

This means we take a regular power plant park which has not reached its technical lifetime in 2020 as given. Consequently, this amount of generation capacity is not part of the optimization process. Instead, the target function is subjected to the plants of a regular power plant park. Hence, we are able to vary the share of the total generation capacity minus the amount of gross capacities referring to old power plants. In other words, we neglect the opportunity to conduct divestments of the specific utility firm. Compared to other goods, markets for power plants are illiquid and they are therefore difficult to sell. The different portfolio combinations of the target year and their corresponding net present value per MW generation capacity are then stored within the model for comparison. Due to the optimization, we are able to gain insights in the optimal composition of generation portfolios in terms of economics. However, the challenge is knowing how to rebalance the generation portfolio. Therefore the model is set up on the idea of flexibility. This means that the results of the optimization process flow directly to the assumptions sheet. By defining the target energy mix leading to economical efficiency, replacements as well as additional investments in generation capacity are conducted, as long as the power plant park is equal to the presetting in the model.

4.5.5 Technical efficiency

Compared to the efficiency from an economical point of view, the expression *technical efficiency* includes feasibility which depends mainly on the characteristics of the electricity grid. Therefore, based on our definition a generation portfolio which is technically efficient is a subset of the feasible generation portfolios, as well as the economically efficient portfolios. While the general optimization process is restricted to short sales in comparison to asset allocation of stocks, we expand the optimization restrictions in order to take technical feasibility into account. Due to the characteristics of the good electricity (see Chapter 2) the electricity generation has to make sure to balance supply and demand for every single minute. Otherwise the network will brake and blackout occurs. Since renewable energies are promoted by fixed tariffs, they seem attractive as investment opportunity compared to fossil plants. However, volatile operating hours due to the dependency on meteorological conditions limits the share of green power plants of total generation capacity.

The incensement of green power plants goes along with additional investments in back-up generation technology which leads to larger power plant parks. Moreover, we have to take geographical restrictions into account. Building new hydro power plant parks require either rich water occurrences in lakes or ascending areas to make use of high differences. Hence, this type of power plant technology is limited in terms of additional investments.[379]

If it turns out that water plants are attractive for profit maximizing utility firms, one strategy for realization might be to purchase existing generation capacity form competitors to avoid geographical restrictions. Very similar to the economical efficiency we take the power plants which have not exceeded technical lifetime till 2020 as given. Therefore the share of potential optimization is target (total) generation capacity less regular power plants.

---

[379] See EWI/ EEFA (2008), pp. 118-119.

Since the analysis aims to identify efficient portfolios which are feasible, the optimization procedure is subjected to an upper limit of wind and photovoltaic power plant capacity of 30% and 15%, respectively. Alongside the restriction of generation capacity from renewable energies, a minimum amount of 10% for base load is provided by coal power plants. A modernization of the European electricity network towards a smart grid, however, allows increasing the share of generation capacity of renewable energies, as generated power can easily be transferred and guarantees balancing load. Table 4.11 represents a comparison of the main criteria regarding technical and economic efficiency.

Table 4.11 Technical and economic efficiency

Criteria	Technical efficiency	Economic efficiency
Short sales	Excluded.	Excluced.
Geographic conditions	Limited additional investments due to geographic conditions (i.e. hydro power plant capacity).	Geographic conditions are not restricting investments in generation capacity.
Restricition of regulatory authority	Security of supply.	No restricitions.
Nuclear energy	It is included as technological option for future investments in power plants due to different electricity markets and its corresponding regulation.	It is part of the optimization procedere.
Grid stability	Grid stability is captured in the optimization procedure with subject to a certain amount (10%) of coal power plant capacity as well as upper limits for wind (30%) and photovoltaic (15%) power plants.	It is not explicitly incorporated in the optimization.

Source: Own table.

The restrictions, discussed in this section are taken into account by formulating proper constraints for the portfolio optimization.

4.6 Summary

In this section we have presented the mode of action of the simulation model. We have used *Excel* in order to set up a model which takes the change of the power plant over time into account. The model identifies the need for replacements automatically, and makes sure that the target generation capacity is built in the target year. Here, commodity prices and meteorological data like wind speed and total sun hours have served as risky variables. Specifically, we have distinguished between base and peak load prices from EEX, APX UK, APX NL and OMEL. Moreover, we have assumed commodity prices (oil, gas, coal, lignite, uranium) as well as carbon certificates as uncertain and have developed respective future price trajectories. Instead of relying on prices, we have taken volume risks into account in terms of wind speed and total sun hours to valuate wind power plants and sun power plants, respectively. To solve the dependencies between these risky variables, we have introduced the methodology of Cholesky. The latter decompose the empirically observed correlations to gain simulated risky variables which correlations tend to be close to the initial matrix.

The simulated price trajectories are then taken as a reference for the valuation procedure which is based on a DCF valuation approach to determine the expected net present value per generation capacity (MW) and the corresponding standard deviation of the respective expected value. As a consequence, the results of the valuation are transferred to the portfolio analysis. Here, we have distinguished between technical and economical efficiency in order to identify generation portfolios and test the research questions.

5 Empirical analyses of European generation portfolios

The purpose of this chapter is to present the simulation results for the optimization of power generation portfolios. However, we will first describe the commodity and meteorological input data. Besides we will show not only the empirical correlation but also the simulated correlation results of these variables. In order to conduct the disaggregated valuation on a single plant basis, we will introduce the sample of power plants and derive an investment strategy to reach the utility's target generation mix over time. This allows identifying the feasible set of generation assets and determining the efficient frontiers for domestic as well as international electricity markets. After that, we will analyze these country specific target generation portfolios Germany, the UK, the Netherlands and Spain. To measure the degree of relative efficiency of the respective generation portfolios, we rely on the performance ratios developed in section 3.4.4. Therefore we will show in this upcoming chapter how efficient utility's target generation portfolios are not only from a domestic but also from an international point of view. These results are taken to adjust the original investment strategy to demonstrate how to rebalance a target power plant portfolio towards the efficient set. This chapter closes with a robustness analysis in order to test the validity of the simulation model and deduces implications.

5.1 Description of the stochastic variables

5.1.1 Data

We have simulated the risky variables by deriving their means and corresponding standard deviations from historical time series. Therefore, we have examined 13 commodity prices from May 31st, 2005 to December 31st, 2009 in order to determine the dependencies of the risky variables properly. Moreover, we have taken data of the *Deutscher Wetterdienst* (DWD) into account to approximate the volume risk of wind and photovoltaic power plants by wind speed and total sun hours, respectively.[380]

All financial data are taken from *Datastream* (Thomson Reuters). Since our sample covers power plants which are located in different countries, we have taken electricity

---

[380] DWD provides these data for free on a monthly basis.

© Springer Fachmedien Wiesbaden GmbH, part of Springer Nature 2011
S. Rothe, *Portfolio Analysis of Power Plant Technologies*, Edition KWV,
https://doi.org/10.1007/978-3-658-24379-1_5

prices from corresponding European power exchanges into account. We rely on spot market base and peak load price changes from the European Energy Exchange (EEX) in Germany, the APX in the United Kingdom, the APX in the Netherlands and the Spanish OMEL.

To gain the data for carbon prices in EU ETS, we rely on EUA future prices with maturity in 2010 from the European Climate Exchange (ECX). The ECX is the predominant marketplace for EUA futures reaching a market share of 43% in 2007[381] and the December 2010 EUA contract is currently the most liquid future. Due to the design of the different trading phases and the induced price jumps of spot prices in the first trading phase, it is more reliable to conduct the analysis with future price data compared to spot market data. The latter collapsed in 2006, when an oversupply of allowances was revealed, after the disclosure of 2005 verified emission data. Finally, in 2007 spot prices moved towards zero, as verified emissions were again below the 2006 yearly allocation.[382] Although future prices were affected from the disclosure as well, they also reflect expectations of market participants with respect to future regulation and the fact that most energy needs are met by forward contracting. Hence, carbon futures are more suitable as proxy for carbon price risk than spot market data.

Even though oil fired power plants have a small impact on power generation in European, the development of oil prices is a crucial factor for power generation. To finance gas infrastructure projects, European natural gas prices are historically linked to the Brent crude oil price. In addition, oil drives energy commodity prices and is therefore captured within the simulation model. Consequently, we control the impact of oil price change by referring to price data of the Brent crude oil forward of the current month.

As demonstrated in Chapter 2, investments in generation capacity are mainly based on natural gas plants leading to strong annual average growth rates in liberalized electricity markets.[383] Therefore, the price changes of monthly gas forwards are taken from the Intercontinental Exchange (ICE) in London. Our sample is not dominated by power plants located in the UK. Yet, ICE gas prices are reliable, as continental and UK gas prices are strongly correlated.[384] Since coal power plants dominate the electricity

---

[381] See Daskalakis et al. (2009), p. 1234.
[382] Please refer to section 2.3.2 for further details.
[383] Please refer to section 2.1.3 for further details.
[384] See Neumann et al., (2006), pp. 729-730.

generation in Central Europe, we take coal price change as an additional risk factor into account. In detail, we refer to the coal price index of Spectron converted into Euro per ton. German power plant parks are particularly characterized by a significant share of lignite power plants. Hence, it is necessary to include lignite price changes to the selection of risky variables. Yet, the non-transparency of lignite prices due to a lack of trading requires approximating lignite prices by the literature.[385]

Irrespective of the controversial discussion of the usage of nuclear power plants, it still represents an important technology for power generation in terms of the European primary energy consumption.[386] Therefore, uranium prices are taken from the Ux Consulting Company provided by Datastream.

In order to incorporate the risk of electricity generation by renewable power plants, we rely on climate data provided by the DWD. This open database provides sun hours and wind speed from 46 weather stations in Germany.[387] We are aware of the fact that not every weather station taken into account is an appropriate area to install a wind or photovoltaic power plant. However, the incorporation of all weather stations serves as a proper index for the climate conditions of the energy market in Central Europe.

---

[385] See Ströbele et al. (2010), p. 99.

[386] See Figure 2.6; for further details, please refer to section 2.1.4.

[387] The weather stations are: Aachen, Augsburg, Bamberg, Berlin-Tempelhof, Bremen, Brocken, Dresden, Düsseldorf, Emden, Erfurt, Fehmarn, Fichtelberg, Frankfurt am Main/ Flughafen, Fritzlar, Görlitz, Greifswald, Hamburg-Fuhlsbüttel, Hannover, Helgoland, Hof, Hohenpeißenberg, Kahler-Asten, Karlsruhe, Kempten, Konstanz, Leipzig, Lindenberg, List-Sylt, Magdeburg, Meiningen, München-Flughafen, Münster, Neuruppin, Nürburg-Barweiler, Nürnberg, Potsdam, Rheinstetten, Rostock, Saarbrücken, Schleswig, Schwerin, Straubing, Stuttgart, Trier, Würzburg, Zugspitze. However, we eliminate Karsruhe, Rheinstetten and Fritzler as these weather stations do not provide a full dataset for the period between May 2005 and December 2009. For further details, please refer to the website of the Deutsche Wetterdienst: http://www.dwd.de/.

5.1.2 Descriptive statistics

We calculate the average monthly mean and corresponding standard deviation of the commodities based on a time series of monthly data from May 31st, 2005 to December 31st, 2010, leading to 56 observations in total. Table 5.1 summarizes the descriptive statistics for the electricity, fuel and carbon prices.

The descriptive statistics summarize the characteristics of energy commodities described in section 2.3.6. A change of meteorological conditions causes sudden price jumps of electricity prices. In addition, the lack of storage opportunities as well as supply shocks lead to volatile power prices compared to other assets. Therefore, the spread between minimum and maximum price level of base and - in particular - peak load prices are higher compared to the spread of fuel prices. In line with the theoretical explanations, electricity prices are more volatile in comparison to ordinary commodity prices.[388] According to the conducted time series analysis, the lowest base load prices are observed at Spanish OMEL (50.57 €/ MWh), whereas the highest level is paid by customers in the UK (59.24 €/ MWh) on average. However the British price level, which might attract investors to build up new generation capacity in this market, goes along with an extraordinary high standard deviation. Volatile prices, however, might deter investors, as pay back periods are insecure.

While the electricity price level for the aforementioned European power markets tends to be close for base load prices, the time series analysis reveals different levels for peak load prices. The latter is almost twice as high in the Netherlands (113.7 €/ MWh) as in the Spanish power market (56.98 €/ MWh). As stated previously, electricity prices are a function of the respective generation system and geographic conditions. Peak load prices, however, indicate the scarcity of the available generation capacity in peak load periods.

---

[388] Please refer to Table 4.3.

Table 5.1 Descriptive statistics: Average monthly commodity prices (May 31st, 2005 to December 31st, 2009)

Risky variables in €/ MWh	Mean	Max.	Min.	Std. Dev.	Skewness	Kurtosis	Jarque-Bera
Base load prices							
APX NL base	57.94	99.87	29.78	19.05	0.42	2.13	3.41
APX UK base	59.24	125.00	28.08	23.49	0.91	2.87	7.74
EEX base	53.59	95.67	28.26	17.22	0.65	2.54	4.39
OMEL base	50.57	77.09	30.35	13.74	0.35	1.87	4.11
Peak load prices							
APX NL peak	113.70	325.83	46.31	62.97	1.72	6.05	49.25
APX UK peak	71.50	149.55	31.40	30.03	0.89	2.67	7.59
EEX peak	67.47	134.59	32.57	23.57	0.82	2.97	6.33
OMEL peak	56.98	89.06	32.93	16.12	0.31	1.91	3.67
Commodity prices							
Carbon*	20.16	29.43	10.03	4.63	-0.05	2.21	1.49
Coal	8.02	16.27	5.42	2.84	1.56	4.43	27.37
Gas	19.81	45.57	8.40	8.28	0.75	3.48	5.84
Oil	30.81	49.91	17.59	6.84	0.84	4.01	8.97
Uranium	3.84	4.99	2.01	0.85	-0.43	2.02	3.92

* in €/ ton.

Source: Own calculation.

By recalling the development of electricity generation in Europe shown in Table 2.1, the Dutch generation system is dominated by gas power plants reaching almost two thirds of total system capacity. Therefore, gas prices drive Dutch power prices leading to price levels which indicate scarcity of the generation system. As a consequence, APX peak prices run above the other European peak load prices (see Figure 5.1).

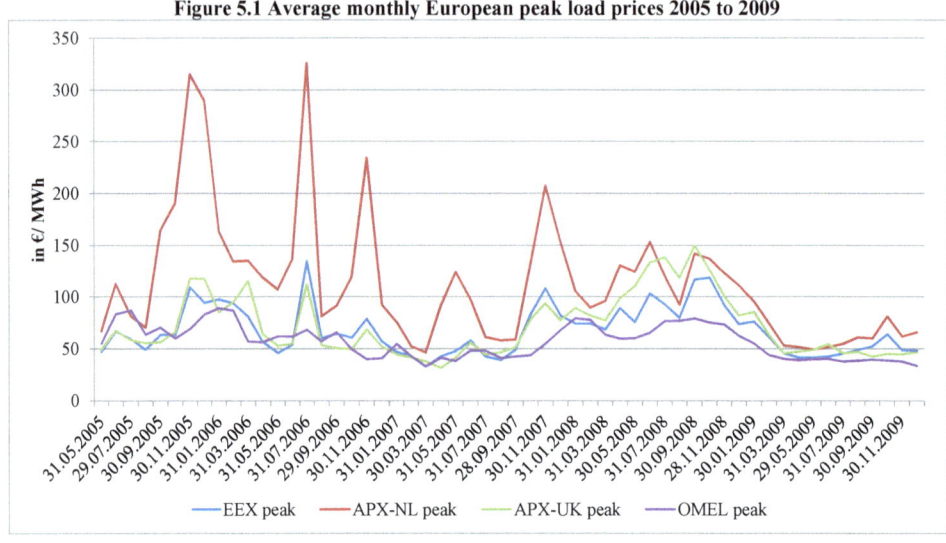

Figure 5.1 Average monthly European peak load prices 2005 to 2009

Source: Own figure.

For a proper empirical methodology we examine the distribution of the power, fuel and carbon prices. The values of skewness and kurtosis of these commodities given in Table 5.1 are not necessarily consistent with the assumption of normal distributed prices. The Bera test statistic rejects the hypothesis of normally distributed prices for values above 4.6 by a significant level of 10%. By relying on Bera test statistic, APX-NL (3.41), EEX (4.39) and OMEL (4.11) base load as well as OMEL peak load prices (3.67) turn out to be normally distributed. In addition, CO_2 future (1.49) and uranium (3.92) prices follow a normal distribution according to the Bera test. In contrast, the test statistics clearly reject the presumption of normally distributed prices for the APX-UK base and Dutch, German as well as Spanish peak load prices. Furthermore, gas, oil and coal prices do not follow a normally distributed price process for the analyzed time period. The test statistics for these commodities, however, is closer to the statistical acceptance in comparison to the power prices. Nevertheless, the theoretical framework requires normally distributed returns.[389] Following *Elton et al.* (2003), the

---

[389] For the assumptions of the theoretical approach, please refer to section 3.4.1.

classical portfolio analysis turns out to deliver at least relatively good results, when returns are not normally distributed. Thus, we generate normally distributed random variables for all commodities following the mean and the corresponding standard deviation, which are given in Table 5.1. In addition, the mean of the specific commodity serves as a starting point for the simulation of the respective projected price pattern, introduced in section 4.3.2.

Even though the volume risk of wind and photovoltaic power plants is taken into account by simulating operating hours as random variables following a triangular distribution, monthly total sun hours and maximum wind speed are needed to analyze interactions with power, commodity and carbon prices. Therefore, Table 5.2 presents the corresponding statistic for these meteorological data.

Table 5.2 Descriptive statistics: Average monthly meteorological data
(May 31st, 2005 to December 31st, 2009)

Risky variables	Mean	Max.	Min.	Std. Dev.	Skewness	Kurtosis	Jarque-Bera
Meteorological data							
Sun in hours	147.38	337.90	39.00	78.72	0.26	2.00	2.98
Wind in m/s	20.77	32.80	16.30	3.12	1.32	6.00	37.36

Source: Own calculation.

5.1.3 Empirical correlations

To explore the mutual dependencies of the risky variables, we calculate continuous compounded monthly returns based on the aforementioned time series of prices. The virtue of relying on returns instead of prices is the fact that all identified risk variables refer to the same dimension. This is especially important for the analysis of the coherency between the meteorological data and commodity prices.

Before running the simulation, we examine the correlation between the returns of the risky variables. Otherwise simulation results would be biased, if the dependencies of the risky variables were neglected. Following the theoretical framework of this thesis, the composition of minimum variance portfolio is mainly determined by the strength of the correlation. If a utility firm aims to minimize the standard deviation of expected returns by a given level of return, low correlated power generation assets should be part of the power plant park leading to a reduction of utility's portfolio risk.

Operating power plants in different electricity markets minimizes risks, if national markets are not perfectly positively correlated. However, we expect, a priori, the correlation of electricity prices between neighboring countries to be higher than that between very distant markets. In other words, due to network interconnection to balance load levels in Europe the correlation of electricity prices in the Netherlands and Germany are supposed to be stronger than in the UK and Spanish markets. Indeed, European electricity price returns are positively (and most of them significantly) correlated according to our results presented in Table 5.3. Contrary, peak load price returns from APX-NL are not statistically significant to Spanish base and peak load price returns. The EEX turns out to be the leading electricity market place, as corresponding price returns correlate as strongest compared to the other power exchanges for base *0.5758* (APX-NL), *0.4784* (APX-UK), 0.4338 (OMEL) as well as peak load levels *0.4242* (APX-NL), *0.4420* (APX-UK), *0.4228* (OMEL). In other words, the correlation among the other power markets is lower.

Since oil and gas are historically priced together we expect a rather high correlation between these two commodities. Even though the correlation coefficient is positive *0.1660*, it turns out to be insignificant [$p = 0.2214$]. One reason might be that the oil gas price link is a Central Europe phenomenon, as gas prices in the UK do not follow oil prices.[390] Still, oil prices seem to influence other fuel prices, as oil price returns are not only positively correlated but also significant to most of the other commodity price returns. This is especially true for the correlation of oil and carbon *(0.3057)* as well as oil and coal price returns *(0.3152)*.

We expect a positive correlation between coal and carbon price returns, as the burning of coal for power generation causes emissions and as a consequence the need to comply with emission regulations. The correlation between carbon and coal price returns amounts to *0.2004*, whereas the respective p-value indicates non-significance [$p = 0.1385$]. However, as the correlation is economic intuitive and the p-value is close to statistical acceptance on a 10% level, we treat the correlation for the following as significant. If carbon prices rise, a power plant operator is better off running gas fired turbines than coal plants. Hence, the price level of emission certificates determines whether the operation of gas power plants is - relative to coal power plants - economical. Consequently, from a theoretical point of view, gas and coal price returns should be negatively related. In contrast, the correlation of coal and gas price

---

[390] Please refer to section 2.3.4 for further details.

returns amounts to *0.1851* and is insignificant [p = 0.1720] for the time period chosen. Very similar, gas and carbon price returns equal *0.0549* and are statistically uncorrelated [p = 0.6876].

In liberalized markets the costs for emission certificates are passed through electricity prices. Consequently, an increase of carbon prices will increase electricity prices. Since the German, the British and the Dutch as well as the Spanish electricity markets are competitive, we expect positive correlation coefficients for electricity price returns and carbon price returns on the specific market. However, we do not identify positive coefficients for all markets. Most importantly, neither the correlation of base load price returns nor peak load price returns and carbon future price returns turn out to be statistically significant.[391]

According to Table 5.3 the correlation between EEX base load price returns and wind speed returns is negative *(-0.1290)*.[392] In periods of high wind supply, wind plant operators feed in the electricity generated into the net which dampen base load price levels. This is in line with the empirical findings and theoretical considerations in the academic literature. Moreover, carbon and coal price returns are negatively correlated with wind speed returns, respectively *-0.0703* and *-0.0593*, as in case of a high wind supply the need for additional operating coal plants to balance load is limited. Consequently, the demand for carbon emission certificates decreases. The coefficients, however, do not turn out to be statistically significant.

---

[391] Testing carbon spot returns does not cause any change of the statistical results.
[392] Since the proxy for wind and sun supply is based on German data, the explanatory power for the relationship between these meteorological returns and European electricity prices is limited.

Table 5.3 Empirical correlations of risky variables

	APX NL Base	APX NL Peak	APX UK Base	APX UK Peak	EEX Base	EEX Peak	OMEL Base	OMEL Peak	Carbon	Coal	Gas	Oil	Uran	Sun	Wind
APX NL Base	1.0000 (-)														
APX NL Peak	0.9105 (0.0000)	1.0000 (-)													
APX UK Base	0.2582 (0.0547)	0.1700 (0.2103)	1.0000 (-)												
APX UK Peak	0.2453 (0.0684)	0.1652 (0.2236)	0.9833 (0.0000)	1.0000 (-)											
EEX Base	0.5758 (0.0000)	0.4242 (0.0011)	0.4784 (0.0002)	0.4420 (0.0006)	1.0000 (-)										
EEX Peak	0.5536 (0.0000)	0.4099 (0.0017)	0.4930 (0.0001)	0.4607 (0.0004)	0.9888 (0.0000)	1.0000 (-)									
OMEL Base	0.2612 (0.0519)	0.1666 (0.2197)	0.3673 (0.0054)	0.3766 (0.0042)	0.4338 (0.0008)	0.4417 (0.0007)	1.0000 (-)								
OMEL Peak	0.3037 (0.0229)	0.2071 (0.1256)	0.2608 (0.0522)	0.2746 (0.0406)	0.4228 (0.0012)	0.4179 (0.0014)	0.5414 (0.0000)	1.0000 (-)							
Carbon	0.1822 (0.1788)	0.2010 (0.1374)	-0.0197 (0.8852)	-0.0308 (0.8219)	-0.0049 (0.9715)	-0.0097 (0.9437)	0.0791 (0.5624)	0.1201 (0.3779)	1.0000 (-)						
Coal	0.0045 (0.9739)	0.0046 (0.9733)	0.3470 (0.0088)	0.3648 (0.0057)	0.0562 (0.6806)	0.0599 (0.6611)	0.1457 (0.2839)	0.0074 (0.9570)	0.2004 (0.1385)	1.0000 (-)					
Gas	0.3788 (0.0040)	0.3466 (0.0089)	0.4963 (0.0001)	0.4259 (0.0011)	0.4047 (0.0020)	0.4158 (0.0014)	0.3078 (0.0210)	0.0778 (0.5685)	0.0549 (0.6876)	0.1851 (0.1720)	1.0000 (-)				
Oil	0.0892 (0.5132)	0.1015 (0.4564)	0.1106 (0.4170)	0.0903 (0.5083)	0.1006 (0.4605)	0.1235 (0.3644)	0.1905 (0.1595)	0.0779 (0.5680)	0.3057 (0.0220)	0.3152 (0.0180)	0.1660 (0.2214)	1.0000 (-)			
Uran	-0.1104 (0.4180)	-0.0648 (0.6351)	0.0757 (0.5791)	0.0426 (0.7554)	-0.0664 (0.6269)	-0.0618 (0.6511)	-0.0598 (0.6613)	-0.1602 (0.2382)	-0.0441 (0.7470)	0.0047 (0.9725)	0.0207 (0.8795)	0.1690 (0.2131)	1.0000 (-)		
Sun	0.1219 (0.3709)	0.2111 (0.1183)	-0.1368 (0.3147)	-0.1470 (0.2796)	0.0852 (0.5322)	0.0817 (0.5496)	-0.0308 (0.8220)	0.0535 (0.6952)	0.2957 (0.0269)	-0.0595 (0.6630)	-0.0132 (0.9229)	0.2885 (0.0311)	-0.0132 (0.9234)	1.0000 (-)	
Wind	0.0388 (0.7767)	0.0998 (0.4643)	0.0664 (0.6266)	0.0885 (0.5164)	-0.1290 (0.3435)	-0.1147 (0.3997)	0.2034 (0.1327)	0.1783 (0.1887)	-0.0703 (0.6067)	-0.0593 (0.6640)	-0.0127 (0.9259)	0.0292 (0.8308)	-0.0577 (0.6728)	-0.3242 (0.0148)	1.0000 (-)

p value in brackets.

Source: Own calculation.

In addition, we have not identified any negative correlation for sun hours' returns and electricity price as well as carbon price returns, *0.0852* [*p* = 0.5322] and *0.2957* [*p* = 0.0269], respectively. One reason might be the fact that the total generation capacity of photovoltaic power plants in Germany is less important in comparison to wind generation capacity. In other words, based on the results presented, photovoltaic power plants have not started to determine base load prices in Central Europe yet.

According to the results, coal, gas, and uranium fuel prices are negatively but insignificantly related to total hours of sun supply. Oil price returns, however, are positively correlated to total sun hours' returns (0.2885). Since oil is particular important for transportation, summer holidays cause usually more traffic and therefore a higher demand for fuel.

To sum up, we confirm in line with the findings in the previous literature that weather conditions influence carbon returns. In addition emission intense variables like coal and oil price returns are positively correlated to carbon price returns.[393] Unlike *Mansanet-Bataller et al.* (2007) we have not detected a significant positive relation between electricity and carbon prices, though. This might be due to the fact that the strength of correlation between commodity price returns depends on the time period taken into account. Our results for the correlations of European electricity price and gas price returns, however, are coinciding with the findings of other studies.[394] Finally, the correlations of the European electricity price returns among each other are in line with the study of *Holler/ Haberfellner* (2006).

Hence, our results are consistent with the findings of other studies, so that we now turn the lens on the simulated correlations among these risky variables in the following section.

---

[393] Mansanet-Bataller et al. (2007); Alberola et al. (2008); Mansanet-Bataller/ Pardo (2008).
[394] Alberola et al. (2008); Mansanet-Bataller et al. (2007).

5.1.4 Simulated correlations

We test the significance of the empirically observed correlation coefficients by relying on the *t-statistic*. Insignificant correlation coefficients are set equal to zero, as these variables are statistically uncorrelated, before generating random variables.[395] In order to gain random variables whose simulated correlation equals the empirical correlation we decompose the correlation matrix (see Table 5.3) using the Cholesky factorization.[396] Since lignite power plants are part of the feasible set of a European utility firm, we assume that lignite and hard coal are almost perfectly correlated in order to generate input fuel prices for the valuation.

As explained in section 4.2.3, multiplying the Cholesky matrix with its transpose leads to the empirically initial matrix. Having generated normally distributed random variables by taking the mean and standard deviation of the respective commodities as well as triangular distributed random variables for the meteorological data, the input parameters are derived to run the Monte Carlo simulation. However, depending on the strength of the correlation coefficient between the risky parameters as well as the magnitude of the commodities standard deviation, negative generated random prices might occur. Even though negative prices are observable on electricity markets, negative commodity prices are not only against the background of this paper but also in general not economically intuitive.

Therefore, we take absolute values of the multiplication of the Cholesky matrix and the matrix of generated random variables. In addition, we compare the simulated mean of the respective commodity with its historical mean. If the simulated mean of any risky input parameter diverges more than 5% in comparison to the historical mean, we multiply the quotients of the historical and simulated means with new generated random variables of the specific commodity. Otherwise results would be biased, as for instance electricity prices of any European sample market reach a far higher price level as empirically observed. Therefore, the modification leads to economic intuitive commodity prices and meteorological data as starting point for the portfolio analyses.

First of all, carbon price movements run alongside with electricity prices, which require a positive algebraic sign of the simulated carbon coefficient. Secondly, electricity and fuel prices should be positively related. Clearly, negative electricity

---

[395] Savvides (1994), p. 11.
[396] Please refer to section 4 for further analytical details.

prices are likely to occur on power exchanges due to balance load level. Besides an increase of renewable energy generation capacity makes negative electricity prices even more likely. Since the expected value per MW generation capacity is quantified for the power plant portfolio on a long term basis, we can neglect these short term price phenomena. Therefore, the simulated electricity and fuel prices are supposed to correlate positively. Lastly, the comparative advantage of coal to gas or vice versa, is currently the critical factor for operative decisions of gas or coal power plants. Due to the age structure of the existing power plant parks and limitation in technologies, it is very likely that this kind of fuel switch will be observable even in 2020.

In contrast to Table 5.3, the following Table 5.4 minimizes information and presents therefore just the statistical significant correlation coefficients, whereas the residuals are set equal to zero. This allows comparing historical coefficients to the simulated correlation of the generated random variables, shown in Table 5.5.

Table 5.4 Adjusted correlation matrix based on empirical data

	APX NL Base	APX NL Peak	APX UK Base	APX UK Peak	EEX Base	EEX Peak	OMEL Base	OMEL Peak	Carbon	Coal	Lignite	Gas	Oil	Uranium	Sun	Wind
APX NL Base	1,0000															
APX NL Peak	0,9105	1,0000														
APX UK Base	0,2582	0,0000	1,0000													
APX UK Peak	0,2453	0,0000	0,9833	1,0000												
EEX Base	0,5758	0,4242	0,4784	0,4607	1,0000											
EEX Peak	0,5536	0,4099	0,4930	0,4420	0,9888	1,0000										
OMEL Base	0,2612	0,0000	0,3673	0,3766	0,4338	0,4417	1,0000									
OMEL Peak	0,3037	0,0000	0,2608	0,2746	0,4228	0,4179	0,5414	1,0000								
Carbon	0,0000	0,0000	0,0000	0,0000	0,0000	0,0000	0,0000	0,0000	1,0000							
Coal	0,0000	0,0000	0,3470	0,3648	0,0000	0,0000	0,0000	0,0000	0,2004	1,0000						
Lignite	0,0000	0,0000	0,3470	0,3648	0,0000	0,0000	0,0000	0,0000	0,2004	0,9900	1,0000					
Gas	0,3788	0,3466	0,4963	0,4259	0,4047	0,4158	0,3078	0,0000	0,0000	0,3152	0,3152	1,0000				
Oil	0,0000	0,0000	0,0000	0,0000	0,0000	0,0000	0,0000	0,0000	0,3057	0,0000	0,0000	0,0000	1,0000			
Uranium	0,0000	0,0000	0,0000	0,0000	0,0000	0,0000	0,0000	0,0000	0,0000	0,0000	0,0000	0,0000	0,0000	1,0000		
Sun	0,0000	0,0000	0,0000	0,0000	0,0000	0,0000	0,0000	0,0000	0,2957	0,0000	0,0000	0,0000	0,2885	0,0000	1,0000	
Wind	0,0000	0,0000	0,0000	0,0000	0,0000	0,0000	0,0000	0,0000	0,0000	0,0000	0,0000	0,0000	0,0000	0,0000	-0,3242	1,0000

Table 5.5 Correlation matrix based on simulation

	APX NL Base	APX NL Peak	APX UK Base	APX UK Peak	EEX Base	EEX Peak	OMEL Base	OMEL Peak	Carbon	Coal	Lignite	Gas	Oil	Uranium	Sun	Wind
APX NL Base	1,0000															
APX NL Peak	0,6939	1,0000														
APX UK Base	0,0960	-0,1535	1,0000													
APX UK Peak	0,1181	-0,1535	0,9760	1,0000												
EEX Base	0,5057	0,2847	0,3711	0,3228	1,0000											
EEX Peak	0,4709	0,2519	0,4077	0,3651	0,9785	1,0000										
OMEL Base	-0,0067	-0,0841	0,0180	0,0214	0,0018	0,0017	1,0000									
OMEL Peak	-0,0991	0,3917	-0,0730	-0,0712	-0,0724	-0,0862	0,4685	1,0000								
Carbon	-0,0546	-0,0468	0,0232	0,0335	0,0002	0,0079	-0,0396	-0,0326	1,0000							
Coal	-0,0293	-0,0318	0,0145	0,0228	-0,0210	-0,0156	-0,0569	-0,0625	0,3688	1,0000						
Lignite	-0,0328	-0,0365	0,0123	0,0201	-0,0246	-0,0205	-0,0528	-0,0618	0,3661	0,9954	1,0000					
Gas	0,3650	0,2423	0,3674	0,3316	0,6637	0,6953	-0,0254	-0,0505	0,0559	0,0216	0,0185	1,0000				
Oil	0,0020	-0,0369	-0,0122	-0,0118	-0,0314	-0,0272	0,0049	-0,0439	0,2670	0,1552	0,1556	-0,0068	1,0000			
Uranium	0,0410	0,0236	0,0482	0,0495	0,0339	0,0410	0,0146	-0,0107	-0,0694	-0,0772	-0,0770	0,0510	-0,0537	1,0000		
Sun	-0,0397	-0,0294	0,4452	0,4402	0,0120	0,0188	-0,0116	-0,0078	-0,0209	-0,0183	-0,0211	0,0146	0,0069	0,0233	1,0000	
Wind	0,0572	0,0260	0,1982	0,2090	0,0389	0,0360	0,0406	0,0011	0,0010	-0,0312	-0,0292	0,0260	0,0138	0,0268	-0,1845	1,0000

Source: Own calculation.

By looking at the aforementioned tables, the simulated correlation tends to be close to the empirically observed correlation. In general, we recognize a relationship which is slightly weaker compared to the historical correlation. This is especially true for the strength of the correlation of base and peak load prices from APX-NL, APX-UK and EEX. In contrast, the simulated correlation coefficient for the Spanish power prices diverges stronger from the empirically observed correlation to European power prices.[397] Fuel and electricity prices, however, tend to be relatively close to the empirical correlation.

Since this relation is consistent with theoretical considerations the portfolio valuation is not be biased. The analyzed generation capacity of Spain is solely based on renewable energies, the negative sign of the correlation coefficient between OMEL electricity prices and carbon is negligible. Besides the correlations of total sun hours and the other input variables are rather slightly negative compared to a low positive correlation which we observed empirically. If we assume that photovoltaic generation capacity will be expanded over time due to the ambitious climate policy targets of the European countries, a negative correlation of sun hours and electricity prices is likely to occur. In the case of adequate sun supply photovoltaic power plants generate electricity which is fed into the grid which lowers the electricity price level. Lastly, the simulated relation between total sun hours and wind speed is clearly negative (-0.185) and therefore in line with the empirically identified correlation between these two methodological parameters.

To sum up, the simulated correlation seems to be suitable for the further portfolio analysis, as generated random price variables capture future trends in the energy mix.

---

[397] As the Spanish sample power plant park does not operate conventional thermal power plants, the evaluation of the target generation portfolio should be reliable.

5.2 Generation portfolio analyses - A disaggregated approach

We have selected the power plant sample based on the following criteria: Firstly, the power plant park of the utility firm should be faced with significant replacements of old plants in the near future as well as investment plans to build up additional generation capacity within a projected period. Secondly, the current generation mix should be heterogeneous in terms of different power plant fuel technologies instead of a utility firm dominated by a single fuel type. Thirdly, the respective utility should operate mainly in Europe, as we aim to shed light on how the change in emission regulation will affect the optimization process of a generation portfolio. Ultimately, we ask for a utility firm which is listed on a stock exchange, as we explore the target power plant park communicated to shareholders of the respective firm. Therefore the issue arises whether the target power plant park turns out to be efficient within a mean-variance framework. While utilities could use the approach for rebalancing their generation portfolios towards efficient power plant parks, investors can make use of the ratios presented to evaluate the degree of efficiency of competitors.

5.2.1 Sample power plant portfolio

The sample power plant data are gained from the Platts energy information database. The latter provides fuel type, gross generation capacity, location and commissioning year of the existing power plants of European utility firms. In addition, the data base comprises power plants that are currently under construction as well as planned. By taking the aforementioned criteria into account, we chose a stock listed German utility firm operating a heterogeneous power plant park in different European countries. The methodology presented, however, can be applied to any utility firm. This data set allows conducting the analysis for a whole range of power plant technologies which frame a utility's specific generation portfolio. As a consequence, our sample power plant park is determined by 255 different power plants adding up to a total gross capacity of 36,492 MW in 2009.[398] Table 5.6 presents the power plant park by distinguishing between location and fuel type.

---

[398] We take solely owned power plants into account and neglect therefore non-owned contractually secured plants. Since water and wind power plants are rather small in terms of gross generation capacity in comparison to conventional thermal power plants, we merge 81 water power plants to 5 hydro power plants and 84 wind turbines to 6 wind power plants. In addition other small power generation units are represented by other power plant technologies.

The majority of the existing generation capacity refers to plants located in Germany summing up to 57.5%. Alongside, generation capacity in the UK, in the Netherlands and Spain amounts to 30.2%, 11.2% and 1.1%, respectively. From a fuel type perspective, the generation mix is characterized by a significant share of coal and lignite plants of 21.3% and 28.5%, respectively. These fourteen conventional thermal power plants, however, are on average 34 years old making extraordinary replacements of generation capacity necessary according to the plants' typical life cycle. In addition, gas and oil plants, respectively, amount to 29% and 5.7% of the group's total generation capacity. While the group of gas power plants is rather modern (27 years on average) compared to the other affiliated conventional thermal power plants, the six oil plants are already close to the end of their life cycle.

Besides 6.9% of the gross generation capacity refers to nuclear power plants. Finally, renewable energies – in particular wind and water power plants – are complementing the sample power plant portfolio within the base year. Other power plant technologies are subsumed as the group of other. The latter primarily consists of waste to energy and biomass plants, however, these plant types are not expected to replace specific power plant technologies nor grow substantially according to the utility's communicated investment plans.

Table 5.6 Power plant portfolio in 2009

Fuel type	Number	Gross capacity in MW	in %
Conventional thermal			
Coal	8	7,767	21.3%
Cogen	2	103	0.3%
Gas	42	10,598	29.0%
Lignite	6	10,387	28.5%
Oil	6	2,078	5.7%
Other	10	1,164	3.2%
Total conventional thermal	74	32,097	88.0%
Non-conventional thermal			
Uranium	1	2,525	6.9%
Total non-conventional thermal	1	2,525	6.9%
Renewables			
Photovoltaic	1	1	0.0%
Water	5	533	1.5%
Wind	6	1,336	3.7%
Total Renewables	12	1,870	5.1%
Total	**87**	**36,492**	**100.0%**

Source: Platts, own calculation.

Figure 5.2 shows the extraordinary need for replacements of the sample power plants during the projected period by illustrating plants respective lifetime curves. In line with previous findings of *Kjärstad/ Johnsson* (2007) and *UBA* (2005) the modeled age structure underlines that the existing generation capacity drops dramatically over the next years. Overall, more than 20 GW or two thirds of generation capacity of the base year have to be replaced to maintain the initial power plant park assuming that power plants under construction will be finished on time.

Figure 5.2 Expiring lifetime curve of sample's power plant park

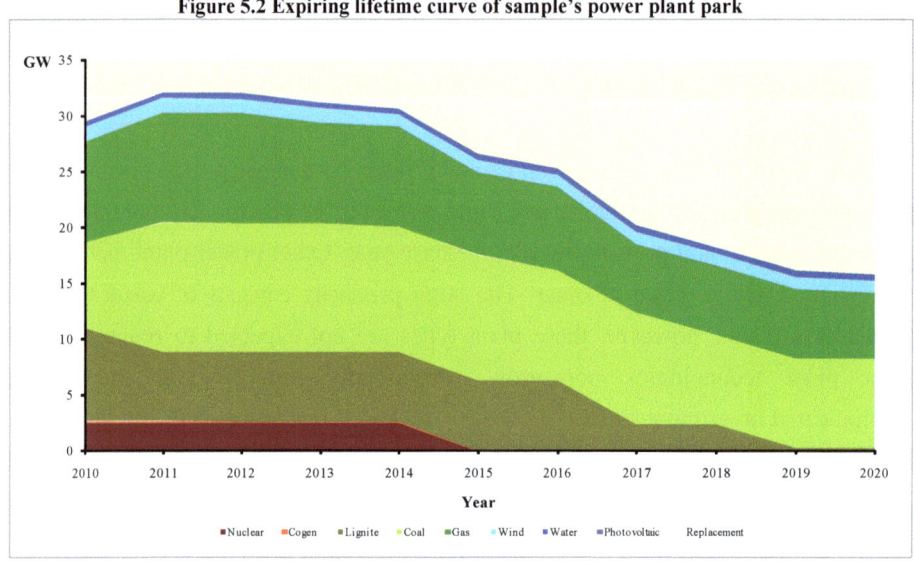

Source: Platts, own calculation.

To maintain generation capacity we identify massive investment needs. Against this background we distinguish between power plants under construction, whereas the year of commissioning given by Platts counteracts the aging initial power plant park and planned generation capacity.

While conventional thermal power dominates the fuel technology of plants under construction, Table 5.7 indicates a change of the investment policy towards a low emission intense power plant park. This is especially true for power plants which are currently planned according to the utility firm, as 14 new wind power plants will account for more than one third (35.2%) of the total planned generation capacity.

Table 5.7 Power plants planned and under construction

Fuel type	Number	Gross capacity in MW	in %
Power plants under construction			
Conventional thermal			
Coal	2	3,800	50.6%
Gas	3	3,094	41.2%
Other	1	320	4.3%
Renewables			
Wind	3	297	4.0%
Total plants under construction	9	7,511	100.0%
Power plants planned			
Conventional thermal			
Coal	2	4,000	34.7%
Gas	6	3,260	28.3%
Other	2	110	1.0%
Renewables			
Water	8	17	0.2%
Wind	14	4,133	35.9%
Total plants planned	32	11,520	100.0%

Source: Platts, own calculation.

Planned power plants are part of the investments in new capacity to reach a generation capacity of 60,471 MW that determine the target portfolio in 2020. In the following section we will present the dynamization of the power plant park and the corresponding investment strategy from the base year to the target year.

5.2.2 Investment strategy

To explore the efficiency of the target generation portfolio, we model for each existing power plant at the end of its estimated economic lifetime a new replacement plant with the same capacity.[399] The decision for the fuel technology of the replacement plant is – in the first step – solely determined by the communicated target generation mix for target year 2020. Figure 5.3 depicts the composition of the respective target portfolio by type of fuel technology.

---

[399] For further details regarding the technical application of replacements within the simulation model, please refer to section 4.4.2.

Figure 5.3 Communicated target portfolio

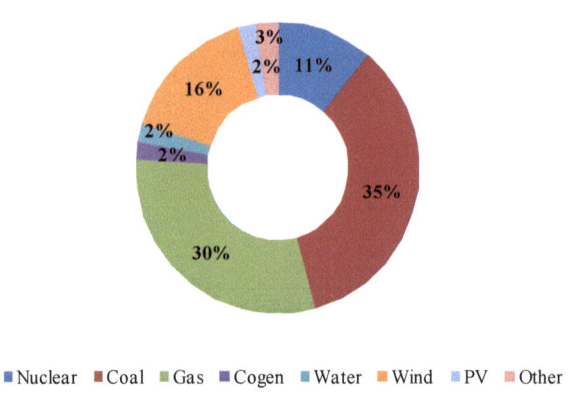

Source: RWE (2008), p. 30.

Consequently, we develop investment plans for replacement plants which with secure the intended target fuel mix. In this respect, the investment plan considers the target generation capacity for the year 2020 and as a consequence necessary buildings. Comparing the power plants of the base year with the target generation capacity for 2020, indicate a massive need for investments. Overall, the generation capacity will almost double to more than 60 GW within the projected planning period, indicating an average annual growth rate of 4%. To reach the target portfolio in 2020, we replace old power plants with the same type, except for lignite, oil and gas plants which are substituted by coal, gas and wind power plants respectively. In general, the model restricts replacements to the country of origin. Yet, new nuclear generation capacity is solely built in the UK due to the passed German directive of phase out of nuclear power plants.[400]

Table 5.8 presents the dynamization of the sample power plant park for the projected planning period covering the decade from the year 2010 to the end of 2020. Following the communicated investment strategy total coal generation capacity will be almost twice as high as in 2010, due to the substitution of lignite capacity. Hence, 12 coal power plants account for 34.6% of total generation capacity in 2020. In contrast, the number of active lignite power plants will diminish from 6 to 2 in the same period. Following the investment plan will lead to 58 gas power plants in 2020, whereas gas gross capacity amounts to 18,141 MW in total. As a consequence, gas becomes the second largest fuel technology in the target year.

---

[400] Please refer to section 2.1.4 for further details.

In addition, wind power plants exhibit strong growth rates causing wind technology to become the third largest generation capacity. Conventional thermal power plants, however, will still account for almost two-thirds of the sample's power plant park in 2020. In addition, nuclear power plants will contribute to the generation mix in 2020 and even increase their importance in terms of total installed capacity compared to 2010 according to the communicated investment plan. Therefore 5 nuclear power plants will account for 11% of total energy generation capacity in 2020.

Following the illustration given in the previous section, the expiring lifetime curves for old plants as well as the ambitious investment plans cause a significant need for building up generation capacity. To demonstrate the huge share of new generation capacity, Table 5.9 shows the building up of new capacity and the replacement of old power plants for the projected planning period. While in 2010 the ratio of new to old power plants amounts to 24.3%, the share increases up to almost 74% at the end of the planning period.

Table 5.8 Development of the power plant park from 2010 to 2020

Plant technology in MW	2010	2011	2012	2013	2014	2015	2016	2017	2018	2019	2020
Coal	9,867	15,767	18,167	18,167	18,258	18,258	16,898	20,724	18,804	20,904	20,904
Cogen	103	103	103	353	353	353	353	603	853	1,103	1,209
Gas	13,144	16,434	16,434	16,934	16,934	16,934	17,434	17,434	17,799	17,799	18,141
Lignite	8,287	6,187	6,187	6,187	6,187	6,187	6,187	2,361	2,361	261	261
Nuclear	2,525	2,525	2,525	3,525	3,525	3,525	3,525	4,525	4,525	4,525	6,652
Photovoltaic	1	1	1	1	501	1,001	1,209	1,209	1,209	1,209	1,209
Water	533	533	533	533	733	950	1,150	1,150	1,150	1,150	1,209
Wind	4,817	4,817	4,817	4,817	5,442	5,442	6,802	6,802	9,373	9,373	9,373
Other	1,164	1,164	1,164	1,164	1,164	1,164	1,164	1,164	1,274	1,274	1,512
Total capacity	40,441	47,531	49,931	51,681	53,097	53,814	54,722	55,972	57,349	57,599	60,471

Source: Own calculation.

Table 5.9 Investments and replacements of power plant technologies from 2010 to 2020

Plant technology in MW	2010	2011	2012	2013	2014	2015	2016	2017	2018	2019	2020
Coal	2,100	4,200	6,600	6,600	7,011	7,011	7,011	10,837	10,837	12,937	12,937
Cogen	0	0	43	293	293	293	293	543	793	1,043	1,149
Gas	4,179	6,605	6,605	7,947	8,007	9,551	10,051	11,329	11,694	11,694	12,291
Lignite	0	0	0	0	0	0	0	0	0	0	0
Nuclear	0	0	0	1,000	1,000	3,525	3,525	4,525	4,525	4,525	6,652
Photovoltaic	0	0	0	0	500	1,000	1,208	1,208	1,208	1,208	1,209
Water	0	0	0	0	200	417	617	617	617	617	676
Wind	3,481	3,481	3,481	3,481	4,283	4,283	5,643	5,643	8,215	8,215	8,215
Other	49	49	49	49	59	69	319	971	1,183	1,273	1,511
Total capacity	9,810	14,336	16,779	19,371	21,354	26,150	28,668	35,674	39,072	41,512	44,641

Source: Own calculation.

Figure 5.4 illustrates the development of the power plant park for the projected planning period. Overall, the generation portfolio in 2020 consists of 126 different power plants which represent 60,471 MW.

Figure 5.4 Development of power plant technologies from 2010 to 2020

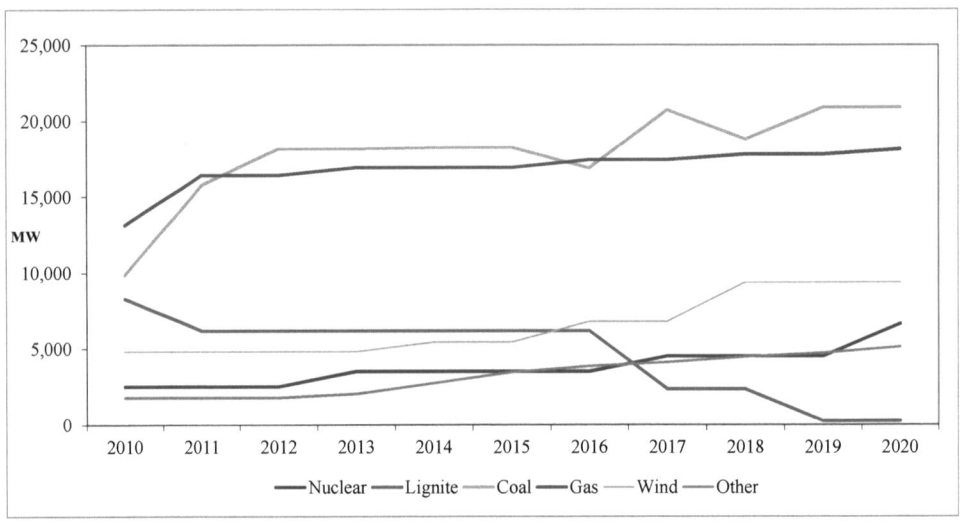

Source: Own figure.

Since photovoltaic, cogen and water power plants generation capacity will be relatively small in comparison to that of the thermal as well as wind power plants, these fuel technologies are subsumed to others just due to reason of illustration. Strong growth rates, e.g., for coal in the beginning of the analyzed period depend mainly on the expiring time of operating lignite plants. Therefore, jumps are due to the replacement of plants by another fuel type as well as investments in new generation capacity. Table 5.10 summarizes the target generation mix in 2020 based on fuel types and respective shares of total generation capacity.

Table 5.10 Power plant portfolio in 2020

Fuel type	Number	Gross capacity in MW	in %
Conventional thermal			
Coal	12	20,904	34.6%
Cogen	7	1,209	2.0%
Gas	58	18,141	30.0%
Lignite	2	261	0.4%
Other	13	1,511	2.5%
Subtotal	92	42,027	69.5%
Non-conventional thermal			
Nuclear	5	6,652	11.0%
Subtotal	5	6,652	11.0%
Renewables			
Photovoltaic	4	1,209	2.0%
Water	11	1,209	2.0%
Wind	14	9,373	15.5%
Subtotal	29	11,792	19.5%
Total	**126**	**60,471**	**100%**

Source: Own calculation.

The bottom line is that the modeling of dynamic power plant portfolios allows us to test the efficiency of the respective target generation portfolio. If the latter turns out to be non-efficient, we demonstrate how to rebalance the portfolio on a disaggregated level. As a consequence, the second step is to adjust the initial investment plan and demonstrate how to improve the degree of efficiency based on the detection of regional distinctions and power plant technologies' financial performance. Even though power plants might operate on the same fuel technology, they differ in terms of age and as a consequence in technical and cost characteristics. In other words, every specific power plant which determines the target generation portfolio represents an individual generation asset. Therefore, we compute the value of each power plant operating in 2020 as today's expected value per MW generation capacity and the corresponding standard deviation of the expected value per MW generation capacity.

As stated in the previous chapter, the regulatory environment of the EU ETS will be tightened leading to a full auctioning of emission certificates for power plant operators. Therefore, the virtue of the valuation approach is additionally to study the dependencies of the power plant portfolios' value and therefore the individual asset value by purchasing the total of all required emission certificates on the market.

5.2.3 Feasibility set

This section presents the results of the simulation based on the DCF results for the individual generation assets. For expository purpose, however, Table 5.11 shows first the results for the individual fuel plant technology, whereas the latter is computed as portfolio of the respective affiliated power plant assets.[401] The weight of the specific generation assets is determined by dividing the gross capacity by the total capacity of the respective asset class.[402]

Table 5.11 Valuation results for power plant technologies

Portfolio of fuel plant technologyy	Mean in K€/ MW	Std. Dev. in K€/ MW	Adjusted Sharpe ratio
Conventional thermal			
Coal	2,013	1,943	1.04
Cogen	1,195	1,867	0.64
Gas	583	867	0.67
Lignite	1,426	2,731	0.52
Other	-5,579	2,531	-2.20
Non conventional thermal			
Nuclear	3,177	1,485	2.14
Renewables			
Water	5,777	2,104	2.75
Wind	1,100	370	2.97
Photovoltaic	2,571	702	3.66

Source: Own calculation.

The portfolio of coal plants exhibits the highest value per MW generation capacity within the group of conventional thermal power plants. This is quite astonishing as operators of coal power plants are obligated to purchase the total demand of emission certificates in 2013 which will have a negative impact on the coal plants' free cash flows and ultimately on the DCF value. The standard deviation of the expected value per MW generation capacity for the coal plant portfolio, however, is relatively high compared to low emission-intense fuel plant technologies like gas. This refers mainly to the dependency of the carbon price pattern.

---

[401] Please refer to section 4.5.1 regarding the calculation of the expected value and standard deviation for each plant. In addition, formulas for computing portfolios return and corresponding risk are presented in section 3.2.3.

[402] The individual weights, values and risks are summarized in Table 5.13 and 5.14 at the end of this section.

Since lignite power plants emit more carbon per MWh generated electricity than coal power plants due to less energy content of this kind of fuel, the impact of future carbon prices is even stronger leading to a lower value per MW generation capacity and higher corresponding standard deviation for the group of lignite power plants. As a consequence, the adjusted Sharpe ratio indicates a low reward for each unit of risk for lignite power plants in comparison to the other thermal power plants. Taking the standard deviation of the expected value per MW generation capacity as adequate risk measure, the portfolio of lignite power plants turns out to be most risky.

In contrast, the group of gas power plants bears the lowest risk in terms of the standard deviation of the expected value. Thanks to low emissions, the impact of future carbon price risk on the profitability is rather low. However, contrary to our expectations, gas power plants' value is rather low compared to coal power plants', even though gas power plants do have a comparative advantage in terms of being less emission intense compared to power generation of coal power plants. Gas prices were relatively high in the past analyzed period, leading to a high gas mean. As the commodity price process is based on high oil prices and therefore high gas prices are captured in the formula of the projected commodity price development, the clean spread diminishes. In addition, historical volatility of gas prices is higher compared to other fuel prices which drive the risk to deviate from the expected simulated price trajectory. Hence, the profitability in terms of expected value per MW generation capacity is lower.

Nuclear power plants do not bear any carbon price risks, however, the portfolio of nuclear plants is not only faced with power and fuel price risks but also with relatively high variable costs which cover a nuclear energy waste fee. Compared to conventional thermal power plant portfolios, the group of nuclear power plants exhibits the highest adjusted Sharpe ratio.

The valuation results for the renewable portfolios indicate that investments are rewarded with high values per MW generation capacity for each unit of risk. A portfolio of photovoltaic power plants reaches the highest adjusted Sharpe ratio of all asset classes, as generated electricity from photovoltaic plants is rewarded with the highest remuneration. Water and wind power plants turn out to be more attractive on a return to risk basis not only compared to conventional thermal but also to the group of non-conventional power plants. This is consistent with our theoretical expectations, as renewable energies do not take fuel and carbon price risks. Instead, the risk for photovoltaic and wind power plants depends on the meteorological conditions which influence operating hours and therefore the amount of generated electricity. In contrast, a water power plant's risk is, according to simulation model, solely revenue based in terms of fluctuating electricity prices. Nevertheless, prices cover variable and fixed costs as well as investment costs for new plants causing relatively high values per MW generation capacity.

Figure 5.5 illustrates power plant assets within the return-standard deviation universe, whereas the fuel plant technologies are considered in individual groups. As we can see, wind and photovoltaic power plants dominate the portfolio of gas and cogen power plants, as they bear higher values per MW generation capacity for a given level of risk. In contrast to the other renewable energies, water power plants do solely dominate lignite power plants, due to its extraordinary high level of standard deviation. The portfolio of nuclear power plants obtains the highest return for a given level of risk for thermal power plants and as a consequence, they lie above cogen, lignite and coal power plants.

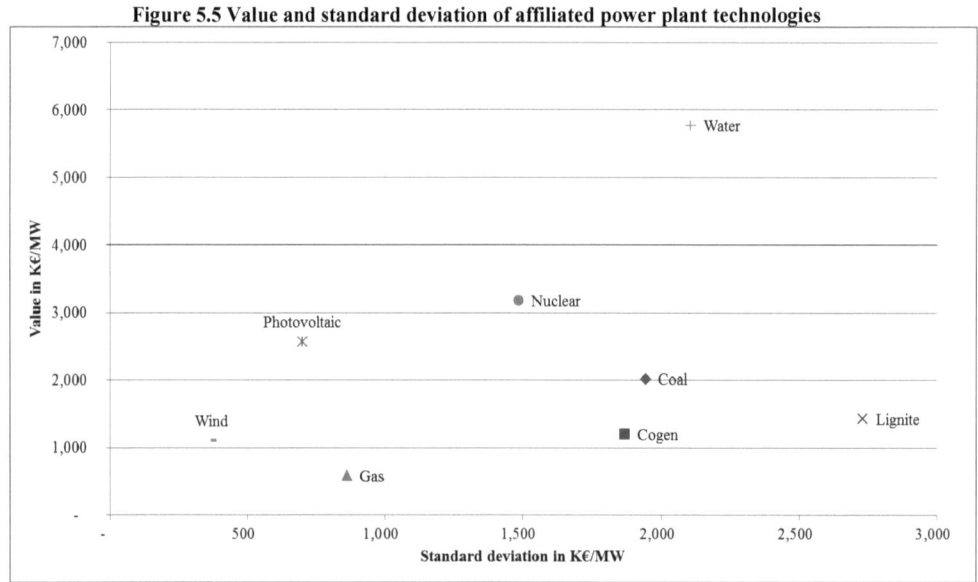

Figure 5.5 Value and standard deviation of affiliated power plant technologies

Source: Own calculation.

As we are interested in testing the efficiency of the communicated target generation mix by the sample utility firm, we analyze the performance of the respective portfolio.

Table 5.12 Composition and weights of sample generation portfolios

Portfolio	Weight	Coal	Cogen	Gas	Lignite	Other	Nuclear	PV	Water	Wind	Total gross capacity in MW
Target portfolio		34.6%	2.0%	30.0%	0.4%	2.5%	11.0%	2.0%	2.0%	15.5%	60,471
National distinction											
Germany		60.5%	4.8%	24.5%	1.0%	0.9%	0.0%	0.0%	4.6%	3.7%	25,390
Netherlands		20.5%	0.0%	65.7%	0.0%	7.3%	0.0%	0.0%	0.2%	6.3%	6,064
UK		15.8%	0.0%	29.1%	0.0%	3.0%	24.3%	0.0%	0.1%	27.7%	27,328
Spain		0.0%	0.0%	0.0%	0.0%	0.0%	0.0%	71.6%	0.3%	28.1%	1,688

Source: Own calculation.

Since the investment plan takes the national location of power plants into account, we consider sub-portfolios of the target portfolio with different combinations of generation assets in order to analyze the performance of each one of them. The composition of the target generation portfolio, as well as the sub-portfolios is presented in Table 5.12.

Additionally, Figure 5.6 shows the return-standard deviation trade-off of the portfolios presented above. The country specific generation portfolios are sub-portfolios of the target fuel mix of the sample's power plant park. As we can appreciate, the generation mix of power plants located in Spain dominates all the other portfolios, as it has the highest expected value per MW generation capacity for the lowest standard deviation. The portfolio bearing the highest standard deviation of the expected return, however, refers to power plants located in Germany.

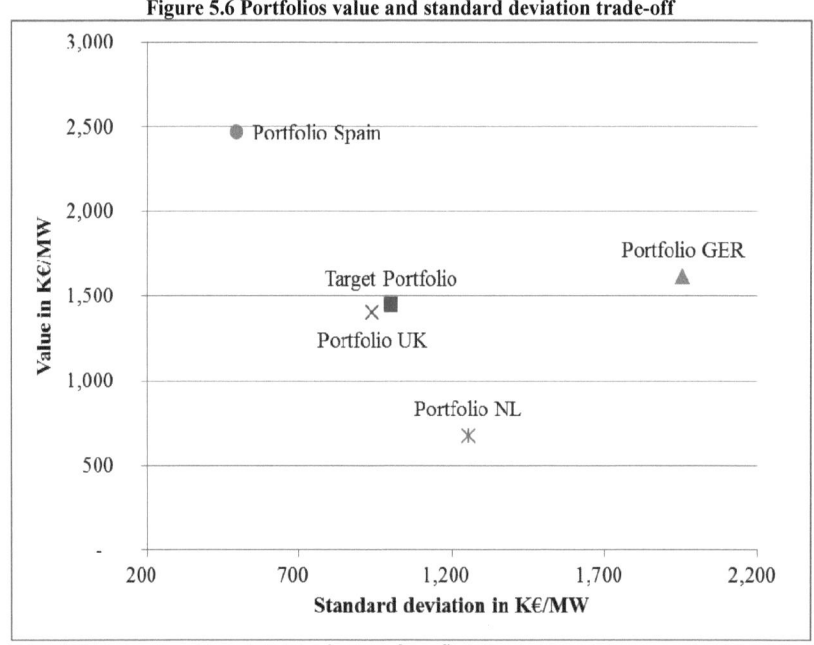

Figure 5.6 Portfolios value and standard deviation trade-off

Source: Own figure.

Remember that the latter mainly consist of conventional thermal power plants which determine 85.9% of the generation capacity. In contrast, the portfolio Spain is solely based on renewable energies, which turned out profitable in relation to the level of risk in comparison to conventional thermal power plants. In other words, the fuel mix explains the location of sample portfolios rather than national power prices. Furthermore, the group of generation assets and therefore national power plants consists of old and new power plants.

Hence, there is need for analyzing these results on a disaggregated level before deriving the efficient frontiers, test the degree of relative efficiency and if portfolios do not turn out to be efficient be able to demonstrate how to rebalance these portfolios. Table 5.13 and 5.14 provide the results on a disaggregated level revealing differences on the load and country level:

Table 5.13 Valuation results for power plant sample

Power plant	Mean	Std. Dev.	Min	Max	Range	Weight	Country
Conventional thermal							
Coal							
2011OLD COAL8	3,883	2,458	-3,482	12,181	15,663	3.64%	GER
2011OLD COAL9	3,642	2,476	-3,857	11,942	15,799	2.65%	GER
2010NEW COAL10	1,972	2,793	-6,720	11,104	17,824	3.47%	GER
2019NEW COAL12	1,187	2,091	-5,064	8,194	13,257	3.47%	GER
2017NEW COAL13	1,319	2,226	-5,369	8,768	14,137	6.33%	GER
2011NEW COAL15	1,845	2,705	-6,534	10,682	17,216	3.47%	GER
COAL TARGET PLANNED	2,373	1,817	-4,509	7,820	12,329	3.97%	UK
COAL TARGET PLANNED	2,086	1,738	-4,347	7,172	11,519	0.68%	UK
Cogen							
2001OLD COGEN1	1,816	2,353	-5,245	11,146	16,391	0.10%	GER
2012NEW COGEN6	1,510	2,098	-4,913	10,093	15,005	0.07%	GER
COGEN TARGET PLANT 1	1,425	2,043	-4,835	9,697	14,532	0.41%	GER
COGEN TARGET PLANT 2	1,152	1,831	-4,466	8,741	13,208	0.41%	GER
COGEN TARGET PLANT 3	1,086	1,785	-4,415	8,467	12,882	0.41%	GER
COGEN TARGET PLANT 4	1,020	1,741	-4,311	8,231	12,542	0.41%	GER
COGEN TARGET PLANT 5	949	1,698	-4,191	7,871	12,063	0.18%	GER
Lignite							
1991OLD LIGNITE2	1,402	2,759	-6,981	9,690	16,671	0.28%	GER
1988OLD LIGNITE3	1,470	2,678	-6,694	9,535	16,229	0.15%	GER
Other							
2017NEW OTHER 121	-6,712	3,391	-17,417	2,739	20,156	0.78%	UK
2016NEW OTHER 122	-6,915	3,448	-17,910	2,825	20,735	0.41%	UK
2018NEW OTHER 124	-6,515	3,508	-17,848	3,744	21,592	0.17%	NL
2017NEW OTHER 129	-6,756	3,609	-18,575	3,725	22,300	0.30%	NL
OTHER TARGET PLANT 1	-6,527	3,466	-17,271	3,200	20,471	0.33%	GER
Non-conventional thermal							
Nuclear							
2015NEW UR1	3,429	1,513	-794	7,782	8,576	4.18%	UK
UR TARGET PLANT 1	3,770	1,552	-541	8,354	8,896	1.65%	UK
UR TARGET PLANT 2	3,103	1,476	-894	7,347	8,241	1.65%	UK
UR TARGET PLANT 3	2,633	1,432	-1,111	6,623	7,734	1.65%	UK
UR TARGET PLANT 4	2,633	1,432	-1,111	6,623	7,734	1.86%	UK

Power plant	Mean	Std. Dev.	Min	Max	Range	Weight	Country
Renewables							
Photovoltaic							
2020NEW PV108	1,822	555	507	3,132	2,625	0.00%	GER
PV TARGET PLANT 1	2,711	728	1,054	4,432	3,378	0.83%	SPAIN
PV TARGET PLANT 2	2,534	695	954	4,176	3,223	0.83%	SPAIN
PV TARGET PLANT 3	2,325	657	830	3,877	3,047	0.34%	SPAIN
Water							
2000OLD WATER41	7,582	2,426	1,140	16,543	15,403	0.34%	GER
1970OLD WATER42	8,198	1,609	4,140	12,931	8,790	0.01%	UK
2010OLD WATER43	7,600	2,431	1,145	16,580	15,435	0.50%	GER
1967OLD WATER44	7,062	5,154	139	37,204	37,065	0.01%	SPAIN
1989OLD WATER45	9,984	2,080	4,055	18,557	14,503	0.02%	NL
WATER TARGET PLANNEI	4,816	1,463	1,344	9,004	7,660	0.02%	UK
WATER TARGET PLANNEI	7,259	1,569	3,303	11,873	8,571	0.01%	UK
WATER TARGET PLANT 1	4,535	2,057	-1,097	12,239	13,336	0.33%	GER
WATER TARGET PLANT 2	4,342	1,989	-1,062	11,911	12,973	0.33%	GER
WATER TARGET PLANT 3	4,152	1,924	-1,041	11,554	12,595	0.33%	GER
WATER TARGET PLANT 4	3,436	1,700	-1,105	9,918	11,022	0.10%	GER
Wind							
2001OLD WIND46	2,367	423	1,196	3,306	2,111	0.02%	GER
2001OLD WIND47	2,367	423	1,196	3,306	2,111	0.77%	UK
2002OLD WIND48	2,367	423	1,196	3,306	2,111	0.64%	SPAIN
2009OLD WIND49	1,243	422	103	2,182	2,079	0.15%	UK
2009OLD WIND50	1,243	422	103	2,182	2,079	0.34%	NL
2016NEW WIND19	775	327	-182	1,491	1,673	0.51%	GER
2014NEW WIND22	892	351	-118	1,669	1,787	0.53%	GER
2018NEW WIND24	706	309	-206	1,379	1,586	3.18%	UK
2016NEW WIND25	812	331	-150	1,540	1,691	1.74%	UK
2014NEW WIND99	885	350	-124	1,659	1,783	0.29%	NL
WIND TARGET PLANNED	1,237	412	134	2,154	2,020	0.15%	SPAIN
WIND TARGET PLANNED	1,233	420	95	2,169	2,074	5.61%	UK
WIND TARGET PLANNED	695	308	-215	1,366	1,581	1.08%	UK
WIND TARGET PLANT 1	892	351	-118	1,669	1,787	0.50%	GER

Source: Own calculation.

Table 5.14 Valuation results for power plant sample contd.

Power plant	Mean	Std. Dev.	Min	Max	Range	Weight	Country
Middle load - conventional thermal							
Coal							
1985OLD COAL4	295	2,074	-5,877	6,809	12,687	1.24%	GER
1984OLD COAL5	1,535	1,836	-4,138	7,617	11,755	1.11%	GER
1976OLD COAL6	1,101	1,334	-4,101	5,053	9,154	2.48%	UK
1987OLD COAL7	2,175	1,662	-4,615	8,152	12,767	2.06%	NL
Gas							
2000OLD GAS10	1,339	1,550	-3,615	8,033	11,648	0.96%	GER
1996OLD GAS12	-422	1,817	-5,880	6,243	12,123	0.54%	GER
2007OLD GAS13	11	1,756	-5,268	6,650	11,918	0.63%	GER
1984OLD GAS14	-5	1,673	-5,115	6,588	11,704	0.19%	GER
1994OLD GAS15	455	1,483	-4,216	4,272	8,488	0.73%	UK
1995OLD GAS24	120	1,782	-5,837	5,653	11,490	0.29%	NL
1999OLD GAS26	538	1,716	-5,234	5,987	11,221	0.26%	NL
1999OLD GAS34	1,219	1,366	-3,274	4,800	8,074	0.22%	UK
2010OLD GAS38	985	1,339	-3,465	4,547	8,012	2.81%	UK
2011OLD GAS39	838	1,542	-4,312	5,997	10,309	1.43%	NL
2009OLD GAS40	569	1,635	-4,472	7,271	11,743	0.88%	GER
2015NEW GAS37	181	1,185	-3,477	4,913	8,390	1.41%	GER
2013NEW GAS38	210	1,249	-3,651	5,242	8,893	1.39%	GER
2020NEW GAS39	93	1,051	-3,076	4,299	7,375	0.42%	GER
2010NEW GAS40	283	1,340	-3,866	5,812	9,678	0.47%	GER
2015NEW GAS41	181	1,185	-3,477	4,913	8,390	1.02%	GER
2010NEW GAS45	696	1,128	-3,044	3,676	6,720	1.49%	UK
2010NEW GAS46	688	1,122	-3,033	3,654	6,687	0.69%	UK
2017NEW GAS52	785	1,097	-2,678	4,364	7,042	2.11%	NL
2010NEW GAS115	703	1,133	-3,055	3,698	6,753	1.71%	UK
2010NEW GAS116	696	1,128	-3,044	3,676	6,720	1.21%	UK
GAS TARGET PLANNED 1	933	1,328	-3,477	4,427	7,904	3.31%	UK
GAS TARGET PLANNED 2	880	1,583	-4,475	6,188	10,664	0.78%	NL
GAS TARGET PLANNED 3	549	1,309	-3,429	4,797	8,225	0.41%	NL
GAS TARGET PLANNED 5	826	1,544	-4,327	5,986	10,313	0.70%	NL
GAS TARGET PLANT 1	393	1,473	-4,185	6,382	10,567	0.83%	GER
GAS TARGET PLANT 2	331	1,365	-3,893	5,886	9,779	0.83%	GER
GAS TARGET PLANT 3	237	1,243	-3,538	5,266	8,804	0.57%	GER

Power plant	Mean	Std. Dev.	Min	Max	Range	Weight	Country
Peak load -conventional thermal							
Gas							
2004OLD GAS11	-145	341	-1,305	883	2,188	0.02%	GER
1995OLD GAS16	757	666	-1,292	3,147	4,439	0.04%	NL
1992OLD GAS17	1,000	631	-1,007	3,334	4,341	0.00%	NL
1994OLD GAS18	876	648	-1,154	3,238	4,392	0.06%	NL
1995OLD GAS19	131	767	-2,231	2,699	4,931	0.07%	NL
1991OLD GAS20	-185	817	-2,743	2,502	5,245	0.07%	NL
1994OLD GAS21	1,002	631	-1,004	3,337	4,341	0.04%	NL
1993OLD GAS22	1,001	631	-1,006	3,336	4,341	0.01%	NL
1988OLD GAS23	995	632	-1,012	3,329	4,341	0.00%	NL
1993OLD GAS25	1,001	631	-1,006	3,336	4,341	0.00%	NL
1993OLD GAS27	1,001	631	-1,006	3,336	4,341	0.00%	NL
1999OLD GAS28	-116	363	-1,084	933	2,018	0.01%	UK
1998OLD GAS29	-780	432	-2,187	626	2,813	0.16%	UK
2000OLD GAS30	-662	419	-1,978	675	2,654	0.07%	UK
1994OLD GAS31	341	313	-534	1,223	1,757	0.01%	UK
2002OLD GAS32	-618	414	-1,901	695	2,596	0.09%	UK
1999OLD GAS33	-1,014	461	-2,611	529	3,140	0.02%	UK
2001OLD GAS35	-751	429	-2,140	640	2,780	0.02%	UK
1993OLD GAS36	-139	328	-1,032	1,149	2,181	0.00%	UK
1996OLD GAS37	-911	448	-2,421	571	2,992	0.06%	UK
2010NEW GAS34	-381	327	-1,481	571	2,051	0.05%	GER
2010NEW GAS48	-179	303	-1,033	682	1,715	0.00%	UK
2014NEW GAS49	365	571	-1,347	2,428	3,775	0.10%	NL
2015NEW GAS54	341	558	-1,311	2,388	3,699	0.12%	NL
2010NEW GAS112	-179	303	-1,033	682	1,715	0.06%	UK
2010NEW GAS113	-179	303	-1,033	682	1,715	0.26%	UK
2010NEW GAS114	-179	303	-1,033	682	1,715	0.17%	UK
2010NEW GAS117	-179	303	-1,033	682	1,715	0.03%	UK
GAS TARGET PLANNED 4	277	529	-1,203	2,186	3,389	0.08%	NL
GAS TARGET PLANNED 6	-372	274	-1,241	410	1,651	0.11%	GER
Other							
2015NEW OTHER 125	-859	765	-3,141	1,702	4,844	0.02%	NL
2010NEW OTHER 126	-937	864	-3,678	1,896	5,574	0.07%	NL
2010NEW OTHER 127	-937	864	-3,678	1,896	5,574	0.01%	NL
2014NEW OTHER 128	-875	783	-3,239	1,792	5,031	0.02%	NL
2019NEW OTHER 130	-797	705	-2,817	1,502	4,318	0.15%	NL
OTHER TARGET PLANNED 1	-1,417	415	-2,572	-182	2,389	0.11%	UK
OTHER TARGET PLANNED 2	-1,417	415	-2,572	-182	2,389	0.07%	UK
OTHER TARGET PLANT 2	-1,510	424	-2,950	-178	2,772	0.06%	GER

Source: Own calculation.

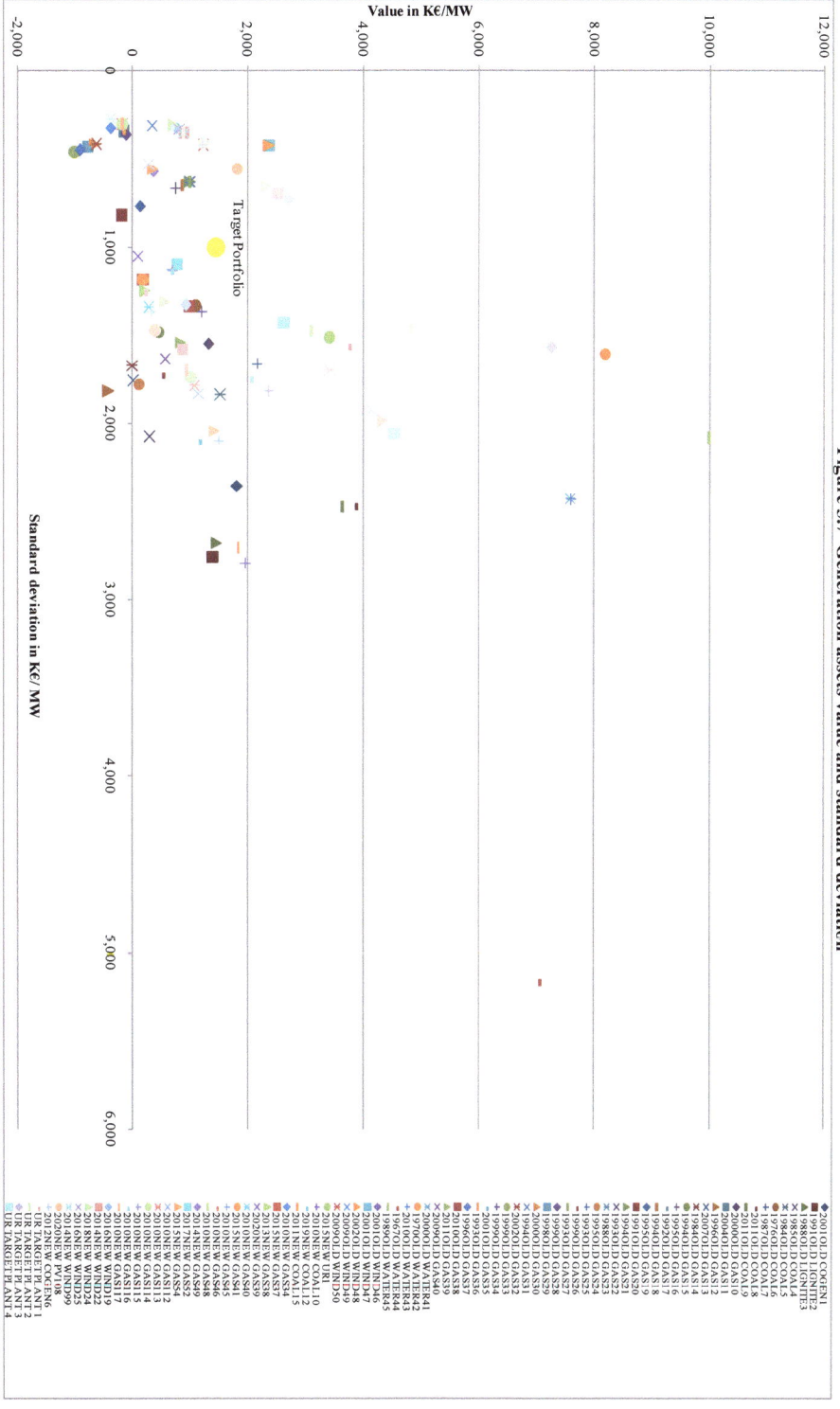

Figure 5.7 Generation assets value and standard deviation

Source: Own figure.

5.2.4 Determining efficient frontiers

Following the simulation results for the set of assets based on the aforementioned investment plan, this section identifies generation portfolios and therefore power plant technologies that are on the efficient set. As noted in Chapter 3, the identification of two efficient portfolios allows determining the frontier where all efficient generation assets are located. Since we have excluded disinvestments of old power plants, the optimization is restricted to a fixed amount of gross generation capacity for the target year. Hence, the optimization potential of the target power plant park amounts to 44,641 MW (73.82%), whereas 15,830 MW (26.18%) refer to the generation capacity of old power plants. Therefore the latter is fixed and cannot be optimized. Thus, any portfolio on the efficient set is a combination of the existing power plants and an efficient portfolio of plants leading either to the location of the minimum variance or maximum return portfolio.

To determine the minimum variance portfolio, we rely on the quadratic programming algorithm introduced in the theoretical section of this paper.[403] In a first step we construct portfolios of affiliated new fuel plant technologies and compute returns and corresponding standard deviations for each kind of fuel technology, whereas the weight of the individual asset is related to its gross generation capacity. Table 5.15 shows the results of the calculation.

Table 5.15 Valuation results for new power plant technologies

Portfolio of fuel plant technologyy	Mean in K€/ MW	Std. Dev. in K€/ MW	Adjusted Sharpe ratio
Conventional thermal			
Coal	1,709	2,045	0.84
Cogen	1,163	1,843	0.63
Gas	560	815	0.69
Other	-5,579	2,531	-2.20
Non conventional thermal			
Nuclear	3,177	1,485	2.14
Renewables			
Water	4,301	1,918	2.24
Wind	963	363	2.65
Photovoltaic	2,571	702	3.66

Source: Own calculation.

---

[403] Please refer to section 3.4.2 for further details.

Compared to the results for the overall portfolio assets given in Table 5.11, the portfolio values for new power plant technologies are on average slightly lower, which is due to the fact that the overall generation portfolio consists not only of new but also of old power plants. Since old plants are typically already depreciated, they are better off in terms of operational costs than new power plants. In addition, investment costs hit new power plants' free cash flow and as a consequence respective plant value per MW generation capacity.

To determine minimum variance generation portfolios, we need power plants' covariance matrix as stated in section 3.2.4. Therefore, we calculate in a second step the respective covariance matrix of these fuel-based portfolios which is presented in Table 5.16:

Against the background of the optimization we distinguish between economic and technical efficiency. While the former is subject to positive weights and the exclusion of short sales, the latter adds constraints to the weights of renewable generation capacity as well as a minimum demand for conventional thermal power plants within the quadratic programming algorithm. In detail, the optimization is subject to an upper limit of wind and photovoltaic power plant capacity of 30% and 15% of total utility's generation capacity, respectively. In addition, at least 10% of generation capacity should refer to coal power plants providing base load. Ultimately, we solve the optimization procedure by using *Solver*.

Table 5.16 Covariance matrix of new power plant technologies

in K€/MW	Coal	Cogen	Gas	Nuclear	PV	Water	Wind	Other
Coal	4,182,941	3,144,046	716,905	836,754	83,635	3,473,605	35,083	2,074,081
Cogen	3,144,046	3,395,504	927,542	210,916	-232	3,185,222	22,064	1,174,608
Gas	716,905	927,542	664,152	521,125	70,625	546,821	17,711	708,684
Nulcear	836,754	210,916	521,125	2,204,507	224,449	507,209	31,450	1,446,172
Photovoltaic	83,635	-232	70,625	224,449	492,969	14,815	-47,317	156,966
Water	3,473,605	3,185,222	546,821	507,209	14,815	3,677,326	31,402	1,337,941
Wind	35,083	22,064	17,711	31,450	-47,317	31,402	131,575	16,244
Other	2,074,081	1,174,608	708,684	1,446,172	156,966	1,337,941	16,244	31,127,389

Source: Own calculation.

Table 5.17 Composition and weights of efficient target generation portfolios

Portfolio / Weight	Coal	Cogen	Gas	Lignite	Other	Nuclear	PV	Water	Wind	Total gross capacity in MW
Target portfolio	34.6%	2.0%	30.0%	0.4%	2.5%	11.0%	2.0%	2.0%	15.5%	100.0%
Age distinction										
Old plants	13.2%	0.1%	9.7%	0.4%	0.0%	0.0%	0.0%	0.9%	1.9%	26.2%
New plants	21.4%	1.9%	20.3%	0.0%	2.5%	11.0%	2.0%	1.1%	13.6%	73.8%
Minimum variance portfolio										
GMVP$_{economic}$	0.0%	0.0%	7.9%	0.0%	0.0%	0.0%	22.2%	0.4%	69.5%	100.0%
GMVP$_{technical}$	10.0%	0.0%	43.6%	0.0%	0.0%	1.4%	15.0%	0.0%	30.0%	100.0%
Minimum risk combination										
Old plants and GMVP$_{economic}$	13.2%	0.1%	15.5%	0.4%	0.0%	0.0%	16.4%	1.2%	53.2%	100.0%
Old plants and GMVP$_{technical}$	20.6%	0.1%	41.9%	0.4%	0.0%	1.0%	11.1%	0.9%	24.1%	100.0%
Maximum return combination										
Old plants and GMRP	13.2%	0.1%	9.7%	0.4%	0.0%	0.0%	0.0%	74.7%	1.9%	100.0%

Source: Own calculation.

A combination of conventional thermal and renewable energies turns out to be efficient. Following the results given in Table 5.17, the global minimum variance portfolio without any constraint consists of gas fired (7.9%), photovoltaic (22.2%), water (0.4%) and wind (69.5%) power plant technologies leading to the lowest standard deviation of the expected value per MW generation capacity of a utility firm. In this respect, an investment strategy towards a low emitting power plant park is in line with operating an efficient power plant park within the mean-variance framework. Taking the fixed amount of generation capacity into account by multiplying the respective fuel weights by 26.2% and the weights of the GMVP by 73.8% determines the generation portfolio characterized by the lowest risk for a given return.

Taking the aforementioned technical criteria into account changes the composition of the global minimum variance portfolio based on technical requirements (GMVP$_{technical}$), even though this efficient generation portfolio is still a combination of conventional thermal and renewable energies. The upper limit of wind and photovoltaic power plants, however, leads to portfolio weights of 30% and 15%, respectively. In addition, nuclear power plants account for 1.4%. Alongside the group of renewable energies, the GMVP$_{technical}$ consists of coal and gas fired fuel technologies with shares of 10% and 43.6%, respectively.

As evidenced by the results in Table 5.15, the portfolio of water power plants is characterized by the highest expected value per MW generation capacity and as a consequence determines a corner portfolio on the efficient set. Hence, the combination of hydroelectricity and existing power plants determine – what we call – the global maximum return portfolio (GMRP).[404]

Figure 5.8 illustrates the run of the efficient frontier from a strictly economic point of view, whereas the first upper dashed line shows the slight shift of the efficient set due to the consideration of the fixed old generation capacity. The incorporation of technical criteria causes a further strong shift, which is illustrated by the second dashed line, of the efficient frontier to the east within the mean-variance-diagram. Even though the shift of the curve converges to the target generation portfolio, the latter is clearly not located on the efficient set, which confirms the overall hypothesis that utility's target generation portfolios are not efficient. However, in the following

---

[404] We do not distinguish between a maximum return portfolio based on economic and technical criteria, as from a perspective of a single utility firm the required share can be realized through acquisition, if hydroelectricity resources are limited.

section we will explore the degree of relative efficiency for different generation portfolios and demonstrate how to rebalance target generation portfolios to the efficient set.

Since technical limits depend on multifarious factors (i.e. network, generation system), we use the efficient frontier derived on technical criteria as approximation. As a consequence, we rely on the efficient set without constraints to determine not only the theoretical optimization potential but also the degree of relative efficiency.

Figure 5.8 Efficient frontiers for target generation portfolio

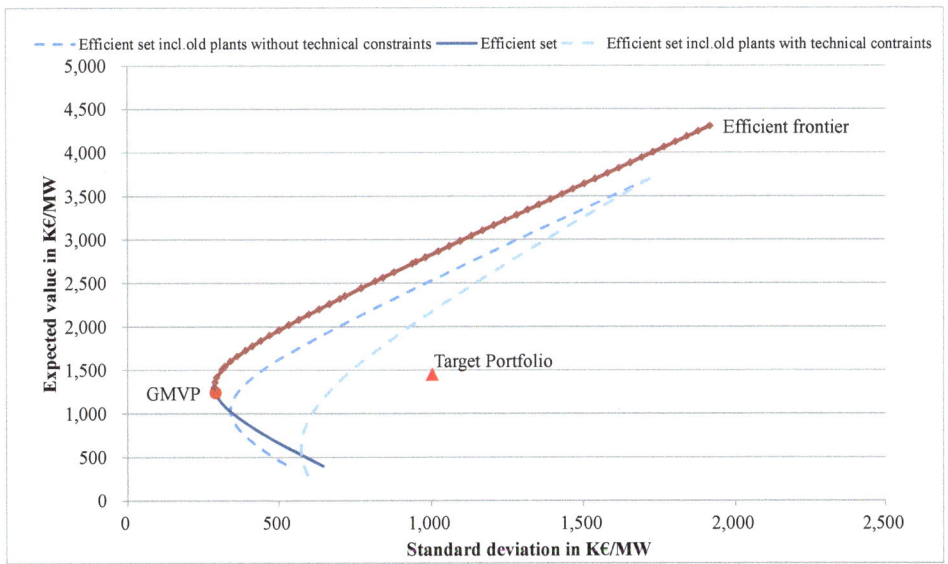

Source: Own figure.

Lastly, Table 5.18 gives an overview of the expected value and corresponding standard deviation of the portfolios defined in Table 5.17. Moreover, we calculate the adjusted Sharpe ratio for respective portfolios. Against this background old power plants exhibit higher expected values per MW generation capacity relative to their risk compared to new power plants. This mainly refers to the fact that old power plants are depreciated and therefore bear a comparative cost advantage. Yet, this group of power plants is faced with larger price risks due to lower average heat rates which require more fuel and emission allowances for generating electricity. Since the target generation portfolio consists of a fixed amount of generation capacity represented by old plants, the adjusted Sharpe ratio of the target mix is higher compared to that of the group of new power plants. New power plants bear the investment costs and as a consequence have to take depreciation cost into account which goes along with a lower adjusted Sharpe ratio.

Nevertheless, the composition of the global minimum variance portfolio not only based on economic but also on technical criteria demonstrates the opportunity to improve the risk-return trade-off.

Table 5.18 Valuation results for efficient target generation portfolios

Portfolio	μ_{PF} K€/MW	σ_{PF} K€/MW	Adjusted Sharpe ratio
Target portfolio	1,449	1,003	1.44
Age distinction			
Old plants	1,994	1,286	1.55
New plants	1,276	939	1.36
Minimum variance portfolio			
GMVP$_{economic}$	1,300	287	4.53
GMVP$_{technical}$	1,133	527	2.15
Minimum risk combination			
Old plants and GMVP$_{economic}$	1,482	439	3.37
Old plants and GMVP$_{technical}$	1,358	696	1.95
Maximum return combination			
Old plants and GMRP$_{economic}$	3,697	1,717	2.15

Source: Own table.

We explore the differences between power plant technologies on a disaggregated level in the following section. Moreover, we shed light on country specific distinctions by measuring the degree of relative efficiency. Ultimately, the findings of the upstream analyses are used to adjust utility's investment planning to rebalance the target generation portfolio.

5.3 Analyzing country-specific generation portfolios

After having presented the results of the individual power plants which represent the target power plant park in 2020, this section identifies national distinctions by constructing portfolios on a country basis. The analysis allows identifying the virtue of operating assets in different European power markets. In addition, we test the degree of efficiency for the communicated target portfolio. The findings on a country as well as on a fuel plant technology level will be taken to formulate recommendations for alternative generation portfolios. Following the remarks given in section 4.5 we evaluate these portfolios first solely based on economic criteria, whereas in a second step we add technical restrictions.

5.3.1 Power plants located in Germany

Figure 5.9 shows the feasible set for the generation assets located in Germany. In addition, the red dot represents the amount of expected return and corresponding standard deviation of the target domestic generation portfolio by taking the weights of the individual power plants. While most of the German generation assets share common risk-return features, the figure detects assets bearing extraordinary risk in terms of the standard deviation of the expected value per MW generation capacity. This is especially true for an old coal plant operating in the middle load with a gross generation capacity of 752 MW, which corresponds to a weight of 2.95% within the country portfolio.

As noted previously, the efficient frontier for power plants located in Germany, can be derived by identifying two efficient portfolios. The total generation capacity amounts to 25,390 MW gross capacity in the target year, whereas 31.5% refer to the group of old and 68.5% to new power plants. Hence, the latter represent the optimization potential. Here, we conduct the optimization strictly to the approach presented in the previous section. As a consequence, we distinguish between economic and technical efficiency.

204

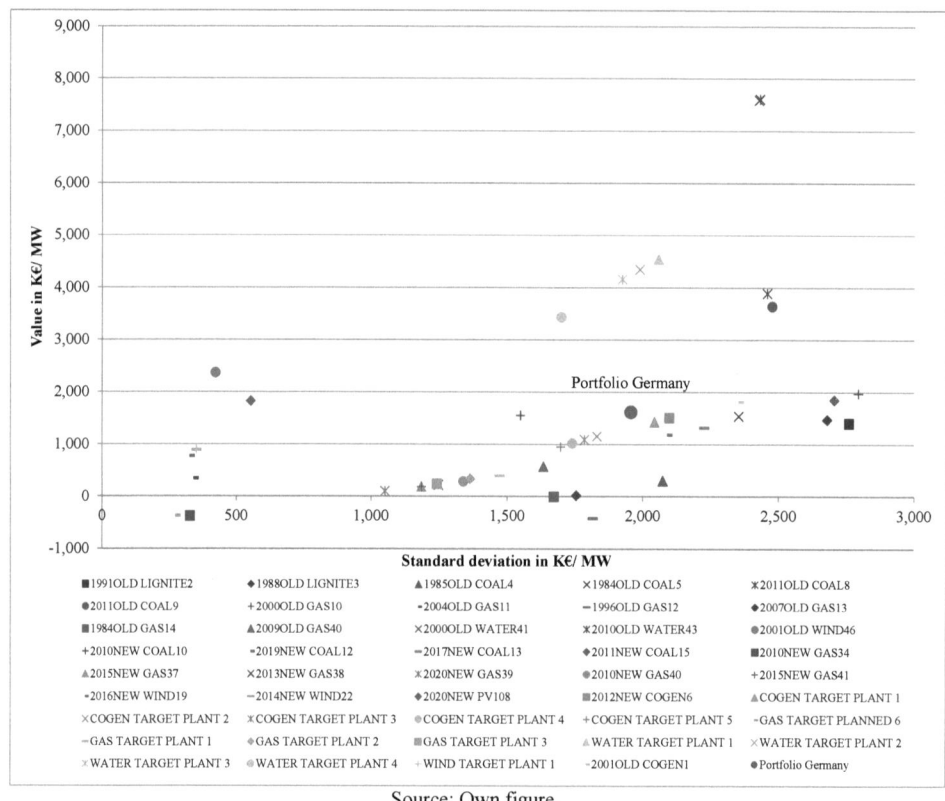

Figure 5.9 Value and standard deviation trade-off for German generation assets

Source: Own figure.

The results are consistent with the findings of the overall optimization. Again, a combination of conventional thermal and renewable energies turns out to be efficient. The weights, however, slightly differ as now on the revenue side solely German power prices determine the profitability and the corresponding level of risk for power generation technologies. Considering the group of old German power plants leads to an efficient portfolio that consists of 32.1% (20.6% coal; 10.3% gas; 1% lignite; 0.2% cogen) conventional thermal and 67.9% (45.4% wind; 20.4% photovoltaic, 2.0% water) renewable energies (see Table 5.19). The share of the latter kind of fuel technology seems high against the background of technical feasibility. Therefore, we re-run the optimization subject to upper limits of renewable and a minimum amount of coal power plants in line with the assumptions defined in the previous section.

Table 5.19 Composition and weights of efficient German generation portfolios

Portfolio / Weight	Coal	Cogen	Gas	Lignite	Other	Nuclear	PV	Water	Wind	Total gross capacity in MW
Germany	60.5%	4.8%	24.5%	1.0%	0.9%	0.0%	0.0%	4.6%	3.7%	100.0%
Age distinction										
Old plants	20.6%	0.2%	7.6%	1.0%	0.0%	0.0%	0.0%	2.0%	0.0%	31.5%
New plants	39.7%	4.5%	17.0%	0.0%	0.9%	0.0%	0.0%	2.6%	3.7%	68.5%
Minimum variance portfolio										
$GMVP_{economic}$	0.0%	0.0%	4.0%	0.0%	0.0%	0.0%	29.8%	0.0%	66.3%	100.0%
$GMVP_{technical}$	10.0%	0.0%	45.0%	0.0%	0.0%	0.0%	15.0%	0.0%	30.0%	100.0%
Minimum risk combination										
Old plants and $GMVP_{economic}$	20.6%	0.2%	10.3%	1.0%	0.0%	0.0%	20.4%	2.0%	45.4%	100.0%
Old plants and $GMVP_{technical}$	27.4%	0.2%	38.5%	1.0%	0.0%	0.0%	10.3%	2.0%	20.6%	100.0%
Maximum return combination										
Old plants and GMRP	20.6%	0.2%	7.6%	1.0%	0.0%	0.0%	0.0%	70.5%	0.0%	100.0%

Source: Own calculation.

Figure 5.10 illustrates the efficient frontier based on economic criteria for German power plants solely. Evidenced by the respective figure, the portfolio of German generation assets is clearly not efficient from an economic and also from a technical perspective. This is mainly due to the significant share of conventional thermal power plants in comparison to renewable generation capacity. In particular coal and gas power plants do account, respectively, for 60.5% and 24.5% of the total German generation capacity. In contrast, renewable generation capacity amounts to less than 10% (4.6% water; 3.7% wind) of the sample national energy mix (see Table 5.19). However, by computing the horizontal, δ and vertical, η distance to the German power plant portfolio, we determine the degree of what we call relative efficiency. The consideration of technical restrictions, however, reduces the distance of the location of the German power plant portfolio to the efficient frontier.

Figure 5.10 Efficient frontiers for German generation portfolios

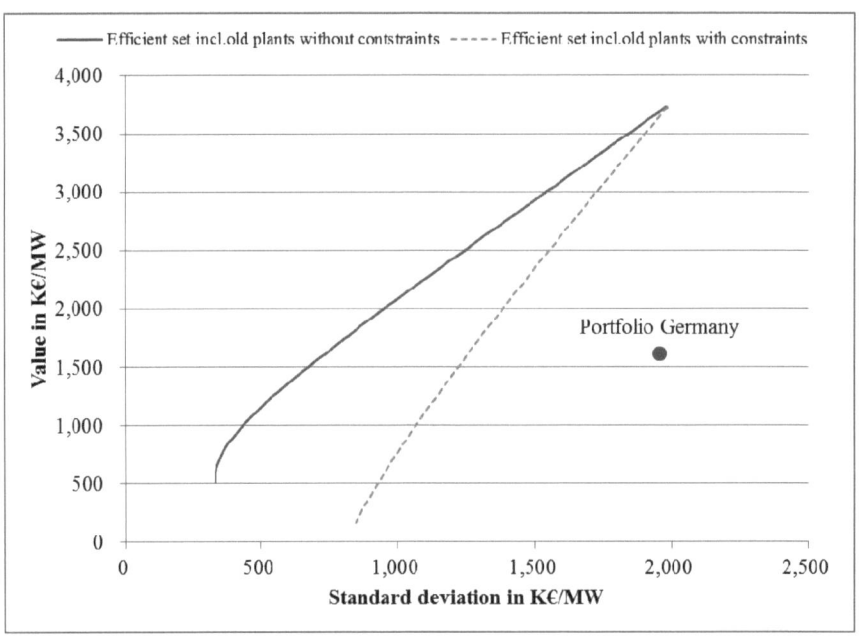

Source: Own calculation.

5.3.2 Power plants located in the United Kingdom

In contrast, the feasible set of power plants located in the UK indicates that return and risk for each generation asset differ leading to a wide spread of the power generation assets (see Figure 5.11). Following the results for British power generation assets the level of individual risk in terms of the corresponding standard deviation is clearly lower in comparison to the German sample. We compute a return of K€ 1,402 and a standard deviation of K€ 941 per MW generation capacity. As a consequence, the respective adjusted Sharpe ratio turns out to be higher (1.49) than in the previous sample (0.83). In other words, operating the fuel mix of the British power plant sample is rewarded with a higher value per unit of risk per MW generation capacity compared to the German generation portfolio. This is due to the composition of the UK generation portfolio that is mainly characterized by nuclear (24.3%) and wind power (27.7%).

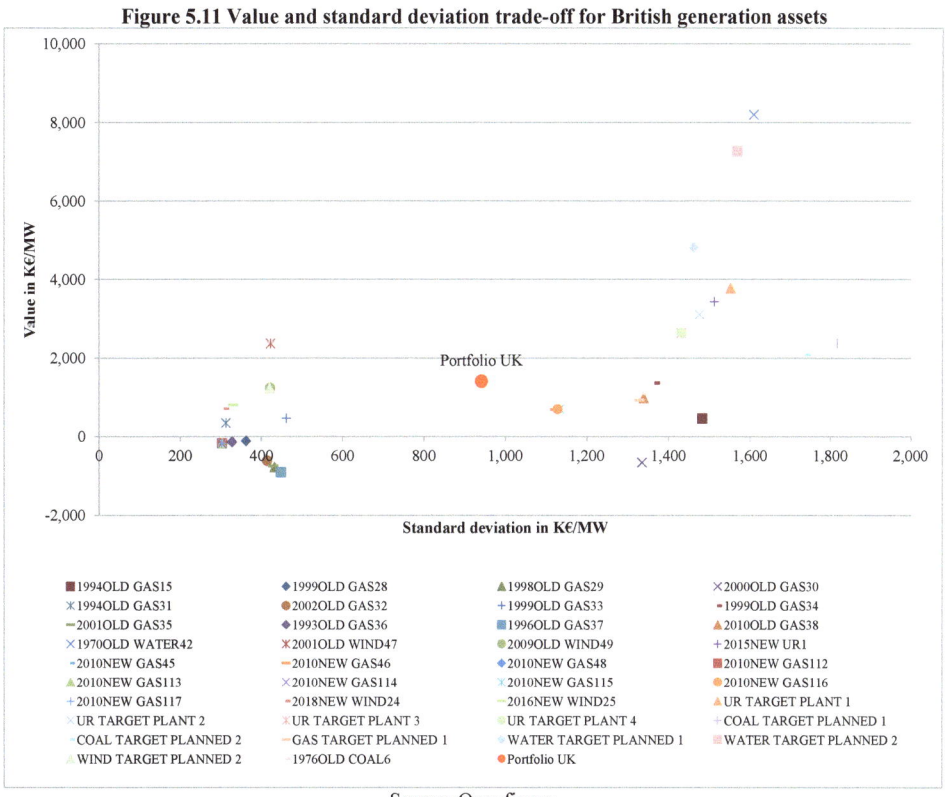

Figure 5.11 Value and standard deviation trade-off for British generation assets

Source: Own figure.

According to the dynamization of the power plant park, 45.2% of the generation capacity refers to power plants located in the UK in the target year. This is due to the substitution of old German nuclear power plants as well as achieving the target amount of nuclear power plant capacity. As a consequence, the share of new power plants is relatively high (83.2%) compared to the proportion of old power plants (16.8%) in the generation portfolio. To obtain the efficient frontiers, we use the mean-variance framework and include the fixed amount of old plants. Table 5.20 presents the respective composition and weights.

Consistent with the previous results, we identify a portfolio of thermal and renewable energies as efficient bearing the lowest standard deviation. Specifically wind (92.1%) and gas (7.9%) power plants determine the global minimum variance portfolio.

Table 5.20 Composition and weights of efficient British generation portfolios

Portfolio / Weight	Coal	Cogen	Gas	Lignite	Other	Nuclear	PV	Water	Wind	Total gross capacity in MW
United Kingdom	15.8%	0.0%	29.1%	0.0%	3.0%	24.3%	0.0%	0.1%	27.7%	100.0%
Age distinction										
Old plants	5.5%	0.0%	9.3%	0.0%	0.0%	0.0%	0.0%	0.0%	2.0%	16.8%
New plants	10.3%	0.0%	19.8%	0.0%	3.0%	24.3%	0.0%	0.1%	25.7%	83.2%
Minimum variance portfolio										
$GMVP_{economic}$	0.0%	0.0%	7.9%	0.0%	0.0%	0.0%	0.0%	0.0%	92.1%	100.0%
$GMVP_{technical}$	10.0%	0.0%	60.0%	0.0%	0.0%	0.0%	0.0%	0.0%	30.0%	100.0%
Minimum risk combination										
Old plants and $GMVP_{economic}$	5.5%	0.0%	15.8%	0.0%	0.0%	0.0%	0.0%	0.0%	78.7%	100.0%
Old plants and $GMVP_{technical}$	13.8%	0.0%	59.2%	0.0%	0.0%	0.0%	0.0%	0.0%	27.0%	100.0%
Maximum return combination										
Old plants and GMRP	5.5%	0.0%	9.3%	0.0%	0.0%	0.0%	0.0%	83.2%	2.0%	100.0%

Source: Own table.

In contrast, photovoltaic plants are not part of the efficient portfolio, as this type of generation asset does not belong to the opportunity set of the national market. The initial efficient frontier is shifted to the east by considering old plants as well as technical requirements, which equals previous optimizations. As we can appreciate, the British generation portfolio does not turn out to be efficient either, which is demonstrated in Figure 5.12.

Figure 5.12 Efficient frontiers for British generation portfolios

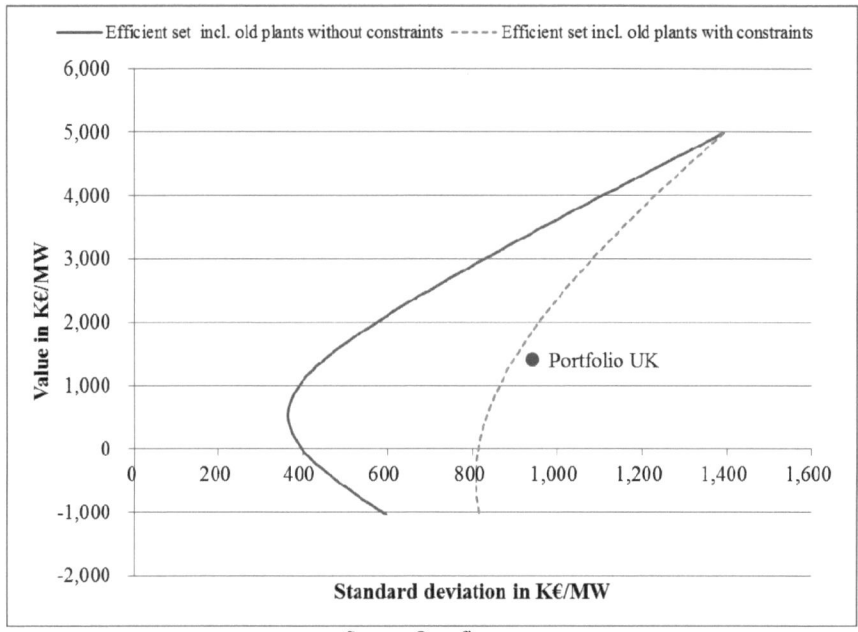

Source: Own figure.

5.3.3 Power plants located in the Netherlands

A significant amount of the Dutch generation capacity is accounted by gas plant technologies, which make up two thirds of the samples energy mix. In addition, coal power plants contribute to more than 20% leading to a sample portfolio of almost 90% of conventional thermal power plants. Since average expected return and corresponding standard deviation differ for these power plant technologies, the feasible set shows a group of assets located far west (mainly gas power plants) and another group of coal plants east as Figure 5.13 illustrates. Very similar to the other power markets, water power plants exhibit the highest returns. In comparison to similar power plant technologies operating in neighboring markets, the expected value per MW generation capacity is the highest, as it is driven by high power prices. Overall, we compute an adjusted Sharpe ratio of 0.54 which is less than the ratio of other non-domestic generation portfolios.

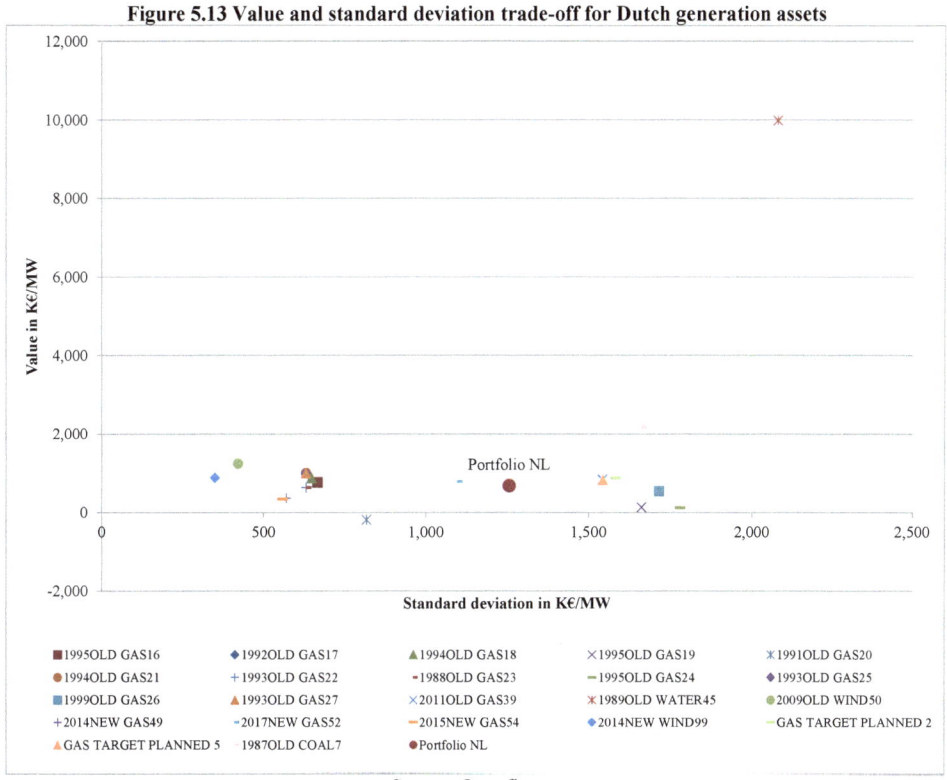

Figure 5.13 Value and standard deviation trade-off for Dutch generation assets

■ 1995OLD GAS16	♦ 1992OLD GAS17	▲ 1994OLD GAS18	✕ 1995OLD GAS19	✳ 1991OLD GAS20
● 1994OLD GAS21	+ 1993OLD GAS22	− 1988OLD GAS23	− 1995OLD GAS24	♦ 1993OLD GAS25
■ 1999OLD GAS26	▲ 1993OLD GAS27	✕ 2011OLD GAS39	✳ 1989OLD WATER45	● 2009OLD WIND50
+ 2014NEW GAS49	− 2017NEW GAS52	− 2015NEW GAS54	♦ 2014NEW WIND99	− GAS TARGET PLANNED 2
▲ GAS TARGET PLANNED 5	1987OLD COAL7	● Portfolio NL		

Source: Own figure.

To obtain the efficient frontier for the opportunity set of the Dutch power plant sample, we compute the minimum variance portfolio. Since 46.8% of generation capacity refers to old power plants operating beyond the target year, the rest amounts to 53.2% and serves for optimization. In line with the previous findings, the minimum variance portfolio without any constraints is based on conventional thermal and renewable power plants. Considering the fixed amount of power plants and technical restrictions, we obtain the efficient frontier for the respective power plant sample. Table 5.21 gives an overview of the weights of the identified portfolios as well as the country-specific target mix.

Table 5.21 Composition and weights of efficient Dutch generation portfolios

Weight Portfolio	Coal	Cogen	Gas	Lignite	Other	Nuclear	PV	Water	Wind	Total gross capacity in MW
Netherlands	20.5%	0.0%	65.7%	0.0%	7.3%	0.0%	0.0%	0.2%	6.3%	100.0%
Age distinction										
Old plants	20.5%	0.0%	22.6%	0.0%	0.0%	0.0%	0.0%	0.2%	3.4%	46.8%
New plants	0.0%	0.0%	43.0%	0.0%	7.3%	0.0%	0.0%	0.0%	2.9%	53.2%
Minimum variance portfolio										
GMVP$_{economic}$	0.0%	0.0%	6.9%	0.0%	0.0%	0.0%	0.0%	0.0%	93.1%	100.0%
GMVP$_{technical}$	10.0%	0.0%	60.0%	0.0%	0.0%	0.0%	0.0%	0.0%	30.0%	100.0%
Minimum risk combination										
Old plants and GMVP$_{economic}$	20.5%	0.0%	26.3%	0.0%	0.0%	0.0%	0.0%	0.2%	52.9%	100.0%
Old plants and GMVP$_{technical}$	25.9%	0.0%	54.6%	0.0%	0.0%	0.0%	0.0%	0.2%	19.4%	100.0%
Maximum return combination										
Old plants and GMRP	20.5%	0.0%	22.6%	0.0%	0.0%	0.0%	0.0%	53.4%	3.4%	100.0%

Source: Own calculation.

According to Figure 5.14, the Dutch sample generation portfolio is not located on the efficient frontier based on economic as well as on technical criteria and is therefore not efficient.

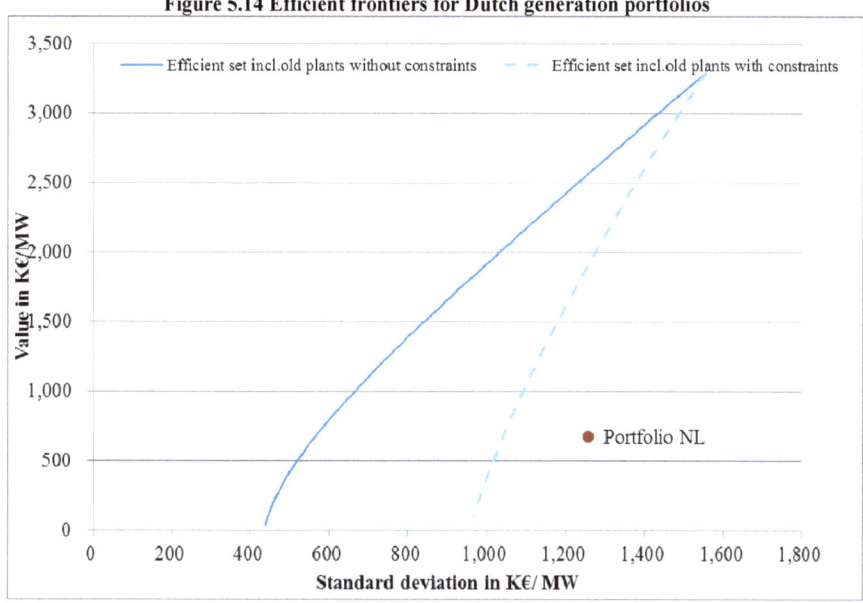

Figure 5.14 Efficient frontiers for Dutch generation portfolios

Source: Own figure.

Ultimately, we explore the portfolio of power plants located in Spain.

5.3.4 Power plants located in Spain

Even though the total Spanish generation capacity is the smallest of the sample portfolios, the energy mix promises interesting results, as the analysis will shed light on the risk-return level of a generation portfolio which is fully composed of renewable energy technologies. In detail, photovoltaic generation capacity amounts to 71.6%, wind generation to 28.1% and 0.3% steam from water power plants. Since all power plants are based on renewable energies, we expect the individual assets to be closely located. Indeed, Figure 5.15 illustrates this. Yet, one photovoltaic power plant lies far east and is dominated by most of the other generation assets. This is mainly due to the assumed remuneration degression rate for power generation of photovoltaic power plants which hits the respective expected value per MW generation capacity.

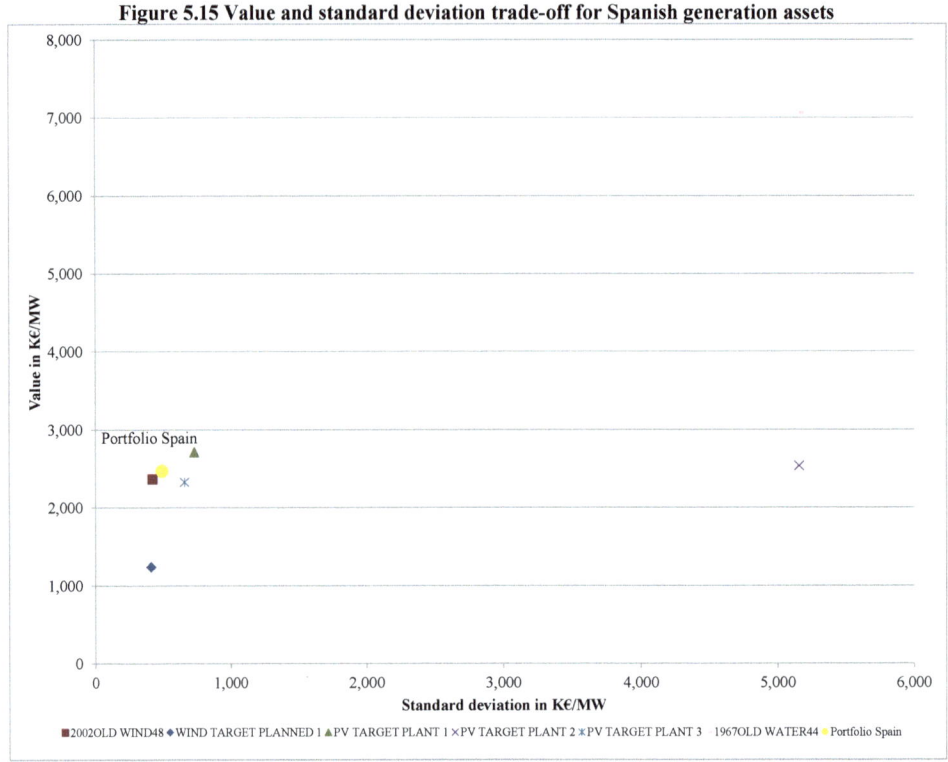

Figure 5.15 Value and standard deviation trade-off for Spanish generation assets

Source: Own figure.

Compared to the other sample power plant parks, the share of the plants located in Spain in the target year is rather scarce, representing 1,688 MW (2.79%) of the generation capacity. Due to the ambitious investment plans to build up photovoltaic generation capacity, new plants account for 76.9% of the Spanish sample.

Table 5.22 Composition and weights of efficient Spanish generation portfolios

Portfolio	Coal	Cogen	Gas	Lignite	Other	Nuclear	PV	Water	Wind	Total gross capacity in MW
Spain	0.0%	0.0%	0.0%	0.0%	0.0%	0.0%	71.6%	0.3%	28.1%	100.0%
Age distinction										
Old plants	0.0%	0.0%	0.0%	0.0%	0.0%	0.0%	0.0%	0.4%	22.7%	23.1%
New plants	0.0%	0.0%	0.0%	0.0%	0.0%	0.0%	71.6%	0.0%	5.3%	76.9%
Minimum variance portfolio										
GMVP$_{economic}$	0.0%	0.0%	0.0%	0.0%	0.0%	0.0%	28.9%	0.4%	70.7%	100.0%
GMVP$_{technical}$	-	-	-	-	-	-	-	-	-	-
Minimum risk combination										
Old plants and GMVP$_{economic}$	0.0%	0.0%	0.0%	0.0%	0.0%	0.0%	22.2%	0.6%	77.2%	100.0%
Old plants and GMVP$_{technical}$	-	-	-	-	-	-	-	-	-	-
Maximum return combination										
Old plants and GMRP	0.0%	0.0%	0.0%	0.0%	0.0%	0.0%	0.0%	77.3%	22.7%	100.0%

Source: Own table.

Hence, we derive the minimum variance portfolio in order to test whether the sample power plant park is located on the efficient frontier. Here, we identify an efficient generation portfolio solely based on renewable, as the national feasible set does not include conventional thermal power plants. Hence, combining wind (70.7%), photovoltaic (28.9%) and water power plants (0.4%) leads to the lowest standard deviation for a given level of return (see Table 5.22). The maximum return is a generation portfolio which solely consists of new water power plant technologies. However, the adjusted Sharpe ratio of the water plant technologies turns out to be lower than the Spanish target generation portfolio. The latter is better off due to the negative correlation of wind and photovoltaic power plants reducing the total standard deviation of the Spanish generation portfolio. As a consequence, the Spanish generation portfolio must be located on the efficient frontier. Varying the share of the two efficient portfolios, we plot the efficient frontier as illustrated in Figure 5.16. The reasons for not determining the efficient frontier based on technical criteria are twofold. First, the sample's feasible set is restricted to renewable plants. Second, the total amount of generation capacity is rather low compared to the other sample markets, so that it is reasonable to assume that other competitors hold more generation capacity and are responsible for grid stability.

Figure 5.16 Efficient frontier for Spanish generation portfolios

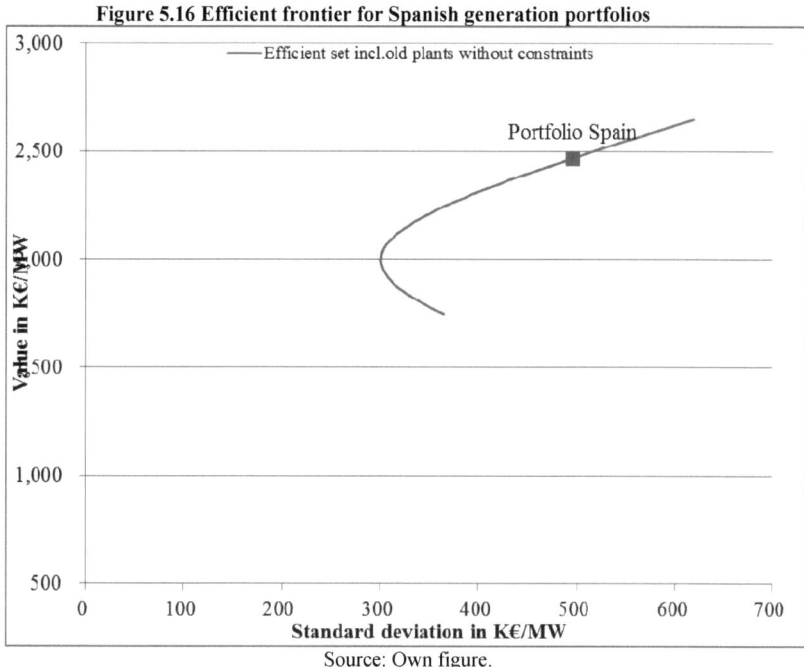

Source: Own figure.

Following the illustration given in Figure 5.16, the sample portfolio is located on the efficient frontier. This is coherent with the previous findings, as the corresponding adjusted Sharpe ratios demonstrate that the Spanish generation mix is the most valuable power plant portfolio. For each unit of risk the reward in terms of the expected value per MW generation capacity is higher in comparison to the other European sample portfolios.

We will determine the portfolios which are vertically and horizontally located towards the national portfolios in order to reveal improvements for the level of return by a given level of risk and vice versa. Specifically, we can derive the respective fuel mix for each European sub-portfolio which is located on the efficient frontier.

5.3.5 Summary

We have computed the expected value per MW generation capacity and the corresponding standard deviation for each national sub-portfolio as well as the adjusted Sharpe ratio. In addition we have distinguished between a portfolio of old and new power plants and computed respective values for efficient generation portfolios in each country. The latter serves to determine the efficient frontiers illustrated in the previous section. Table 5.23 represents these results:

We find that the Spanish power plant sample solely based on renewable power generation dominates the other country specific fuel mixes. The results for the adjusted Sharpe ratios demonstrate the opportunity to improve the risk-return trade-off compared to the initial fuel mix. However, the country specific differences are rather due to respective fuel mixes than electricity prices. Against this background we re-run simulations for individual power plant investments in the sample markets in section 5.5.

Even though the results show the merit of specific national energy markets for power generation investments, please mark that the results do not allow to deduce any evidence regarding the degree of efficiency for the national power markets. Therefore, the following section will determine the degree of relative efficiency of country-specific generation assets.

Table 5.23 Country-specific overview of valuation results for efficient generation portfolios

Country	Germany			United Kingdom			Netherlands			Spain		
Portfolio of fuel plant technology	Mean in K€/	Std. Dev. in K€/	Adjusted Sharpe ratio	Mean in K€/	Std. Dev. in K€/	Adjusted Sharpe ratio	Mean in K€/	Std. Dev. in K€/	Adjusted Sharpe ratio	Mean in K€/	Std. Dev. in K€/	Adjusted Sharpe ratio
Samples nationl mix	1,616	1,956	0.83	1,402	941	1.49	677	1,256	0.54	2,469	495	4.99
Age distinction												
Old plants	2,617	2,109	1.24	1,036	1,029	1.01	1,409	1,353	1.04	2,132	882	2.42
New plants	1,151	1,865	0.62	1,476	935	1.58	33	1,204	0.03	2,479	499	4.97
Minimum variance portfolio												
GMVP economic	1,117	261	4.28	956	353	2.71	876	339	2.58	1,633	323	5.05
GMVP technical	783	777	1.01	966	833	1.16	957	739	1.30	na	na	na
Minimum risk combination												
Old plants and GMVP economic	1,589	722	2.20	970	390	2.49	1,125	708	1.59	1,748	364	4.80
Old plants and GMVP technical	1,361	1,177	1.16	978	863	1.13	1,168	1,120	1.04	na	na	na
Maximum return combination												
Old plants and GMRP economic	3,744	1,989	1.88	4,989	1,393	3.58	3,292	1,552	2.12	3,615	3,377	1.07

Source: Own calculation.

5.4 Determining the degree of relative efficiency of generation assets

To determine the degree of relative efficiency for the country-specific and the target portfolio, Table 5.24 presents the portfolios and the corresponding weights. Note that the table summarizes first of all benchmark portfolios which are composed of old plants of the respective sample and efficient portfolios derived from an economic perspective. That is why we allow holding significant shares of renewable power plant capacity, for instance. For expository purposes, we add affiliated weights of fuel technologies which are derived from results of the disaggregated single plant valuation. In addition, the table distinguishes between efficient portfolios that are horizontally (henceforth: Z_{HE}) and vertically (henceforth: Z_{VE}) positioned with respect to the portfolio which is evaluated. The efficient frontier, however, is a combination of two portfolios. While the first portfolio consists of the group of old plants and the generation assets bearing the lowest standard deviation, the second portfolio combines old plants with the generation assets showing the highest expected return per MW generation capacity.

Table 5.24 Composition and weights for vertical and horizontal efficient generation portfolios

Portfolio / Weight	Coal	Cogen	Gas	Lignite	Other	Nuclear	PV	Water	Wind
Target portfolio									
Z_{Target}	34.6%	2.0%	30.0%	0.4%	2.5%	11.0%	2.0%	2.0%	15.5%
Z_{VE}	13.2%	0.1%	12.7%	0.4%	0.0%	0.0%	8.6%	36.0%	28.9%
Z_{HE}	13.2%	0.1%	15.5%	0.4%	0.0%	0.0%	16.4%	1.2%	53.2%
National distinction									
Germany									
$Z_{Germany}$	60.5%	4.8%	24.5%	1.0%	0.9%	0.0%	0.0%	4.6%	3.7%
Z_{VE}	20.6%	0.2%	7.7%	1.0%	0.0%	0.0%	0.7%	68.1%	1.6%
Z_{HE}	20.6%	0.2%	10.3%	1.0%	0.0%	0.0%	20.1%	2.8%	44.9%
Netherlands									
$Z_{Netherlands}$	20.5%	0.0%	65.7%	0.0%	7.3%	0.0%	0.0%	0.2%	6.3%
Z_{VE}	20.5%	0.0%	23.9%	0.0%	0.0%	0.0%	0.0%	35.5%	20.1%
Z_{HE}	20.5%	0.0%	26.3%	0.0%	0.0%	0.0%	0.0%	0.2%	52.9%
United Kingdom									
$Z_{United Kingdom}$	15.8%	0.0%	29.1%	0.0%	3.0%	24.3%	0.0%	0.1%	27.7%
Z_{VE}	5.5%	0.0%	11.9%	0.0%	0.0%	0.0%	0.0%	50.4%	32.2%
Z_{HE}	5.5%	0.0%	15.1%	0.0%	0.0%	0.0%	0.0%	8.9%	70.4%
Spain									
Z_{Spain}	0.0%	0.0%	0.0%	0.0%	0.0%	0.0%	71.6%	0.3%	28.1%
Z_{VE}	0.0%	0.0%	0.0%	0.0%	0.0%	0.0%	13.7%	30.2%	56.2%
Z_{HE}	0.0%	0.0%	0.0%	0.0%	0.0%	0.0%	20.1%	8.0%	71.9%

Source: Own calculation.

5.4.1 Efficiency of the target portfolio

In a first step, we test the communicated target generation portfolio for its degree of efficiency. Figure 5.17 illustrates the location of the target generation mix within the μ–σ diagram. It appears that the target portfolio is not placed on the efficient frontier and as a consequence is not efficient. Thus, the results approve hypothesis (1) stating that utility's generation portfolios are not efficient. The asterisks highlighted on the efficient frontier, however, indicate portfolios which are horizontally and vertically efficient to the target generation portfolio. By measuring the distance, the degree of relative efficiency can be computed to shed light on the question how efficient the target energy mix is in comparison to alternative generation portfolios.

Figure 5.17 Horizontal and vertical distance of the target generation portfolio to the efficient frontiers

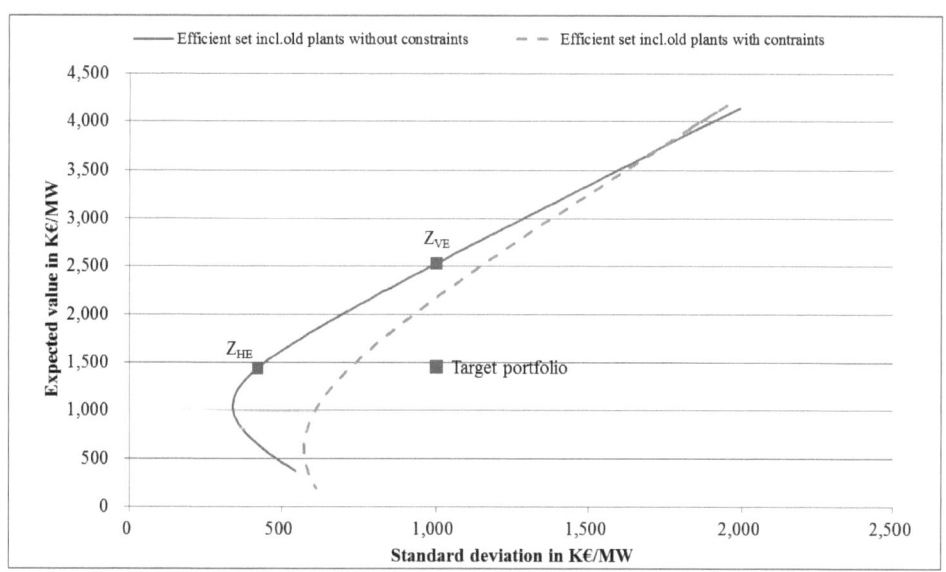

Source: Own figure.

We find an adjusted Sharpe ratio of 1.45 for the respective portfolio indicating that one Euro additional risk is rewarded with 1.45 Euro extra returns in terms of value per MW generation capacity (see Table 5.25). The degree of efficiency is based on the ratios η and δ that measure, respectively, the vertical and horizontal distance to the efficient frontier by relying on the adjusted Sharpe ratio introduced in Chapter 4. The vertical distance to the efficient frontier amounts to 0.57 for the target portfolio indicating non-efficiency. Apparently, a generation portfolio exists which bears the same amount of risk, but rewards investments in power generation technologies with a return of 2.5 times higher than the target generation mix. Yet, the question arises whether this portfolio is not only efficient from an economic but also from a technical point of view. Referring to the weights and keeping in mind that water plants drive expected returns, a realization requires operating a power plant park whose generation capacity refers to 36% to hydroelectricity. While the exploitation of new hydroelectricity resources is limited, the required number of water power plants could be gained in practice by acquisitions. However, the generation mix which is located on the efficient set lying horizontally in comparison to the target portfolio seems more feasible even from a technical perspective. The majority (53.2%) of the generation portfolio refers to wind power plants, whereas 29.2% of total generation is generated by conventional thermal power plants. Since wind power generation assets bear the lowest standard deviation of the expected return relative to other asset classes, an operator aiming to reduce risk should invest in wind power plant technologies. The degree of horizontal efficiency amounts to 0.43 so that the holder of this efficient portfolio is rewarded with 3.36 units return for each unit of risk. Therefore this ratio clearly indicates that the target generation mix can be optimized towards lower risk by achieving the same level of return. Comparing the ratio of vertical efficiency (0.57) to horizontal efficiency (0.43), however, suggests that the communicated target generation mix is less efficient from a risk point of view than to the level of return. Apparently, the diversification potential by combining wind and photovoltaic power plants is insufficiently realized.

Table 5.25 Degree of efficiency for sample generation portfolios based on economic criteria

Portfolio	μ_{PF}	σ_{PF}	Z_{PF}	Z_{VE}	Z_{HE}	η	δ
Target portfolio	1,449	1,003	1.4442	2.5215	3.3660	0.5728	0.4291
National distinction							
Germany	1,616	1,956	0.8259	1.8895	2.1933	0.4371	0.3766
Netherlands	677	1,256	0.5389	2.0418	1.5901	0.2639	0.3389
United Kingdom	1,402	941	1.4890	3.6192	3.1042	0.4114	0.4797
Spain	2,468	495	4.9879	4.9879	4.9879	1.0000	1.0000

Source: Own calculation.

The following sections shed light on the performance of the generation assets within their power markets.

5.4.2 Efficiency of the domestic portfolio

After having analyzed the efficiency degree of the target generation mix, in this section we explore the results for power plants operating in the German power market. The power plant sample mainly consists of conventional thermal power plants, whereas coal fired technologies dominate representing almost two thirds of the respective generation mix. In contrast, the amount of renewable energies is rather small representing 8.4% of the generation mix. Against this background and after having presented Figure 5.10 which shows the German generation portfolio relative to the efficient frontier, it is not astonishing that the respective generation mix does not turn out to be efficient. As a further evidence the adjusted Sharpe ratio amounts to less than one (0.83), indicating that each extra unit of risk is not fully rewarded (see Table 5.25). The degree of relative efficiency, however, is based on the distance to the efficient frontier, which shows the efficient generation portfolios of the respective national power markets. As stated previously, the precise combination of generation assets that determine the efficient frontier is a function of old plants which already operated before the base year. Consistent with the previous findings[405], the ratios of the German power plant sample, η and δ, demonstrate that the efficiency degree is clearly lower than the target portfolio. This is true not only from a risk but also from a return perspective.

Very similar to the results related to the whole portfolio of power plants assets, the sample's national mix is relatively more efficient from a return perspective than from a risk perspective. Hence, the respective η ratio which measures the vertical distance is larger than the δ ratio. As a consequence, instead of investing in new conventional thermal power plants, a significant amount of capacity should either be based on wind power technology to reduce the amount of corresponding generation risk or substituted – as far as technically possible – by hydroelectricity plant technologies. Irrespectively, the results demonstrate that the use of coal power plant technologies should be massively cut.

Since we have identified a higher degree of efficiency for the target generation portfolio in comparison with the national power generation mix, the power plant technologies operating on the other European power markets must have contributed positively to the degree of efficiency of the target portfolio. Hence, we can deduce that

---

[405] Please refer to section 5.4.1.

operating power plants on different markets leads to an overall reduction of risk and as a consequence improves the risk-return trade-off from a utility's perspective.

Thus, the results support hypothesis (2.1) stating that international diversification of electricity generation portfolios leads to holding a higher degree of relative efficient portfolios in comparison to purely domestic generation portfolios. Within the following section we explore the driving forces in detail.

5.4.3 Efficiency of international generation portfolios

Alongside the power plant sample operating in the domestic power market, more than 35,000 MW generation capacities refer to plants operating in non-domestic markets. Following the weights on a fuel type technology basis given in Table 5.24 each generation mix differs leading to unequally efficient degrees.

Starting with power technologies located in the UK, as they represent the lion's share (80% or 27,328 MW) of non-domestic gross generation capacity, we find an adjusted Sharpe ratio for UK generation sample assets of 1.49 (see Table 5.25) which is slightly more than the corresponding ratio of the target portfolio (1.44). Even though the performance ratio indicates a similar reward for each unit of risk, the degree of relative efficiency differs. This is due to the specific efficient frontier which depends on the respective feasible set of generation assets. According to the respective values for η and δ, the target generation portfolio is relatively more efficient from a return (0.57 to 0.38) as well as from a risk point of view (0.43 to 0.41) compared to the British power plant sample.

Furthermore, our results refute the findings of *Roques et al.* (2008), who state that investors holding pure gas power portfolios are better off compared to operating diversified generation portfolios. Considering the composition of the global minimum variance portfolio for the whole power plant sample leads to an adjusted Sharpe ratio of 4.53 (see Table 5.18), which is higher compared to the results for new single fuel type technologies. Hence, a utility firm is better off operating a diversified power plant park in comparison to a pure portfolio of a single type of fuel with respect to the risk return trade-off. Against this background, we confirm hypothesis (2.2).

The results for power generation assets operating in the Netherlands show, that each unit of risk is rewarded with less value per MW generation capacity in comparison to the UK market (see Table 5.23). The adjusted Sharpe ratio amounts to less (0.54) than the respective ratio for the UK market (1.49) and in addition the ratios indicating the degree of relative efficiency turn out to be lower for the Dutch generation assets from a risk as well as from a return perspective. Nevertheless, the efficient generation portfolio which is horizontally positioned to the Dutch sample portfolio consists of 46.3% of conventional thermal power plants and therefore this portfolio should even be feasible from a technical point of view.

Ultimately, the Spanish generation mix turns out to be efficient (see Table 5.25). Since the composition of the Spanish sample generation portfolio solely based on renewable energies turns out to be efficient, its hypothesis (2.3), which posits the reverse, cannot be clearly confirmed. However, the Spanish investment opportunity set does not consist of conventional thermal power plants. Considering the whole sample of power plant technologies, we identify a combination of conventional thermal and renewable energy generation assets as efficient leading to the lowest level of risk with respect to the Markowitz portfolio theory.

According to the results it seems that a power plant mix avoiding conventional as well as non-conventional thermal power plants turns out to be efficient within a mean-variance framework. This can be seen as evidence for investors as well as utilities to rethink their investment plans and strengthen their efforts to enlarge the share of renewable energy capacity in the total generation capacity as far as technically feasible.

While we consider volume risk for wind and photovoltaic power plants, we take the price risk for water power plants into account. Therefore, the question arises whether implications change, if we face the operator of renewable energy capacity with price risk in terms of volatile power prices observed on energy exchanges. However, the presumed degression rate leads to a price level which is almost equal to the base load price at the beginning of the perpetuity. Nevertheless, results and the model should be tested for robustness.

For the sake of completeness, we show the portfolio weights from a technical perspective in Table 5.26.

Table 5.26 Degree of efficiency for sample generation portfolios based on technical criteria

Portfolio	μPF	σPF	ZPF	ZVE	ZHE	η	δ
Target portfolio	1,449	1,003	1.4442	2.1702	2.0045	0.6655	0.7205
National distinction							
Germany	1,616	1,956	0.8259	1.8631	1.6756	0.4433	0.4929
Netherlands	677	1,256	0.5389	1.5150	1.0433	0.3557	0.5165
UK	1,402	941	1.4890	1.9630	1.5676	0.7585	0.9499
Spain	2,468	495	4.9879	4.9879	4.9879	1.0000	1.0000

Source: Own calculation.

5.4.4 Robustness

In this section we test the results for robustness. Thinking critically about the underlying assumptions of our simulation model, so far we have neglected the fact that power plant technologies vary in terms of the time needed to build the respective plant due to the capacity size or regulative approvals (e.g. coal, nuclear or hydroelectricity plants). Since the realization of not only non-conventional thermal but also hydroelectricity power plants investment projects need more time in comparison to gas power plants for instance, respective cash flows are lagged and as consequence this has an impact on the profitability of the power plant.

We assume a time lag of 3 years for hydroelectricity and nuclear power plants so that cash flows of the respective plants will be realized three years later after having invested. In addition, we presume a time lag of 2 years for coal fired power plants, whereas the construction time of the remaining power plant technologies still holds (1 year). As a consequence, gas, cogen, wind and photovoltaic power plants exhibit a comparative advantage, since the realization of lagged cash flows causes a negative impact on the expected value. Nevertheless, water power plants turn out to be most profitable. In addition, the portfolio of new coal fired power plants exhibits the highest value per MW generation capacity within the group of conventional thermal power plants. Considering the time lag of building power plants has rather an impact on the expected value than on the level of standard deviation of the expected value. Hence, the composition of the minimum variance portfolio without any technical constraints does not alter, whereas the affiliated weights slightly change. Specifically, the share of gas power plants decreases from 7.9% to 7.7%, whereas the reduction of wind and photovoltaic amounts to 0.09% and 0.3%, respectively. In contrast, the share of water power plants within the minimum variance portfolio slightly increases from 0.4% to 0.7%. This finding is interesting, as water plants exhibit a comparative disadvantage due to the construction time lag, but the respective portfolio weight rises, though. Fewer years of cash inflows cause a lower price uncertainty in terms of the dispersion from the simulated to the expected price trajectory and therefore an increase of the respective portfolio weight.

In line with our previous findings, the composition of the minimum variance portfolio from a technical perspective does not change by taking construction time lags into account.

In addition, we consider volume instead of price risk for wind and photovoltaic power plants. As our results state the attractiveness of these renewable power plant technologies in comparison to conventional thermal plants, it is reasonable to question whether we have incorporated the risk profile of these plants properly. Since we have assumed a fixed remuneration, the profitability of wind and photovoltaic plants depends solely on operating hours. As a consequence the standard deviation of the expected value per MW generation capacity turns out lower in comparison to the other plant technologies. Hence we will re-run the simulation by taking price and volume risks for the aforementioned plant technologies into account.

Instead of the fixed remuneration for wind and photovoltaic power plants, we assume now that in the perpetuity the respective plants have to compete on electricity markets. Therefore, generated electricity is sold into the market and as a consequence the operator receives the base load price of the specific electricity market. We find that wind power plants operate profitable in 2020, whereas the expected value of a portfolio of new photovoltaic power plants has massively diminished. Alongside the negative impact on the expected value per MW generation capacity, we identify higher levels of the standard deviation of the respective power plant technologies. Specifically, the standard deviation of the expected value per MW generation capacity for new wind and photovoltaic power plants amount to 534 K€ (363 K€) and 781 K€ (702 K€), respectively.

However, the composition of the minimum variance portfolio without any technical constraints still holds. The price risks for wind and photovoltaic power plants lead to lower shares within the minimum variance portfolio for the former, whereas the share of gas power plants has increased. Specifically, wind and gas plants account for 58% (69.5%) and 13.2% (7.9%), respectively. We had expected a lower share of photovoltaic power plants within the minimum variance portfolio a priori. Instead, we find astonishingly an increase of 6.6% compared to the previous optimization so that photovoltaic power plants account for 28.8% (22.2%) by considering price risks.

As noted, the level of standard deviation increases for renewable energies, if price risks are taken into account. However, the level of risk is still – relative to the other power plant technologies – low so that these technologies account for the minimum variance portfolio. In addition, due to the negative correlation between photovoltaic and wind power plants respective weights remain high within a portfolio bearing the lowest risk.

We deduce therefore that an efficient generation portfolio is a combination of conventional thermal and renewable energies leading to the lowest standard deviation of the expected value per MW generation capacity.

5.5 Rebalancing

In this section, we explore in which electricity market power plant investments turn out to be most economically sound and in addition to shed light on national differences to rebalance the target mix. For this purpose, we have re-run the simulation for six selected thermal power plant technologies. Renewable energies are not part of this analysis, as we have assumed equal remuneration for green power plant technologies. Table 5.27 compares investments in new generation capacity between the sample European power markets:

Following the results represented in Table 5.27, an investment in a new coal fired power plant before 2013 should be conducted in the United Kingdom, as this generation asset dominates a similar plant located in the other European power markets in terms of expected value and risk. Hence, the respective Sharpe ratio amounts to 1.37 and is therefore higher than the ones from Germany (0.68), the Netherlands (1.03) and Spain (0.17). The reasons for this finding are threefold: First, comparing historical base load prices, the APX-UK price level turns out to be the highest within the sample. Secondly, we find a significant positive correlation between respective APX and coal prices in the UK in comparison to those of other markets. Hence, an increase in coal prices goes along with an increase of power prices for the UK and as a consequence profitability of a coal plant investment within the simulation model.

Ultimately, carbon prices and coal prices are positively correlated so that coal power plant operators in the UK are better off, as respective power prices move together with coal and carbon prices. In contrast, a low power price level -as observed in Spain- causes a lower than expected value and due to no correlation among the risky variables an extraordinarily high standard deviation.

Table 5.27 Valuation results for selected single power plant technologies in Europe

Country	Germany			United Kingdom			Netherlands			Spain		
Portfolio of fuel plant technology	Mean in K€/	Std. Dev. in K€/	Adjusted Sharpe ratio	Mean in K€/	Std. Dev. in K€/	Adjusted Sharpe ratio	Mean in K€/	Std. Dev. in K€/	Adjusted Sharpe ratio	Mean in K€/	Std. Dev. in K€/	Adjusted Sharpe ratio
Conventional thermal												
Coal 2011	1,845	2,705	0.68	2,526	1,845	1.37	2,391	2,329	1.03	970	5,554	0.17
Coal 2013	1,647	1,854	0.89	2,268	1,787	1.27	2,149	2,196	0.98	835	5,158	0.16
Cogen	546	5,113	0.11	1,762	1,426	1.24	1,667	1,706	0.98	480	4,501	0.11
Gas middle load	677	1,116	0.61	678	1,115	0.61	596	1,324	0.45	- 341	3,420	-0.10
Gas peak load	- 381	327	-1.16	- 179	303	-0.59	471	- 623	0.76	- 528	803	-0.66
Non conventional thermal												
Nuclear	3,214	2,233	1.44	3,770	1,552	2.43	3,670	1,905	1.93	2,568	4,818	0.53

Source: Own calculation.

Taking into account the change of the regulative environment after 2013, the profitability of a coal power plant ceteris paribus diminishes, irrespective of the country-specific location. We find a total reduction of -10.13%, -10.20%, -10.73% and -13.97% for a new coal power plant built in 2013 compared to a similar plant built in 2011 in the Netherlands, the UK, Germany and Spain, respectively. While from a profitability point of view, a coal power plant built up in the Netherlands after 2012 leads to the highest value per MW generation capacity, from a risk perspective – similar to the results obtained for coal power plants built before 2013 – a utility firm should invest in the UK.

Looking at the results for non-conventional thermal power plants new nuclear power plants should be conducted in the UK, as the respective price level causes a shorter payback period than similar investments in Germany, the Netherlands and Spain. Very similar to the results of a coal power plant investment before 2013, a new nuclear power generation asset in the UK dominates a similar generation assets located in the sample power markets. Remember, in contrast to other commodity prices, we do not detect any correlation between uranium and European power prices.

Finally, we distinguish between gas power plants running as middle and peak load power plants. Taking the Sharpe ratio as criterion for investments, a utility firm would be indifferent between Germany and the UK for the investment of a middle load gas power plant, while the Dutch and – in particular - the Spanish power market should not be considered for a gas plant investment at all. The results for the latter refer to the low price level observed on the Spanish power market. However, taking a look at results for investments in gas fired peak load plants shows that the Dutch market causes the highest expected value per MW generation capacity. In addition, here we find a positive adjusted Sharpe ratio in comparison to the other European markets. Corresponding Sharpe ratios are not only lower but also negative for a gas peak load investment in Germany, the UK or Spain, which is due to lower peak load prices. However, the results should not prevent investments in peak load plants in general, because just the mean turned out negative and in addition the simulation model cannot incorporate all technical characteristics, especially the value of flexibility. Since Dutch peak prices turned out to be extraordinarily high and volatile in the past, the positive expected plant value goes along with a high standard deviation of the expected value per MW generation capacity.

Having tested the advantages of single power plant investments and against the background of the efficient frontier, we are able to adjust the proposed investment plan in order to realize an efficient target generation portfolio. Specifically, we choose a fuel mix which leads to the lowest standard deviation of the expected value per MW generation portfolio. Hence, the fuel mix is located on the efficient frontier. Following the presumptions of technical efficiency, the adjusted target generation portfolio is composed of 41.9% gas and 20.6% coal fired power plants, respectively. Alongside these conventional thermal power plants, the efficient fuel mix consists of wind (24.1%), photovoltaic (11.1%) and water (0.9%) power plant technologies. In addition, 0.4% of total generation capacity refers to lignite power plants and lastly the remainder refers to cogen power plants (0.1%).

To achieve this generation portfolio in the target year, we recommend adjusting the ordinary investment strategy in the following way: First, substitute old – meaning beyond the economic lifecycle - lignite fired power plants by coal power plants. If the respective plant is built before 2013, the utility firm should invest in a coal power plant located in the UK. Otherwise, the investment should be made in the Netherlands for new coal power plants operating after 2012. Since the adjusted target generation mix does not include nuclear power plant technology, coal fired plants replace old nuclear power plants until the share of coal power generation amounts to 20.5% in total. Furthermore, coal power plants reaching the end of their economic lifecycles are substituted by wind, photovoltaic and gas power plant technologies. The latter are located in the UK to benefit from the higher adjusted Sharpe ratio. As noted previously, gas fired plants running on peak load are located in the Netherlands.

All other power plant technologies should be replaced by the same kind of fuel technology after reaching their economic lifecycles. To benefit from the highest European base load prices, water plants are most valuable in the UK. For wind and photovoltaic power plants we do not distinguish between country specific remunerations. As a consequence, the selection of the power markets has no impact on the degree of efficiency of the target generation portfolio. No additional investments in lignite power plants are needed, as the target mix is achieved by the old fixed amount of the respective fuel technologies. Ultimately, the higher share of renewable energies adding up to 36.1% of the adjusted target fuel mix in comparison to 19.5% of the initial investment plan might cause additional conventional thermal back up technologies in practice.

5.6 Implications

The simulation results demonstrate that utilities should verify their investment plans for power generation capacity by using the suggested procedure to optimize their power plant park in terms of efficiency. Having identified an efficient target generation portfolio enables the respective utility firm to rebalance its energy mix at time. Replacements as well as investments in additional generation capacity go along with a massive need for financing these large scale investment projects. While typically the average cost of debt rises by the level of the total amount of debt due to default risk, the equity costs depend on the relative systematic risk of the individual utility firm. Hence, a utility firm opting for efficient generation capacity should be rewarded by lower risk premiums in comparison to competitors in capital markets. As a consequence, lower equity costs should enable the utility firm to realize its investment plans. In contrast, from a capital market perspective financial analysts should take the degree of efficiency of the utilities' generation mix into account to better understand industry risks and to improve standard valuation methodologies.

In addition, we have shown that diversification from a fuel based technology as well as from a revenue perspective in terms of operating in different markets pay back. Relying on the adjusted Sharpe ratio, a diversified generation portfolio leads to a higher reward in terms of present value per MW generation capacity for each unit of risk. Thus, a utility firm should make use of the virtue of open markets caused by liberalization of European power markets and add-up generation capacity not only in domestic but also in non-domestic markets.

In line with previous studies we confirm that gas prices and European base load prices are positively correlated, so that gas power plants seem to be attractive from an investor's perspective, as their cash flows are "self hedged". In fact, gas power plants bear the lowest standard deviation of the expected return per MW generation capacity among the group of conventional thermal power plants. As a consequence, gas power plant technologies are part of efficient generation portfolios from a strictly economic perspective. However, and that is one astonishing finding, a portfolio based on coal plants leads to a higher adjusted Sharpe ratio compared to gas power plants, even though coal plants exhibit a higher carbon price risk due to the emission intensity of the power generation process. The reasons are threefold. First, gas is used not only for power generation but also for heating. Therefore the flexibility of usage as well as the clean combustion in a tightening environmental regulation drive the demand for gas in particular and as a consequence the gas price. Moreover, the oil price peg determines the gas price level, so that gas prices depend on oil price development. Since the oil price risk is systematic, gas prices are indirectly faced with higher uncertainty compared to fossil based fuels. Alongside the mentioned facts, higher than expected oil prices cause high gas prices as well as high gas price standard deviation leading to a simulated price pattern which diverges stronger from the expected price path. As a consequence, the price process has a negative impact on the gas power plant's free cash flow and therefore its expected value. In addition, new gas power plants of competitors further increase the overall price pressure.

After all, our results show that a utility firm should adjust its target generation capacity towards a minimum amount of conventional thermal power plants. Since gas power plants bear the lowest standard deviation of the expected value per MW generation capacity, they reduce overall portfolio risks. In addition the operation of gas turbines in peak load times causes benefits from short ramp-up times which enable to generate electricity especially in periods of high power prices.

Coal power plant operators have to comply with the EU ETS emission certificates so that respective prices have a negative impact on the profitability of coal power plants beyond 2013. Nevertheless the adjusted Sharpe ratio for a portfolio of coal power plants turns out to be higher than that of gas power plants. As a consequence, utilities should rather choose clean coal power plants among the asset class of conventional thermal power plant technologies opting for return.

Ultimately, the non-emission of carbon within the power generation process of nuclear power plants leads to an adjusted Sharpe ratio which is higher compared to the respective ratio of the conventional thermal power plants. As long as the electricity network does not manage to distribute generated power from renewable energies without high conduction losses and be able to handle volatile operating hours for renewable energy capacities, nuclear power plants should take the function of basic services. Construction periods for renewable energy capacities are shorter compared to conventional thermal and in particular to new nuclear generation capacity. This comparative advantage should enable utilities to increase the share of renewable energy capacity in their total energy mix quickly. Against the background of social welfare consideration, the increase in renewable energy capacity within an electricity system might increase power prices and therefore has a negative impact on energy intensive industries like aluminum, chemical and the automotive industry.

5.7 Summary

In this chapter we have analyzed in a first step the risky variables based on empirical commodity data and their mutual dependencies which have an impact on the profitability of power plant technologies. Alongside conventional thermal plant technologies, we have taken renewable energies into account, whereas their operation depends on meteorological conditions.

Furthermore, we have presented the change of the initial power plant park over time demonstrating that the generation mix communicated by the sample utility firm in the target year is not efficient. Since the target portfolio consists of four sub-portfolios based on power plant technologies operating in different countries, we have tested not only the target but also four additional generation portfolios.

Efficient generation portfolios are a combination of renewable energies, namely wind, water and photovoltaic together with gas as conventional thermal power plant technology leading to the lowest standard deviation of the expected value per MW generation capacity. In line with previous findings in the literature, we have confirmed a high correlation of gas and power prices in European power markets, which reduces the level of standard deviation of the expected value per MW generation capacity of this fuel technology. In addition, and that is one major finding, renewable energies should not only be part of a utility's power plant park but also –depending on technical constraints - be a predominant source of energy of a utility's overall fuel mix. As we have demonstrated the inclusion of renewable energies leads to a better combination in terms of expected value and risk per MW generation capacity.

Therefore the proposed investment strategy does not coincide with an efficient power plant park. Instead, the initial investment plan should be adjusted. In a nutshell, we recommend adjusting the ordinary investment strategy in the following way: Substitute old lignite fired plants by coal power plants, whereas old coal power plants should be replaced by a combination of wind, water and photovoltaic power plants. All other power plant technologies should be replaced by the same kind of fuel technology after their economic lifecycle.

6 Conclusions

This chapter responds to the underlying research questions by summarizing the main results of the simulation model. Based on the results, we derive implications for management and research practice and give an outlook for future research.

6.1 Summary

Alongside the liberalization of electricity markets, the introduction of the EU ETS has caused significant carbon price risks for utility firms. As a consequence, power generators nowadays bear the risks of volatile electricity, fuel and carbon prices. Therefore, we have characterized the price determinants of energy commodities and analyzed interactions among them. As European utilities are faced with aging power plants, which implies a massive need for investments in the near future, we have studied the merits of different types of power plant technologies.

For evaluating these power generation assets, we have developed a theoretical framework with respect to *Markowitz's* (1952) traditional portfolio selection process. In doing so, we have conducted a comprehensive portfolio analysis form a utility's perspective. Specifically, we have turned our lens on the issue to opt for an efficient fuel mix by taking a cross-national approach. In addition, we have tested utility's communicated target generation mix for efficiency and have discovered how efficient these portfolios are. The identification of two efficient portfolios allows to measure the vertical and horizontal distance from the target portfolio towards the efficient frontier. Since we have considered the economic profitability of power plants, the distance to the efficient frontier reveals the level of improvement in terms of additional value per MW generation capacity through the same level of risk. Or, if the objective is to reduce risks, the potential risk reduction for a given level of return can be quantified. To determine the degree of efficiency, we have relied on performance ratios following the suggestion of *Bar-Lev/ Katz* (1976), which we have adjusted to account for competitive markets.

Based on this framework, we have developed a dynamic simulation model for real power plant data covering conventional, non-conventional and renewable power plant technologies. Each power plant's expected value per MW generation capacity and its corresponding standard deviation is computed by using a DCF valuation technique. Therefore, we have estimated thermal power plants' free cash flows by taking

© Springer Fachmedien Wiesbaden GmbH, part of Springer Nature 2011
S. Rothe, *Portfolio Analysis of Power Plant Technologies*, Edition KWV,
https://doi.org/10.1007/978-3-658-24379-1_6

simulated non-linear price patterns for electricity, carbon and fuel into account. Here, we have distinguished between base and peak load prices from power markets of Germany, the United Kingdom, the Netherlands and Spain. Alongside electricity prices, we assume uncertain oil, gas, coal, lignite and uranium commodity prices as well as carbon emission certificate prices. Empirical mean and corresponding price standard deviation for the underlying price trajectory are computed from price data of European Energy Exchanges. However, all risky price variables are forward-looking, as their growth-rates are derived by relying on an equilibrium commodity price projection given by *EWI/ EEFA* (2008). The historical standard deviation of the respective variable determines the divergence from the expected price pattern over time. Since renewable energies do not bear any price risks due to fixed remunerations for generated green electricity, we have considered volume risk by taking meteorological data in terms of wind speed and total sun hours from DWD into account. The interaction of these risky variables is incorporated within the model so that the empirical correlation tends to be close to the simulated correlation. Lastly, we have used *Solver*, which is based on a quadratic programming algorithm to identify the composition of efficient generation portfolios. In this process, we have also considered technical restrictions to be able to distinguish between technical and economic efficiency of generation portfolios.

We have built up this simulation model to explore the dynamic change of a sample's power plant park over time towards a target generation mix taking the perspective of a utility firm operating on liberalized European electricity markets. We have found that the communicated target generation portfolio is not located on the efficient set. Against this background, we have demonstrated how to adjust investment plans to rebalance the generation asset portfolio of the respective utility firm by considering economic lifecycles of power plants and, as a consequence the need for replacements in time. In addition, we have discovered the impact of the emission regulation change in 2013 not only from a profitability but also from a risk point of view by computing a corresponding standard deviation of the expected value. Furthermore, we have shown the merits of operating in different European electricity markets, by conducting the analysis not only in domestic but also in international electricity markets. Following the simulation results, we are able to answer the research questions defined in the beginning:

Firstly, an efficient portfolio of power plant technologies is a combination of conventional thermal and renewable energies, whereas the former group of fuel technologies is based on gas power plants and the latter consists of wind, water and photovoltaic power plants this combination leading to the lowest standard deviation of the expected value per MW generation capacity by a given level of return. Considering technical requirements in terms of upper limits of renewable energies as well as a minimum generation capacity of coal power plants massively increases the share of gas power plants in comparison to the share of renewable energies. Besides, we find that nuclear power plants are part of this efficient generation portfolio which causes the lowest standard deviation. However, if an investor opts to maximize return for a given level of risk, hydroelectricity is most profitable. Due to the limits of building new hydroelectricity water plants, the respective kind of fuel type should be combined with thermal power plants. In this respect, nuclear power plants might be an option.

Secondly, we shed light on an efficient generation portfolio for the target year. Since we have demonstrated the non-efficiency of the communicated target portfolio of the sample power plant park in 2020, we deduce to adjust the target mix, as its possible to reduce the amount of risk for a given level of return. Specifically, the adjusted target portfolio without technical constraints should consist of gas (15.5%) and coal (13.2%) fired power plants as well as wind (53.2%), photovoltaic (16.4%) and water (1.2%) power plants. The rest of the target generation capacity should refer to cogen (0.1%) and lignite (0.4%) power plants. In contrast, taking technical restrictions into account, we identify an efficient generation mix as follows: gas (41.9%), coal (20.6%), nuclear (1.0%), wind (24.1%), photovoltaic (11.1%) and water (0.9%) power plants, whereas the share of cogen and lignite plants remains constant.

Thirdly, against this background follows that the initial investment strategy should be changed. Specifically, old lignite and nuclear fired plants should be substituted by coal power plants, whereas old coal power plants should be replaced by a combination of gas, wind, and photovoltaic power plants. All other power plant technologies should be replaced by the same kind of fuel technology after their economic lifecycle. In comparison to the other European power markets, Dutch electricity prices reveal the highest level and therefore gas power plants - in particular - are likely to operate profitability. In addition, the high volatility of Dutch peak power prices increases the value of flexibility of gas power plants, as the time needed to heat up is low in comparison to other thermal power plants and therefore enables to realize high prices.

Fourthly, full auctioning of emission certificates will hit emission intense power plants' free cash flows and therefore expected value per MW generation capacity. In addition, since carbon prices exhibit a high relative standard deviation which is captured in the projected price pattern, the risk of deviation of the expected value per MW generation capacity will increase. As a consequence, not only the profitability but also the level of risk will increase making this group of fuel technologies less attractive for utilities compared to low emission intense power plant technologies. In addition, financing new emission intense generation capacity is more expensive compared to low emission intense power plants, as carbon risk premiums can be observed on capital markets.[406]

Ultimately, operating in different power markets pays off. We have confirmed that European power markets are positively correlated and against the background of an improvement of power exchange with neighboring countries will be even stronger in the near future. Thus, from a risk perspective no diversification potential solely based on prices exists. However, each country offers different meteorological conditions and this should be taken into account to realize a specific investment time to operate efficient generation portfolios. Utilities generating electricity in non-domestic countries can benefit from higher prices levels (i.e. APX-NL) and take advantage of fluctuating prices by investing in flexible power plant technologies.

6.2 Implications for management and research

This section derives the implications of the results presented not only for the management but also for the further research practice. Starting first with the utilities' management practice, we recommend the following:

Re-think investment plans towards holding a larger share of renewable energies within the generation portfolio. According to our results a combination of conventional thermal and renewable energies turns out to be efficient in terms of expected value and risk per MW gross generation capacity. Therefore, implementing a strategy based on renewable energies which causes less CO_2 per MWh generated electricity clearly pays off. This is even true, if not only volume but also price risks for wind and photovoltaic power plants are taken into account. In comparison to the other conventional and non-conventional power plant technologies, the level of risks in terms of the standard deviation for wind and photovoltaic plants has turned out lower and as a consequence these technologies still account for the minimum variance portfolio. In addition, meteorological data from DWD have shown a negative coherence for wind speed and

---

[406] See Bassen et al. (2010); Bassen/ Rothe (2009b).

total sun hours which drive wind and photovoltaic energy yield, respectively. As a consequence, we have detected a negative correlation for wind and photovoltaic power generation asset returns. Holding a combination of these two types of generation assets therefore enables operators to diminish generation risk for a given level of return.

Appraising an investment project solely based on its respective expected value neglects the corresponding impact on the overall firms' assets risks. Hence, the decision to invest in a specific type of generation capacity should be based on the trade-off between return in terms of expected value and the corresponding standard deviation for the whole portfolio of assets. Against this background, the adjusted ratios assist utility firms to control the performance of specific power plant portfolios and generation stakes operating in liberalized electricity markets. Taking these ratios as indicators of efficiency causes a reduction of the vertical or horizontal distance to the efficient set, if investment plans are accordingly adjusted. In addition, financial analysts should take the degree of efficiency of the utilities' generation mix into account to enlarge standard valuation methodologies.

Alongside management practice, this thesis contributes to the existing research in the following way: From the methodological side we model target power plant portfolios that are actually planned by a European utility firm operating on liberalized electricity markets in order to explore the degree of efficiency. We have suggested adjusted performance ratios which are - unlike existing studies - able to evaluate the risk-return reward for common power plant assets. In addition, these ratios quantify the degree of relative efficiency by measuring the distance to the efficient frontier of power plant portfolios.

In contrast to the existing literature[407], which rather chooses a static approach to evaluate existing generation assets, we conduct an analysis over a specific period of time to account for the respective power plant age structure and therefore the need for replacements. The virtue of this dynamic approach is the possibility to take the change of a power plant park and therefore the feasible set into account over time. As a consequence, this dynamic approach demonstrates how to rebalance generation portfolios from a base to a target year by appraising plant technologies on a micro level.

In addition, we analyze not only conventional and non-conventional thermal but also renewable energy power plants which are located in different European electricity

---

[407] Roques et al. (2008).

markets. The latter allows studying the merits of international diversification for power plant generation assets, which has not been explored yet. Therefore, to the best of our knowledge, this is the first study, which provides a comprehensive portfolio analysis taking the whole power plant park of a utility firm as well as the corresponding dependencies of meteorological conditions and commodity price returns into account. The analysis provides valuable insights on the impact of operating different power plant technologies on portfolio risk and return with respect to the running Kyoto commitment period.

Specifically, we have emphasized the importance of holding renewable energies within a generation portfolio compared to conventional thermal power plants. Therefore valuation methodologies should be expanded to take the unique characteristics of renewable energies into account. Considering weather data is just the starting point. More important seems improving not only technical restrictions but also presumptions to increase the impact of the simulation model in practice.

At last, we give reasons why utility's target generation portfolios have not turned out to be efficient. Firstly, the non-efficiency of target generation portfolios might be explained by the aftereffects of the pre-liberalization area on the European electricity markets. Competitive markets force suppliers to operate efficiently, as otherwise rivals might squeeze non-efficient firms out of the market. Secondly, related to our first point, investments are often evaluated, whether projects' expected return is larger than the respective firm's cost of capital.[408] However, as explained before, this is just half the truth as investment projects – irrespective of their nature – should be appraised by taking the overall impact on the total portfolio into account. Against this background, remember the results for portfolios of new coal power plants for instance, presented in section 5.2.4. The latter have shown the highest expected value per MW generation capacity, however, the optimization taking even technical constraints into account has suggested holding a far smaller share of coal power generation assets compared to the initial investment plan.

Our results have shed light on the degree of efficiency for a specific target generation and four related sub-portfolios based on real power plant data of a utility firm. Nevertheless, since we have derived the optimization based on data for new power plant technologies before taking the fixed amount of existing plant capacity into account, the general implications do also hold true for other European utility firms.

---

[408] See Glachant (2006), p.73; also Weber/ Swider (2006), p.15.

6.3 Future outlook and concluding remarks

As noted previously, the allocation mechanism of the EU ETS will change to full auction system starting in 2013. In addition, other industry branches will be incorporated into the EU ETS and will therefore comply with emission certificates. Obtaining more historical data in particular of Phase II will be interesting to see, whether the dependency of the commodity variables will change and with it the mean-variance optimization of the utilities fuel mix. Furthermore, a valuable extension of the simulation model would be to explore the composition of utility's power plant park by assuming endogen electricity prices. This includes studying the strategic behavior of competitors. In addition, the assumptions regarding technical constraint depend -in contrast to the economic results- on the utility's individual service areas and therefore the respective electricity grid. Thus, improving technical restrictions and presumptions will help to increase the impact of the simulation model in practice.

From a capital market perspective it would be interesting to study individual discount rates for power plant technologies and estimate fair risk premiums. Alongside ageing European power plant parks, the sample investment plan has demonstrated not only a massive need for replacement of old power plants but also for additional investments in new generation capacity and as a consequence an extraordinary need for financing utilities' investment programs. The development of the power plant park towards the target year has shown that 75% of the target generation capacity refers to new power plants which correspond with a total amount of 44,000 MW. With respect to the investment costs per MW generation capacity noted in the model assumptions, it reveals the strong need for financing opportunities. Thus, utilities will have to raise not only equity capital but also debt. With respect to the degree of efficiency of generation portfolios, we leave the appreciation from capital markets and in particular bond holders for future research.

Nevertheless, from an environmental perspective it would be desirable if utilities re-thought their investment plans, as we have demonstrated that generation portfolios based on low emission intense conventional thermal (gas fired plants) and renewable energies turn out to be efficient within a value and risk framework. Following the suggested energy mix will lead to a lower level of risk in terms of standard deviation by the same level of expected value per MW generation capacity. Hence, policy makers as well as other stakeholders (i.e banks) should aim to provide a reliable framework in order to increase the likelihood of realizing efficient and environmental-friendly generation portfolios in practice.

References

Abadie, L. M., Chamorro, J. M. (2008): Valuing flexibility: The case of an integrated gasification combined cycle power plant, in: Energy Economics 30, pp. 1850-1881.

Alberola, E., Chevallier, J., Chèze, B. (2008): Price drivers and structural breaks in European carbon prices 2005-2007, in: Energy Policy 36, pp. 787-797.

Alberola, E., Chevallier, J. (2009): European carbon prices and banking restrictions: Evidence from phase I (2005-2007), in: The Energy Journal, 30, pp. 51-80.

Alberola, E., Chevallier, J., Chèze, B. (2009): The EU emission trading scheme: Disentangling the effects of industrial production and CO_2 emission on carbon prices, in: Economie Internationale 116, pp. 93-125.

Anger, N. (2008): Emission trading beyond Europe: Linking schemes in a post-Kyoto world, in: Energy Economics 30 (2008), pp. 2028-2049.

Arocena, P. (2008): Cost and quality gains from diversification and vertical integration in the electricity industry: A DEA approach, in: Energy Economics 30 (2008), pp. 39-58.

Atherton, P., Simms, A. M., Savvantidou, S., Hunt, S. B. (2009): New nuclear – The economics say no, Citi Investment Research & Analysis.

Averch, H., Johnson, L. L. (1962): Behavior of the firm under regulatory constraint, in: American Economic Review 52, pp. 1053-1069.

Awerbuch, S. (1993): The surprising role of risk and discount rates in utility integrated resource planning, in: The Electricity Journal 6, pp. 20-33.

Awerbuch, S. (1995): Market-based IRP – It's easy! in: The Electricity Journal 8, pp. 50-67.

Awerbuch, S., Berger, M. (2003): Applying portfolio theory to EU electricity planning and policy making, Report number EET/2003/03, International Energy Agency.

Awerbuch, S. (2004): Towards a finance-oriented valuation of conventional and renewable energy sources in Ireland, Report, Sustainable Energy Ireland.

Awerbuch, S. (2006): Portfolio-based electricity generation planning- policy implications for renewables and energy security, in: Dixon, R. (Ed.), Mitigation and Adaptation Strategies for Global Change 11, pp. 693-710.

© Springer Fachmedien Wiesbaden GmbH, part of Springer Nature 2011
S. Rothe, *Portfolio Analysis of Power Plant Technologies*, Edition KWV,
https://doi.org/10.1007/978-3-658-24379-1

Bar-Lev, D., Katz, S. (1976): A portfolio approach to fossil fuel procurement in the electric utility industry, in: Journal of Finance 31, pp. 933-947.

Bassen, A., Rothe, S. (2009a): CO_2 und Unternehmensbewertung, in: Finanz Betrieb 11, pp. 240-246.

Bassen, A., Rothe, S. (2009b): Incorporating CO_2 risks in valuation practice: A capital market approach for European utilities, in: Online Proceedings of the 32nd IAEE International Conference San Francisco, California, US.

Bassen, A., Koch, N., Rothe, S. (2010): Is a carbon beta born? Valuing fuel mix strategies of European utilities, Working Paper, University of Hamburg.

Benninga, S. (2008): Financial Modeling, 3rd Edition, The MIT Press, Massachusetts.

Benz, E., Trück, S. (2009): Modelling the price dynamics of CO_2 emission allowances, in:
Energy Economics 31, pp. 4-15.

Berger, M., Awerbuch, S., Haas, R. (2003): Versorgungssicherheit und Diversifizierung der Energieversorgung in der EU – Mean-Variance Portfolioanalyse des Stromerzeugungsmix und Auswirkungen auf die Bedeutung erneuerbarer Energieträger, in: Berichte aus Energie- und Umweltforschung, Bundesministerium für Verkehr, Innovation und Technologie, Wien.

Bettzüge, M. O., Lochner, S. (2009): Der russisch-ukrainische Gaskonflikt im Januar 2009 - eine modellgestützte Analyse, in: Energiewirtschaftliche Tagesfragen 7, pp. 26-30.

Black, F. (1972): Capital market equilibrium with restricted borrowing, in: The Journal of Business 45, pp. 444-455.

Black, F., Litterman, R. (1991): Asset allocation: Combining investor views with market equilibrium, in: The Journal of Fixed Income 1, pp. 7-18.

Black, F., Litterman, R. (1992): Global portfolio optimization, in: Financial Analysts Journal 48, pp. 28-43.

Bode, S. (2006): On the impact of renewable energy support schemes on power prices, HWWI Research Paper.

Böcking, H.-J., Nowak, K. (1998): Der Beitrag der Discounted Cashflow-Verfahren zur Lösung der Typisierungsproblematik bei Unternehmensbewertungen: eine Warnung vor „naiven" Übertragung modelltheoretischer Erkenntnisse auf die Bewertungspraxis, in: DB 51/ 1998), pp. 685-690.

Böhringer, C. (2008): Europäische Klimapolitik: Zwischen Anspruch und Wirklichkeit, in: Zeitschrift für Energiewirtschaft 4, pp. 235-240.

Böske, J. (2007): Zur Ökonomie der Versorgungssicherheit in der Energiewirtschaft, Dissertation, University of Münster.

Bonacina, M., Gulli, F. (2007): Electricity pricing under carbon emissions trading: a dominant firm with competitive fringe model, in: Energy Policy 35, pp. 4200-4220.

Bonacina, M., Cozialpi, S. (2009): Carbon allowances as inputs or financial assets: Lesson learned from the pilot phase of the EU ETS, IEFE Working Paper No. 19.

Botterud, A., Ilic, M. D., Wangensteen, I. (2005): Optimal investments in power generation under centralized and decentralized decision making, IEEE Transactions on Power Systems 20, pp. 254-263.

Bower, D. H., Bower, R. S., Logue, D. E. (1984): Arbitrage pricing theory and utility stock returns, in: Journal of Finance 39, pp. 1041-1054.

Boyer, M., Filion, D. (2007): Common and fundamental factors in stock returns of Canadian oil and gas companies, in: Energy Economics 29, pp. 428-453.

BP (2009): Statistical review of world energy, London.

Brealey, R. A., Stewart, C. M., Allen, F. (2010): Principles of corporate finance, 10th Edition, McGraw-Hill, New York.

Bunch, J. R., Parlett, B. N. (1971): Direct methods for solving symmetric indefinite systems of linear equations, in: SIAM Journal on Numerical Analysis 8, pp. 639-655.

Burger, M., Graeber, B., Schindlmayer, G. (2007): Managing energy risk - An integrated view on power and other energy markets, John Wiley & Sons Ltd., West Sussex.

Cahyadi, R., Min, K. J., Wang, C.-H., Abi-Samra, N. (2003): Generation unit selection via capital asset pricing model for generation planning, in: International Journal of Energy Research 27, pp. 1251-1263.

Chao, H.-P., Oren, S., Wilson, R. (2008): Reevaluation of vertical integration and unbundling in restructured electricity markets, in: Sioshansi, F. (Ed.), Competitive electricity market – Design, implementation, performance, Elsevier Global Energy Policy and Economic Series, New York, pp. 27-65.

Chen, N.-F., Roll, R., Ross, S. A. (1986): Economic forces and the stock market, in: Journal of Business 59, pp. 383-403.

Clewlow, L., Strickland, C. (2000): Energy derivatives: Pricing and risk management, Lacima Publications, London.

Cohen, K. J., Elton, E. J. (1967): Inter-temporal portfolio analysis based on simulation of joint returns, in: Management Science, 14, pp. 5-18.

Constantini, V., Gracceva, F., Markandya, A., Vicini, G. (2007): Security of energy supply: Comparing scenarios from a European perspective, in: Energy Policy 35, pp. 210-226.

Cornwall, N. (2008): Achieving electricity market integration in Europe, in: Sioshansi, F. (Ed.), Competitive electricity market – Design, implementation, performance, Elsevier Global Energy Policy and Economic Series, New York, pp. 95-135

Cox, M. G., Siebert, B. L. (2006): The use of a Monte Carlo method for evaluating uncertainty and expanded uncertainty, in: Publishing Metrologia 43, pp. 178-188.

Dalebroux, J. (2008): Evolution of certain M&A deal terms in energy transactions, in: The Electricity Journal 21, pp. 19-23.

Damodaran, A. (1996): Investment valuation – Tools and techniques for determining the value of any asset, John Wiley & Sons, Inc., New York.

Dannenberg, H. (2009): Berücksichtigung von Abhängigkeiten im Risikomanagement – Nutzung von Microsoft Excel, in: Controller Magazin, 6/2009, pp. 63-70.

Daskalakis, G., Psychoyios, D., Markellos, R. N. (2009): Modelling CO_2 emission allowance price and derivatives: Evidence from the European trading scheme, in: Journal of Banking and Finance 33, pp. 1230-1241.

Delarue, E., Voorspools, K., D'heaseleer, W. (2008): Fuel switching in the electricity sector under the EU ETS: Review and prospective, in: Journal of Energy Engineering 134, pp. 40-46.

Deng, S.-J., Oren, S. S. (2006): Electricity derivatives and risk management, in: Energy 31, pp. 940-953.

Dietrich, J. K., Heckerman, D.G. (1983): Determinants of the systematic risk of electric utilities: Theory and estimation, in: Applied Economics 15, pp. 619-633.

Dimson, E. (1989): The discount rate for a power station, in: Energy Economics 11, pp. 175-180.

Drobetz, W. (2002): Einsatz des Black-Litterman Verfahrens in der Asset Allocation, in: Dichtl, H., Kleeberg, J., Schlenger, C. (Ed.): Innovative Konzepte zur systematischen Portfolioplanung, Uhlenbruch Verlag, pp. 203-240.

Drukarczyk, J./ Schüler, A. (2009): Unternehmensbewertung, 6th Edition, Franz Vahlen, München.

Dyner, I., Larsen, E. R. (2001): From planning to strategy in the electricity industry, in: Energy Policy 29, pp. 1145-1154.

EEX/ EUREX (2008): EEX-EUREX Product Cooperation Emission Trading, November 2008, Leipzig.

Ellerman, D., Buchner, B. (2008): Over-allocation or abatement? A preliminary analysis of the EU ETS based on the 2006-06 emission data, in: Environmental and Resource Economics 41, pp. 267-287.

Elton, E. J., Gruber, M. J., Brown, S. J., Goetzmann, W. N. (2003): Modern portfolio theory and investment analysis, 6th Edition, John Wiley & Sons, New York.

Erdmann, G., Zweifel, P. (2008): Energieökonomik – Theorie und Anwendungen, Springer Berlin.

EU (1996): Directive 96/92/EC of the European Parliament and of the Council of 19 December 1996 concerning common rules for the internal market in electricity, Official Journal of the European Union.

EU (2003): Directive 2003/54/EC of the European Parliament and of the Council of 26 June 2003 concerning common rules for the internal market in electricity and repealing Directive 96/92/EC, Official Journal of the European Union.

EU (2003): Directive 2003/87/EC of the European Parliament and of the Council of 13 October 2003 establishing a scheme for greenhouse gas emission allowance trading within the Community and amending Council Directive 96/61/EC, Official Journal of the European Union.

EU (2008): Directive 2008/101/EC of the European Parliament and of the Council of 19 November 2008 amending Directive 2003/87/EC so as to include aviation activities in the scheme for greenhouse gas emission allowance trading within the Community, Official Journal of the European Union.

EU (2009): Directive 2009/31/EC of the European Parliament and of the Council of 23 April 2009 of the geological storage of carbon dioxide and amending Council Directive 85/337 EEC, European Parliament and Council Directives 2000/60/EC, 2001/80/EC, 2004/35/EC, 2006/12/EC, 2008/1/EC and Regulation (EC) No 1013/2006, Official Journal of the European Union.

Eurostat (2010): Energy yearly statistics 2008, 2010 Edition, Luxembourg.

EWI/ EEFA (2008): Energiewirtschaftliches Gesamtkonzept 2030, Universität zu Köln.

Eydeland, A., Wolyniec, K. (2003): Energy and power risk management - New developments in modelling, pricing and hedging, John Wiley & Sons Inc., New Jersey.

Fama, E. F. (1969): Efficient capital markets: A review of theory and empirical work, in: Journal of Finance 25, pp. 383-417.

Fama, E. F., French, K. R. (1993): Common risk factors in the returns on stocks and bonds, in: Journal of Financial Economics 33, pp. 3-56.

Felder, F. A. (1996): Integrating financial thinking with strategic planning to achieve competitive success, in: The Electricity Journal 9, pp. 62-67.

Ferson, W. E., Harvey, C. R. (1994): Sources of risks and expected returns in global equity markets, Journal of Banking and Finance 18, pp. 775-803.

Fiorenzani, S. (2006): Quantitative methods for electricity trading and risk management - Advanced mathematical and statistical methods for energy finance, Palgrave Macmillan Ltd., New-York.

Ford, A. (1999): Cycles in competitive electricity markets: A simulation study of the Western United States", in: Energy Policy 27, pp. 637-658.

Ford, A. (2001): Waiting for the boom: A simulation study of power plant construction in California", in: Energy Policy 29, pp. 847-869.

Francis, J.C. (1986): Investments: Analysis and Management, 4th Edition, McGraw-Hill, New York.

Frondel, M., Schmidt, C. (2008): CO_2-Emissionshandel: Auswirkungen auf Strompreise und energieintensive Industrie, in: Energiewirtschaftliche Tagesfragen 11, pp. 53-57.

Geman, H. (2005): Commodities and commodity derivatives – Modeling and pricing for agriculturals, metals and energy, 1st Edition, John Wiley & Sons, West Sussex.

Glachant, J.-M. (2006): Generation technology mix in competitive electricity markets, in: Lévêque, F. (Ed.), Competitive electricity markets and sustainability, Edward Elgar, Northampton, pp. 54-86.

Green, R. (2006): Investment and generation capacity, in: Lévêque, F. (Ed.), Competitive electricity markets and sustainability, Edward Elgar, Northampton, pp. 21-53.

Gup, B. E. (1983): The basic of investing, 2nd Edition, John Wiley & Sons, New-York.

Hacura, A., Jadamus-Hacura, M., Kocot, A. (2001): The risk analysis in investment appraisal based on the Monte Carlo simulation technique, in: The European Physical Journal 20, pp. 551-553.

Härle, P. (2006): Rechtliche Bewältigung des Handels an der EEX, in: Schwintowski, H.-P. (Ed.), Handbuch Energiehandel, 1st Edition, Schmidt, Berlin, pp. 355-416.

Hansen, U. (1998): Technological options for power generation, in: Energy Journal 19, pp. 63-88.

Hau, E. (2008): Windkraftanlagen – Grundlagen, Technik, Einsatz, Wirtschaftlichkeit, 4th Edition, Springer, Berlin.

Helfat, C. E. (1988): Investment choices in industry, Massachusetts Institute of Technology.

Herbst, A. (1990): The handbook of capital investing, Harper-Business, New-York.

Hertz, D. B. (1964): Risk analysis in capital investment, in: Harvard Business Review 42, pp. 95-106.

Hoffman, V.H. (2007): EU ETS and investment decisions: The case of the German electricity industry, in: European Management Journal 25 pp. 464-474.

Holler, J., Haberfellner, M. (2006): Divergenz oder Konvergenz europäischer Großhandels-märkte?, Working Paper, Energie-Control.

Hotelling (1931): The Economics of exhaustible resources, in: Journal of Political Economy 39, pp. 137-175.

Humphreys, H., McClain, K. (1998): Reducing the impacts of energy price volatility through dynamic portfolio selection, in: Energy Journal 19, pp. 107-132.

Hundt, M., Barth, R., Sun, N., Wissel, S., Voss, A. (2009): Verträglichkeit von erneuerbaren Energien und Kernenergie im Erzeugungsportfolio, Report, Institut für Energiewirtschaft und Rationelle Energieanwendung, University of Stuttgart.

International Energy Agency (2007): Climate policy uncertainty and investment risk, 1st Edition, Paris.

International Energy Agency (2008a): World energy outlook 2008, Paris.

International Energy Agency (2008b): Deploying renewable – Principles for effective policies, 1st Edition, Paris.

Jansen, J., Beurskens, L., Tilburg, X. (2006): Application of portfolio analysis to the Dutch generation mix", Report c-05-100, ECN.

Jensen, M. C. (1968): The performance of mutual funds in the period 1945-1964, in: Journal of Finance 23, pp. 389-416.

Jensen, M.C. (1986): Agency costs of free cash flow, corporate finance and takeover, in: American Economic Review 76, pp. 323-329.

Jorion, P. (2003): Financial risk manger handbook, 2nd Edition, John Wiley & Sons, Inc., Hoboken, New Jersey.

Kaldor, N. (1939): Speculation and economic stability, in: Review of Economic Studies 7, pp. 1-27.

Kaltschmitt, M., Streicher, W., Wiese, A. (2006): Erneuerbare Energien – Systemtechnik, Wirtschaftlichkeit, Umweltaspekte, 4th Edition, Springer, Berlin.

Kanen, J. L. M. (2006): Carbon trading & pricing, Environmental Finance, Publications, London.

Kara, M., Syri, S., Lehtilä, A., Helynen, S., Kekkonen, V., Ruska, M., Forsström, J. (2008): The impacts of EU CO_2 emission trading on electricity markets and electricity consumers in Finland, in: Energy Economics 30 pp. 193-211.

Kat, H. M., Oomen, R. C. (2006): What every investor should know about commodities, part I: Univariate return analysis, Working Paper, Alternative Investment Research Centre, Cass Business School, London.

Keppler, J.II., Mansanct-Bataller, M. (2010): Causalities between CO_2, electricity, and other energy variables during phase I and phase II of the EU ETS, Energy Policy 38, pp. 3329-3341.

Kjärstad, J., Johnsson, F., (2007): The European power plant infrastructure. Presentation of the Chalmers energy infrastructure database with applications, in: Energy Policy 35, pp. 3643-3664.

Knight, E. R. W. (2010): The economic geography of carbon market trading: How legal regimes and environmental performance influence share performance under a carbon market, Working Paper, Oxford University Centre for the Environment.

Kobes, S. (2008): Eckpunkte des EU-Klimapaketes, in: Dow Jones TradeNews Emissions, 26.

Koller, T., Goedhart, M., Wessels, D. (2005): Valuation – measuring and managing the value of companies, McKinsey & Company, 4th Edition, John Wiley & Sons, New Jersey.

Konstantin, P. (2007): Praxisbuch Energiewirtschaft, Energieumwandlung, -transport, und -beschaffung im liberalisierten Markt, Springer, Berlin.

Krey, B. (2008): Five essays in energy economics, Dissertation, University of Zurich.

Krey, B. B., Zweifel, P. (2008): Efficient and secure power for the United States and Switzerland, in: Krey, B. (Ed.), Five essays in energy economics, Dissertation, University of Zurich, pp.7-34.

Kulatilaka, N., Balasubramanian, P., Storck, J. (1999): Using real options to frame the IT investment problem, in: Trigeorgis, L. (Ed.), Real options and business strategy – Applications to decision making, Risk Books, London.

Lehmann, F. (1966): Allgemeiner Bericht über Monte Carlo Methoden, in: Blätter der Deutschen Gesellschaft für Versicherungs- und Finanzmathematik (DGVFM) 8, pp. 431-456.

Lewellen, W. G., Long, M. S. (1972): Simulation versus single-value estimates in capital expenditure analysis, in: Decision Sciences, 3, pp. 19-33.

Lintner, J. (1965): The valuation of risk assets and the selection of risky investments in stock portfolios and capital budgets, in: Review of Economics and Statistics, 47, pp. 13-27.

Litzenberger, R., Ramaswamy, K., Sosin, H. (1980): On the CAPM approach to the estimation of a public utility's cost of equity capital, in: Journal of Finance, 35, pp. 369-383.

Loitz, R. (2000): Konzeption und Einsatz des Shareholder Value Ansatzes für die Bewertung und Steuerung von Unternehmen, in: Betrieb und Wirtschaft 54, pp. 701-705.

Lutz v. C., Kalina, R. (2010): Best-Practice-Standards zur Erstellung von Finanzmodellen, in: Finanz-Betrieb, pp. 75-83.

Madlener, R., Kaufmann, M. (2002): Power exchange spot market trading in Europe: theoretical considerations and empirical evidence, Working Paper.

Madlener, R., Glensk, B. Raymond, P. (2009): Applying mean-variance portfolio analysis to E.ON's power generation portfolio in the UK and Sweden, Conference Paper 6. Internationale Energiewirtschaftstagung, TU Wien.

Mansanet-Bataller, M., Pardo, A., Valor, E. (2007): CO_2 prices, energy and weather, in: The Energy Journal 28, pp. 67-86.

Mansanet-Bataller, M., Pardo, A. (2008): CO_2 prices and portfolio management, Working Paper, University of Valencia.

Markowitz, H. (1952): Portfolio selection, in: Journal of Finance 7, pp. 77-91.

Markowitz, H. (1959): Portfolio selection: Efficient diversification of investments, Cowles Foundation Monograph, Yale University Press, New Haven.

McLeish, D. L. (2004): Monte Carlo Simulation and Finance, John Wiley and Sons Inc., New Jersey.

Merton, R. C. (1972): An analytical derivation of the efficient portfolio frontier, in: Journal of Financial and Quantitative Analysis 7, pp. 1851-1872.

Meyer, B. H. (2005): Stochastische Unternehmensbewertung – Der Wertbeitrag von Realoptionen, Dissertation, University of Göttingen.

Michaud, R. O. (1998): Efficient asset management: A practical guide to stock portfolio optimization and asset allocation, Harvard Business School Press, Boston.

Milojcic, G. (2009): Anmerkungen zur europäischen Energiepolitik – Versorgungssicherheit durch CO_2-Infrastruktur, in: Energiewirtschaftliche Tagesfragen 10, pp. 30-32.

MIT (2003): The future of nuclear power – An interdisciplinary MIT study, Massachusetts Institute of Technology.

Modigliani, F., Miller, M. (1958): The cost of capital, corporate finance, and the theory of investment, in: American Economic Review 48, pp. 261-297.

Mossin, J. (1966): Equilibrium in a capital asset market, in: Econometrica 34, pp. 768-783.

Müller, D. (2005): Investitionsentscheidungen in der Elektrizitätswirtschaft eine betriebswirtschaftliche Entscheidung, in: Zeitschrift für Energiewirtschaft 1, pp. 65-76.

Naylor, T. N. (1971): Computer simulation experiments with models of economic systems, John Wiley & Sons, Inc., New York.

Neuhoff, K., Martinez, K. K., Sato, M. (2006): Allocation, incentives and distortions: the impact of EU ETS emissions allowance allocations to the electricity sector, Climate Policy 6, pp. 73-91.

Neuhoff, K. (2007): Investment decisions under climate policy uncertainty, EPRG Working Paper Series.

Neumann, v. J. (1951): Various techniques used in connection with random digits, in: Applied Mathematic Sciences 12, pp. 36-38.

Neumann, A., Siliverstovs, B., Hirschausen, v. C. (2006): Convergence of European spot market prices for natural gas? A real-time analysis of market integration using the Kalman Filter, in: Applied Economics Letters 13, pp. 727-732.

Neubarth, J., Woll, O., Weber, C., Gerecht, M. (2006): Beeinflussung der Spotmarktpreise durch Windstromerzeugung, in: Energiewirtschaftliche Tagesfragen 56, pp. 42-45.

Newbery, D., Green, R. (1996): Regulation, public ownerships, and privatization of the English electricity industry, in: Gilbert, R. J., Kahn, E. P. (Ed.), International comparison of electricity regulation, Cambridge University Press, pp. 25-81.

Oberndorfer, U. (2009): EU emission allowances and the stock market: Evidence from the electricity industry, Ecological Economics, 68, pp. 1116-1126.

Pavlak, A. (2008): The economic value of wind energy, in: The Electricity Journal 21, pp. 46-50.

Pilgram, T. (2006): Formen des Handels an der EEX, in: Schwintowski, H.-P. (Ed.), Handbuch Energiehandel, 1st Edition, Schmidt, Berlin.

Qin, Y. (2007): Discount rates for energy investments: A CAPM approach, Working Paper, Econ Pöyry, Norway.

Rademacher, M. (2008): Development and perspectives on supply and demand in the global hard coal market, in: Zeitschrift für Energiewirtschaft 2, pp. 67-87.

Reinaud, J. (2003): Emission trading and its possible impacts on investment decisions in the power sector, International Energy Agency (IEA) Information Paper.

Riddick, L. A. (1992): The effects of regulation on stochastic systematic risk, in: Journal of Regulatory Economics 4, pp. 139-157.

Robichek, A. A., Myers, S. C. (1966): Conceptual problems in the use of risk-adjusted discount rates, in: Journal of Finance 21, pp. 727-730.

Roques, F. A., Newbery, D. M., Nuttal, W. J. (2008): Fuel mix diversification incentives in liberalized electricity markets - A mean variance portfolio theory approach, in: Energy Economics 30, pp. 1831-1849.

Roques, F. A., Newbery, D. M., Nuttal, W. J., Neufville, R., Connors, S. (2006): Nuclear power a hedge against uncertain gas and carbon prices? in: The Energy Journal, International Association for Energy Economics 27, pp. 1-24.

Rosenkranz, F., Missler-Behr, M. (2005): Unternehmensrisiken erkennen und managen-Einführung in die quantitative Planung, Springer, Berlin.

Ross, S. A. (1976): The arbitrage theory of capital asset pricing, in: Journal of Economic Theory 13, pp. 341-360.

Ross, S. A., Westerfield, R. W., Jaffe, J. (2005): Corporate finance, 5th Edition, McGraw-Hill, New York.

RWE (2008): Facts and figures 2008, Essen.

Sadorsky, P. (2001): Risk factors in stock returns of Canadian oil and gas companies, in: Energy Economics 23, pp. 17-28.

Savvides, S. C. (1994): Risk analysis in investment appraisal, in: Project Appraisal 9, pp. 3-18.

Schnabel, R. B., Eskow, E. (1990): A new modified Cholesky factorization, in: SIAM Journal on Numerical Analysis 11, pp. 1136-1158.

Seifert, J., Uhrig-Homburg, M., Wagner, M. (2008): Dynamic behavior of CO_2 spot prices, in: Journal of Environmental Management 56, pp. 180-194.

Seitz, N. (1990): Capital budgeting and long-term financing decisions, Dryden Press.

Sharpe, W. F. (1964): Capital asset prices: A theory of market equilibrium under conditions of risk, in: Journal of Finance 19, pp. 425-442.

Sharpe, W. F. (1966): Mutual fund performance, in: Journal of Business 39, pp. 119-138.

Sharpe, W. F. (1994): The Sharpe ratio, in: The Journal of Portfolio Management 21, pp. 49–58.

Sharpe, W. F., Alexander, G. J., Bailey, J. V. (1999): Investments, 6th Edition, Prentice Hall, New Jersey.

Sijm, J., Neuhoff, K., Chen, Y., (2006): CO_2 cost pass through and windfall profits in the power sector, in Climate Policy 6, pp. 49-72.

Simonsen, I. (2005): Volatility of power markets, in: Physica A 355, pp. 10-20.

Skea, J. (2010): Valuing diversity in energy supply, in: Energy Policy 38, pp. 3608-3621.

Solnik, B. H. (1974): Why not diversify internationally rather than domestically? in: Financial Analysts Journal 30, pp. 48-52.

Spinney, P. J., Watkins, G. C. (1996): Monte Carlo simulation techniques and electric utility resource decisions, in: Energy Policy 24, pp. 155-163.

Statman, M. (1987): How many stocks make a diversified portfolio? in: Journal of Financial and Quantitative Analysis 22, pp. 353-363.

Stirling, A. (1994): Diversity and ignorance in electricity supply investment – Addressing the solution rather than the problem, in: Energy Policy 22, pp. 195-216.

Ströbele, W., Pfaffenberger, W., Heuterkes, H. (2010): Energiewirtschaft – Einführung in Theorie und Politik, 2nd Edition, Oldenbourg, München.

Sun, N., Swider, D. J., Voß, A. (2006): A comparison of methodologies incorporating uncertainties into power plant investment evaluations, in: Proceedings of the IAEE International Conference, Potsdam.

Sunderkötter, M., Weber, C. (2009): Valuing fuel diversification in optimal investment policies for electricity generation portfolios, Working Paper, University of Duisburg-Essen.

Takashima, R., Goto, M., Kimura, H., Madarme, H. (2008): Entry into the electricity market: Uncertainty, competition, and mothballing option, in: Energy Economics 30, pp. 1809-1830.

Tolley, G., Jones, D. (2004): The economic future of nuclear power, Report, University of Chicago.

Treynor, J. L. (1965): How to rate management of investment funds, in: Harvard Business Review 43, pp. 63-75.

Tseng, C.-L., Barz, G. (2002): Short-term generation asset valuation: A real options approach, in: Operations Research 50, pp. 297-310.

Turton, H., Barreto, L. (2006): Long-term security of energy supply and climate change, in: Energy Policy 34, pp. 2232-2250.

UBA (2005): Die Zukunft in unseren Händen. 21 Thesen zur Klimaschutzpolitik des 21. Jahrhunderts und ihre Begründungen, Umweltbundesamt.

Ulreich, S. (2005): Der Emissionshandel in der EU-25: Erste Erfahrungen mit einem neuen Instrument, in: Zeitschrift für Energiewirtschaft 4, pp. 279-288.

Viebig, J., Poddig, T., Tancar, R. (2009): Das Black/ Litterman-Modell: Portfoliosteuerung in der Praxis, in: Finanz Betrieb 12, pp. 727-732.

van Horne, J. C. (1966): Capital budgeting decisions involving combinations of risky investments, in: Management Science 13, pp. 84-92.

Wagner, M. (2007): CO_2-Emissionszertifikate - Preismodellierung und Derivatebewertung, Dissertation, University of Karlsruhe, 2007.

Wang, J., Liu, C. (2006): Generating multivariate mixture of normal distributions using a modified Cholesky decomposition, in: Proceedings of the 2006 Winter Simulation Conference, pp. 342-347.

Weber, C., Swider, D. J. (2006): Power plant investments under fuel and carbon price uncertainty, Working Paper, Institute of Energy Economics and the Rational Use of Energy (IER), University of Stuttgart.

Wissen, R., Nicolosi, M. (2007): Anmerkung zur akutellen Diskussion zum Merit-Order Effekt der erneuerbaren Energien", EWI Working Paper 07/03.

Yang, M., Blyth, W., Bradely, R., Bunn, D., Clarke, C., Wilson, T. (2008): Evaluating the power investment options with uncertainty in climate policy, in: Energy Economics 30, pp. 1933-1950.

Zachmann, G., von Hirschausen, C. (2008): First Evidence of Asymmetric Cost Pass-through of EU Emissions Allowances: Examining Wholesale Electricity Prices in Germany, Economics Letters 99, pp. 465-469

Zangari, P. (1996): Routines to simulate correlated normal random variables, in: Risk Metrics[TM] –Technical Document, J.P. Morgan/ Reuters, 4th Edition, New York.

Ziesing, H.-J. (2009): Differenzierte Entwicklung bei insgesamt weiter steigenden welt-weiten CO_2-Emissionen, in: Energiewirtschaftliche Tagesfragen 9, pp. 56-65.

Appendix

Macro - Power plant park

This macro is written in VBA to value each power plant by conducting a Monte Carlo Simulation.

```
Application.ScreenUpdating = False
Sheets("New Plant 1").Activate
If Cells(3, 5).Value = "1" And Cells(3, 7).Value = "1" And Cells(3, 9).Value = "1"
And Cells(3, 11).Value = "1" Then
For i = 1 To 1000
Sheets("Correlations").Activate
Range(Cells(i + 5, 4), Cells(i + 5, 14)).Select
Selection.Copy
Sheets("New Plant 1").Activate
Range("C16").Select
Selection.PasteSpecial Paste:=xlPasteValues, Operation:=xlNone, SkipBlanks _
    :=False, Transpose:=False
Sheets("Correlations").Activate
Range(Cells(i + 5, 40), Cells(i + 5, 50)).Select
Selection.Copy
Sheets("New Plant 1").Activate
Range("C21").Select
Selection.PasteSpecial Paste:=xlPasteValues, Operation:=xlNone, SkipBlanks _
    :=False, Transpose:=False
Sheets("Correlations").Activate
Range(Cells(i + 5, 28), Cells(i + 5, 38)).Select
Selection.Copy
Sheets("New Plant 1").Activate
Range("C26").Select
Selection.PasteSpecial Paste:=xlPasteValues, Operation:=xlNone, SkipBlanks _
    :=False, Transpose:=False
Calculate
Range("C49").Select
Selection.Copy
```

© Springer Fachmedien Wiesbaden GmbH, part of Springer Nature 2011
S. Rothe, *Portfolio Analysis of Power Plant Technologies*, Edition KWV,
https://doi.org/10.1007/978-3-658-24379-1

```
Cells(65 + i, 2).Select
Selection.PasteSpecial Paste:=xlPasteValues, Operation:=xlNone, SkipBlanks _
    :=False, Transpose:=False
Next i


ElseIf Cells(3, 5).Value = "1" And Cells(3, 7).Value = "2" And Cells(3, 9).Value = "1"
And Cells(3, 11).Value = "1" Then
For i = 1 To 1000
Sheets("Correlations").Activate
Range(Cells(i + 5, 4), Cells(i + 5, 14)).SelectCells(23 + i, 40).Select
Selection.Copy
Sheets("New Plant 1").Activate
Range("C16").Select
Selection.PasteSpecial Paste:=xlPasteValues, Operation:=xlNone, SkipBlanks _
    :=False, Transpose:=False
Sheets("Correlations").Activate
Range(Cells(i + 5, 52), Cells(i + 5, 62)).Select
Selection.Copy
Sheets("New Plant 1").Activate
Range("C21").Select
Selection.PasteSpecial Paste:=xlPasteValues, Operation:=xlNone, SkipBlanks _
    :=False, Transpose:=False
Sheets("Correlations").Activate
Range(Cells(i + 5, 28), Cells(i + 5, 38)).Select
Selection.Copy
Sheets("New Plant 1").Activate
Range("C26").Select
Selection.PasteSpecial Paste:=xlPasteValues, Operation:=xlNone, SkipBlanks _
    :=False, Transpose:=False
Calculate
Range("C49").Select
Selection.Copy
Cells(65 + i, 2).Select
Selection.PasteSpecial Paste:=xlPasteValues, Operation:=xlNone, SkipBlanks _
    :=False, Transpose:=False
Next i
```

```
ElseIf Cells(3, 5).Value = "1" And Cells(3, 7).Value = "3" And Cells(3, 9).Value = "1"
And Cells(3, 11).Value = "1" Then
For i = 1 To 1000
Sheets("Correlations").Activate
Range(Cells(i + 5, 4), Cells(i + 5, 14)).Select
Selection.Copy
Sheets("New Plant 1").Activate
Range("C16").Select
Selection.PasteSpecial Paste:=xlPasteValues, Operation:=xlNone, SkipBlanks _
    :=False, Transpose:=False
Sheets("Correlations").Activate
Range(Cells(i + 5, 64), Cells(i + 5, 74)).Select
Selection.Copy
Sheets("New Plant 1").Activate
Range("C21").Select
Selection.PasteSpecial Paste:=xlPasteValues, Operation:=xlNone, SkipBlanks _
    :=False, Transpose:=False
Sheets("Correlations").Activate
Range(Cells(i + 5, 28), Cells(i + 5, 38)).Select
Selection.Copy
Sheets("New Plant 1").Activate
Range("C26").Select
Selection.PasteSpecial Paste:=xlPasteValues, Operation:=xlNone, SkipBlanks _
    :=False, Transpose:=False
Calculate
Range("C49").Select
Selection.Copy
Cells(65 + i, 2).Select
Selection.PasteSpecial Paste:=xlPasteValues, Operation:=xlNone, SkipBlanks _
    :=False, Transpose:=False
Next i

ElseIf Cells(3, 5).Value = "1" And Cells(3, 7).Value = "5" And Cells(3, 9).Value = "0"
And Cells(3, 11).Value = "1" Then
For i = 1 To 1000
```

```
Sheets("Correlations").Activate
Range(Cells(i + 5, 4), Cells(i + 5, 14)).Select
Selection.Copy
Sheets("New Plant 1").Activate
Range("C16").Select
Selection.PasteSpecial Paste:=xlPasteValues, Operation:=xlNone, SkipBlanks _
    :=False, Transpose:=False
Sheets("Correlations").Activate
Range(Cells(i + 5, 88), Cells(i + 5, 98)).Select
Selection.Copy
Sheets("New Plant 1").Activate
Range("C21").Select
Selection.PasteSpecial Paste:=xlPasteValues, Operation:=xlNone, SkipBlanks _
    :=False, Transpose:=False
Calculate
Range("C49").Select
Selection.Copy
Cells(65 + i, 2).Select
Selection.PasteSpecial Paste:=xlPasteValues, Operation:=xlNone, SkipBlanks _
    :=False, Transpose:=False
Next i




ElseIf Cells(3, 5).Value = "2" And Cells(3, 7).Value = "3" And Cells(3, 9).Value = "1"
And Cells(3, 11).Value = "1" Then
For i = 1 To 1000
Sheets("Correlations").Activate
Range(Cells(i + 5, 16), Cells(i + 5, 26)).Select
Selection.Copy
Sheets("New Plant 1").Activate
Range("C16").Select
Selection.PasteSpecial Paste:=xlPasteValues, Operation:=xlNone, SkipBlanks _
    :=False, Transpose:=False
```

```
Sheets("Correlations").Activate
Range(Cells(i + 5, 64), Cells(i + 5, 74)).Select
Selection.Copy
Sheets("New Plant 1").Activate
Range("C21").Select
Selection.PasteSpecial Paste:=xlPasteValues, Operation:=xlNone, SkipBlanks _
    :=False, Transpose:=False
Sheets("Correlations").Activate
Range(Cells(i + 5, 28), Cells(i + 5, 38)).Select
Selection.Copy
Sheets("New Plant 1").Activate
Range("C26").Select
Selection.PasteSpecial Paste:=xlPasteValues, Operation:=xlNone, SkipBlanks _
    :=False, Transpose:=False
Calculate
Range("C49").Select
Selection.Copy
Cells(65 + i, 2).Select
Selection.PasteSpecial Paste:=xlPasteValues, Operation:=xlNone, SkipBlanks _
    :=False, Transpose:=False
Next i


ElseIf Cells(3, 5).Value = "2" And Cells(3, 7).Value = "4" And Cells(3, 9).Value = "1"
And Cells(3, 11).Value = "1" Then
For i = 1 To 1000
Sheets("Correlations").Activate
Range(Cells(i + 5, 16), Cells(i + 5, 26)).Select
Selection.Copy
Sheets("New Plant 1").Activate
Range("C16").Select
Selection.PasteSpecial Paste:=xlPasteValues, Operation:=xlNone, SkipBlanks _
    :=False, Transpose:=False
Sheets("Correlations").Activate
Range(Cells(i + 5, 76), Cells(i + 5, 86)).Select
Selection.Copy
```

```
Sheets("New Plant 1").Activate
Range("C21").Select
Selection.PasteSpecial Paste:=xlPasteValues, Operation:=xlNone, SkipBlanks _
    :=False, Transpose:=False
Sheets("Correlations").Activate
Range(Cells(i + 5, 28), Cells(i + 5, 38)).Select
Selection.Copy
Sheets("New Plant 1").Activate
Range("C26").Select
Selection.PasteSpecial Paste:=xlPasteValues, Operation:=xlNone, SkipBlanks _
    :=False, Transpose:=False
Calculate
Range("C49").Select
Selection.Copy
Cells(65 + i, 2).Select
Selection.PasteSpecial Paste:=xlPasteValues, Operation:=xlNone, SkipBlanks _
    :=False, Transpose:=False
    Next i


ElseIf Cells(3, 5).Value = "1" And Cells(3, 7).Value = "6" And Cells(3, 9).Value = "0"
And Cells(3, 11).Value = "1" Then
Sheets("Correlations").Activate
Range(Cells(6, 173), Cells(16, 173)).Select
Selection.Copy
Sheets("New Plant 1").Activate
Range("C16").Select
Selection.PasteSpecial Paste:=xlPasteValues, Operation:=xlNone, SkipBlanks _
    :=False, Transpose:=True
For i = 1 To 1000
Sheets("Correlations").Activate
Cells(5 + i, 171).Select
Selection.Copy
Sheets("New Plant 1").Activate
Range("G6").Select
Selection.PasteSpecial Paste:=xlPasteValues, Operation:=xlNone, SkipBlanks _
```

```
        :=False, Transpose:=False
Range("C21").Select
ActiveCell.Value = 0
Range("C26").Select
ActiveCell.Value = 0
Calculate
Range("C49").Select
Selection.Copy
Cells(65 + i, 2).Select
Selection.PasteSpecial Paste:=xlPasteValues, Operation:=xlNone, SkipBlanks _
        :=False, Transpose:=False
Next i




ElseIf Cells(3, 5).Value = "1" And Cells(3, 7).Value = "7" And Cells(3, 9).Value = "0"
And Cells(3, 11).Value = "1" Then
Sheets("Correlations").Activate
Range(Cells(6, 174), Cells(16, 174)).Select
Selection.Copy
Sheets("New Plant 1").Activate
Range("C16").Select
Selection.PasteSpecial Paste:=xlPasteValues, Operation:=xlNone, SkipBlanks _
        :=False, Transpose:=True
For i = 1 To 1000
Sheets("Correlations").Activate
Cells(5 + i, 172).Select
Selection.Copy
Sheets("New Plant 1").Activate
Range("G6").Select
Selection.PasteSpecial Paste:=xlPasteValues, Operation:=xlNone, SkipBlanks _
        :=False, Transpose:=False
Range("C21").Select
ActiveCell.Value = 0
```

```
Range("C26").Select
ActiveCell.Value = 0
Calculate
Range("C49").Select
Selection.Copy
Cells(65 + i, 2).Select
Selection.PasteSpecial Paste:=xlPasteValues, Operation:=xlNone, SkipBlanks _
    :=False, Transpose:=False
Next i


ElseIf Cells(3, 5).Value = "1" And Cells(3, 7).Value = "8" And Cells(3, 9).Value = "0"
And Cells(3, 11).Value = "1" Then
For i = 1 To 1000
Sheets("Correlations").Activate
Range(Cells(i + 5, 4), Cells(i + 5, 14)).Select
Selection.Copy
Sheets("New Plant 1").Activate
Range("C16").Select
Selection.PasteSpecial Paste:=xlPasteValues, Operation:=xlNone, SkipBlanks _
    :=False, Transpose:=False
Range("C21").Select
ActiveCell.Value = 0
Range("C26").Select
ActiveCell.Value = 0
Calculate
Range("C49").Select
Selection.Copy
Cells(65 + i, 2).Select
Selection.PasteSpecial Paste:=xlPasteValues, Operation:=xlNone, SkipBlanks _
    :=False, Transpose:=False
Next i


ElseIf Cells(3, 5).Value = "1" And Cells(3, 7).Value = "1" And Cells(3, 9).Value = "1"
And Cells(3, 11).Value = "2" Then
For i = 1 To 1000
Sheets("Correlations").Activate
```

```
Range(Cells(i + 5, 100), Cells(i + 5, 110)).Select
Selection.Copy
Sheets("New Plant 1").Activate
Range("C16").Select
Selection.PasteSpecial Paste:=xlPasteValues, Operation:=xlNone, SkipBlanks _
     :=False, Transpose:=False
Sheets("Correlations").Activate
Range(Cells(i + 5, 40), Cells(i + 5, 50)).Select
Selection.Copy
Sheets("New Plant 1").Activate
Range("C21").Select
Selection.PasteSpecial Paste:=xlPasteValues, Operation:=xlNone, SkipBlanks _
     :=False, Transpose:=False
Sheets("Correlations").Activate
Range(Cells(i + 5, 28), Cells(i + 5, 38)).Select
Selection.Copy
Sheets("New Plant 1").Activate
Range("C26").Select
Selection.PasteSpecial Paste:=xlPasteValues, Operation:=xlNone, SkipBlanks _
     :=False, Transpose:=False
Calculate
Range("C49").Select
Selection.Copy
Cells(65 + i, 2).Select
Selection.PasteSpecial Paste:=xlPasteValues, Operation:=xlNone, SkipBlanks _
     :=False, Transpose:=False
Next i

ElseIf Cells(3, 5).Value = "1" And Cells(3, 7).Value = "3" And Cells(3, 9).Value = "1"
And Cells(3, 11).Value = "2" Then
For i = 1 To 1000
Sheets("Correlations").Activate
Range(Cells(i + 5, 100), Cells(i + 5, 110)).Select
Selection.Copy
Sheets("New Plant 1").Activate
Range("C16").Select
```

```
Selection.PasteSpecial Paste:=xlPasteValues, Operation:=xlNone, SkipBlanks _
    :=False, Transpose:=False
Sheets("Correlations").Activate
Range(Cells(i + 5, 64), Cells(i + 5, 74)).Select
Selection.Copy
Sheets("New Plant 1").Activate
Range("C21").Select
Selection.PasteSpecial Paste:=xlPasteValues, Operation:=xlNone, SkipBlanks _
    :=False, Transpose:=False
Sheets("Correlations").Activate
Range(Cells(i + 5, 28), Cells(i + 5, 38)).Select
Selection.Copy
Sheets("New Plant 1").Activate
Range("C26").Select
Selection.PasteSpecial Paste:=xlPasteValues, Operation:=xlNone, SkipBlanks _
    :=False, Transpose:=False
Calculate
Range("C49").Select
Selection.Copy
Cells(65 + i, 2).Select
Selection.PasteSpecial Paste:=xlPasteValues, Operation:=xlNone, SkipBlanks _
    :=False, Transpose:=False
Next i

ElseIf Cells(3, 5).Value = "1" And Cells(3, 7).Value = "5" And Cells(3, 9).Value = "0"
And Cells(3, 11).Value = "2" Then
For i = 1 To 1000
Sheets("Correlations").Activate
Range(Cells(i + 5, 100), Cells(i + 5, 110)).Select
Selection.Copy
Sheets("New Plant 1").Activate
Range("C16").Select
Selection.PasteSpecial Paste:=xlPasteValues, Operation:=xlNone, SkipBlanks _
    :=False, Transpose:=False
Sheets("Correlations").Activate
Range(Cells(i + 5, 88), Cells(i + 5, 98)).Select
```

```
Selection.Copy
Sheets("New Plant 1").Activate
Range("C21").Select
Selection.PasteSpecial Paste:=xlPasteValues, Operation:=xlNone, SkipBlanks _
    :=False, Transpose:=False
Calculate
Range("C49").Select
Selection.Copy
Cells(65 + i, 2).Select
Selection.PasteSpecial Paste:=xlPasteValues, Operation:=xlNone, SkipBlanks _
    :=False, Transpose:=False
Next i

ElseIf Cells(3, 5).Value = "2" And Cells(3, 7).Value = "3" And Cells(3, 9).Value = "1"
And Cells(3, 11).Value = "2" Then
For i = 1 To 1000
Sheets("Correlations").Activate
Range(Cells(i + 5, 112), Cells(i + 5, 122)).Select
Selection.Copy
Sheets("New Plant 1").Activate
Range("C16").Select
Selection.PasteSpecial Paste:=xlPasteValues, Operation:=xlNone, SkipBlanks _
    :=False, Transpose:=False
Sheets("Correlations").Activate
Range(Cells(i + 5, 64), Cells(i + 5, 74)).Select
Selection.Copy
Sheets("New Plant 1").Activate
Range("C21").Select
Selection.PasteSpecial Paste:=xlPasteValues, Operation:=xlNone, SkipBlanks _
    :=False, Transpose:=False
Sheets("Correlations").Activate
Range(Cells(i + 5, 28), Cells(i + 5, 38)).Select
Selection.Copy
Sheets("New Plant 1").Activate
Range("C26").Select
Selection.PasteSpecial Paste:=xlPasteValues, Operation:=xlNone, SkipBlanks _
```

```
    :=False, Transpose:=False
Calculate
Range("C49").Select
Selection.Copy
Cells(65 + i, 2).Select
Selection.PasteSpecial Paste:=xlPasteValues, Operation:=xlNone, SkipBlanks _
    :=False, Transpose:=False
Next i

ElseIf Cells(3, 5).Value = "2" And Cells(3, 7).Value = "4" And Cells(3, 9).Value = "1"
And Cells(3, 11).Value = "2" Then
For i = 1 To 1000
Sheets("Correlations").Activate
Range(Cells(i + 5, 112), Cells(i + 5, 122)).Select
Selection.Copy
Sheets("New Plant 1").Activate
Range("C16").Select
Selection.PasteSpecial Paste:=xlPasteValues, Operation:=xlNone, SkipBlanks _
    :=False, Transpose:=False
Sheets("Correlations").Activate
Range(Cells(i + 5, 76), Cells(i + 5, 86)).Select
Selection.Copy
Sheets("New Plant 1").Activate
Range("C21").Select
Selection.PasteSpecial Paste:=xlPasteValues, Operation:=xlNone, SkipBlanks _
    :=False, Transpose:=False
Sheets("Correlations").Activate
Range(Cells(i + 5, 28), Cells(i + 5, 38)).Select
Selection.Copy
Sheets("New Plant 1").Activate
Range("C26").Select
Selection.PasteSpecial Paste:=xlPasteValues, Operation:=xlNone, SkipBlanks _
    :=False, Transpose:=False
Calculate
Range("C49").Select
Selection.Copy
```

```
Cells(65 + i, 2).Select
Selection.PasteSpecial Paste:=xlPasteValues, Operation:=xlNone, SkipBlanks _
    :=False, Transpose:=False
Next i

ElseIf Cells(3, 5).Value = "1" And Cells(3, 7).Value = "6" And Cells(3, 9).Value = "0"
And Cells(3, 11).Value = "2" Then

Sheets("Correlations").Activate
Range(Cells(6, 173), Cells(16, 173)).Select
Selection.Copy
Sheets("New Plant 1").Activate
Range("C16").Select
Selection.PasteSpecial Paste:=xlPasteValues, Operation:=xlNone, SkipBlanks _
    :=False, Transpose:=True
For i = 1 To 1000
Sheets("Correlations").Activate
Cells(5 + i, 171).Select
Selection.Copy
Sheets("New Plant 1").Activate
Range("G6").Select
Selection.PasteSpecial Paste:=xlPasteValues, Operation:=xlNone, SkipBlanks _
    :=False, Transpose:=False
Range("C21").Select
ActiveCell.Value = 0
Range("C26").Select
ActiveCell.Value = 0
Calculate
Range("C49").Select
Selection.Copy
Cells(65 + i, 2).Select
Selection.PasteSpecial Paste:=xlPasteValues, Operation:=xlNone, SkipBlanks _
    :=False, Transpose:=False
Next i
```

```
ElseIf Cells(3, 5).Value = "1" And Cells(3, 7).Value = "7" And Cells(3, 9).Value = "0"
And Cells(3, 11).Value = "2" Then
Sheets("Correlations").Activate
Range(Cells(6, 174), Cells(16, 174)).Select
Selection.Copy
Sheets("New Plant 1").Activate
Range("C16").Select
Selection.PasteSpecial Paste:=xlPasteValues, Operation:=xlNone, SkipBlanks _
    :=False, Transpose:=True
For i = 1 To 1000
Sheets("Correlations").Activate
Cells(5 + i, 172).Select
Selection.Copy
Sheets("New Plant 1").Activate
Range("G6").Select
Selection.PasteSpecial Paste:=xlPasteValues, Operation:=xlNone, SkipBlanks _
    :=False, Transpose:=False
Range("C21").Select
ActiveCell.Value = 0
Range("C26").Select
ActiveCell.Value = 0
Calculate
Range("C49").Select
Selection.Copy
Cells(65 + i, 2).Select
Selection.PasteSpecial Paste:=xlPasteValues, Operation:=xlNone, SkipBlanks _
    :=False, Transpose:=False
Next i
```

```
ElseIf Cells(3, 5).Value = "1" And Cells(3, 7).Value = "8" And Cells(3, 9).Value = "0"
And Cells(3, 11).Value = "2" Then
For i = 1 To 1000
Sheets("Correlations").Activate
Range(Cells(i + 5, 100), Cells(i + 5, 110)).Select
Selection.Copy
Sheets("New Plant 1").Activate
Range("C16").Select
Selection.PasteSpecial Paste:=xlPasteValues, Operation:=xlNone, SkipBlanks _
    :=False, Transpose:=False
Range("C21").Select
ActiveCell.Value = 0
Range("C26").Select
ActiveCell.Value = 0
Calculate
Range("C49").Select
Selection.Copy
Cells(65 + i, 2).Select
Selection.PasteSpecial Paste:=xlPasteValues, Operation:=xlNone, SkipBlanks _
    :=False, Transpose:=False
Next i

ElseIf Cells(3, 5).Value = "1" And Cells(3, 7).Value = "1" And Cells(3, 9).Value = "1"
And Cells(3, 11).Value = "3" Then
For i = 1 To 1000
Sheets("Correlations").Activate
Range(Cells(i + 5, 124), Cells(i + 5, 134)).Select
Selection.Copy
Sheets("New Plant 1").Activate
Range("C16").Select
Selection.PasteSpecial Paste:=xlPasteValues, Operation:=xlNone, SkipBlanks _
    :=False, Transpose:=False
Sheets("Correlations").Activate
Range(Cells(i + 5, 40), Cells(i + 5, 50)).Select
Selection.Copy
Sheets("New Plant 1").Activate
```

```
Range("C21").Select
Selection.PasteSpecial Paste:=xlPasteValues, Operation:=xlNone, SkipBlanks _
    :=False, Transpose:=False
Sheets("Correlations").Activate
Range(Cells(i + 5, 28), Cells(i + 5, 38)).Select
Selection.Copy
Sheets("New Plant 1").Activate
Range("C26").Select
Selection.PasteSpecial Paste:=xlPasteValues, Operation:=xlNone, SkipBlanks _
    :=False, Transpose:=False
Calculate
Range("C49").Select
Selection.Copy
Cells(65 + i, 2).Select
Selection.PasteSpecial Paste:=xlPasteValues, Operation:=xlNone, SkipBlanks _
    :=False, Transpose:=False
Next i

ElseIf Cells(3, 5).Value = "1" And Cells(3, 7).Value = "3" And Cells(3, 9).Value = "1"
And Cells(3, 11).Value = "3" Then
For i = 1 To 1000
Sheets("Correlations").Activate
Range(Cells(i + 5, 124), Cells(i + 5, 134)).Select
Selection.Copy
Sheets("New Plant 1").Activate
Range("C16").Select
Selection.PasteSpecial Paste:=xlPasteValues, Operation:=xlNone, SkipBlanks _
    :=False, Transpose:=False
Sheets("Correlations").Activate
Range(Cells(i + 5, 64), Cells(i + 5, 74)).Select
Selection.Copy
Sheets("New Plant 1").Activate
Range("C21").Select
Selection.PasteSpecial Paste:=xlPasteValues, Operation:=xlNone, SkipBlanks _
    :=False, Transpose:=False
Sheets("Correlations").Activate
```

```
Range(Cells(i + 5, 28), Cells(i + 5, 38)).Select
Selection.Copy
Sheets("New Plant 1").Activate
Range("C26").Select
Selection.PasteSpecial Paste:=xlPasteValues, Operation:=xlNone, SkipBlanks _
    :=False, Transpose:=False
Calculate
Range("C49").Select
Selection.Copy
Cells(65 + i, 2).Select
Selection.PasteSpecial Paste:=xlPasteValues, Operation:=xlNone, SkipBlanks _
    :=False, Transpose:=False
Next i

ElseIf Cells(3, 5).Value = "1" And Cells(3, 7).Value = "5" And Cells(3, 9).Value = "0"
And Cells(3, 11).Value = "3" Then
For i = 1 To 1000
Sheets("Correlations").Activate
Range(Cells(i + 5, 124), Cells(i + 5, 134)).Select
Selection.Copy
Sheets("New Plant 1").Activate
Range("C16").Select
Selection.PasteSpecial Paste:=xlPasteValues, Operation:=xlNone, SkipBlanks _
    :=False, Transpose:=False
Sheets("Correlations").Activate
Range(Cells(i + 5, 88), Cells(i + 5, 98)).Select
Selection.Copy
Sheets("New Plant 1").Activate
Range("C21").Select
Selection.PasteSpecial Paste:=xlPasteValues, Operation:=xlNone, SkipBlanks _
    :=False, Transpose:=False
Calculate
Range("C49").Select
Selection.Copy
Cells(65 + i, 2).Select
Selection.PasteSpecial Paste:=xlPasteValues, Operation:=xlNone, SkipBlanks _
```

```
    :=False, Transpose:=False
Next i


ElseIf Cells(3, 5).Value = "2" And Cells(3, 7).Value = "3" And Cells(3, 9).Value = "1"
And Cells(3, 11).Value = "3" Then
For i = 1 To 1000
Sheets("Correlations").Activate
Range(Cells(i + 5, 136), Cells(i + 5, 146)).Select
Selection.Copy
Sheets("New Plant 1").Activate
Range("C16").Select
Selection.PasteSpecial Paste:=xlPasteValues, Operation:=xlNone, SkipBlanks _
    :=False, Transpose:=False
Sheets("Correlations").Activate
Range(Cells(i + 5, 64), Cells(i + 5, 74)).Select
Selection.Copy
Sheets("New Plant 1").Activate
Range("C21").Select
Selection.PasteSpecial Paste:=xlPasteValues, Operation:=xlNone, SkipBlanks _
    :=False, Transpose:=False
Sheets("Correlations").Activate
Range(Cells(i + 5, 28), Cells(i + 5, 38)).Select
Selection.Copy
Sheets("New Plant 1").Activate
Range("C26").Select
Selection.PasteSpecial Paste:=xlPasteValues, Operation:=xlNone, SkipBlanks _
    :=False, Transpose:=False
Calculate
Range("C49").Select
Selection.Copy
Cells(65 + i, 2).Select
Selection.PasteSpecial Paste:=xlPasteValues, Operation:=xlNone, SkipBlanks _
    :=False, Transpose:=False
Next i
```

```
ElseIf Cells(3, 5).Value = "2" And Cells(3, 7).Value = "4" And Cells(3, 9).Value = "1"
And Cells(3, 11).Value = "3" Then
For i = 1 To 1000
Sheets("Correlations").Activate
Range(Cells(i + 5, 136), Cells(i + 5, 146)).Select
Selection.Copy
Sheets("New Plant 1").Activate
Range("C16").Select
Selection.PasteSpecial Paste:=xlPasteValues, Operation:=xlNone, SkipBlanks _
    :=False, Transpose:=False
Sheets("Correlations").Activate
Range(Cells(i + 5, 76), Cells(i + 5, 86)).Select
Selection.Copy
Sheets("New Plant 1").Activate
Range("C21").Select
Selection.PasteSpecial Paste:=xlPasteValues, Operation:=xlNone, SkipBlanks _
    :=False, Transpose:=False
Sheets("Correlations").Activate
Range(Cells(i + 5, 28), Cells(i + 5, 38)).Select
Selection.Copy
Sheets("New Plant 1").Activate
Range("C26").Select
Selection.PasteSpecial Paste:=xlPasteValues, Operation:=xlNone, SkipBlanks _
    :=False, Transpose:=False
Calculate
Range("C49").Select
Selection.Copy
Cells(65 + i, 2).Select
Selection.PasteSpecial Paste:=xlPasteValues, Operation:=xlNone, SkipBlanks _
    :=False, Transpose:=False
Next i

ElseIf Cells(3, 5).Value = "1" And Cells(3, 7).Value = "6" And Cells(3, 9).Value = "0"
And Cells(3, 11).Value = "3" Then
Sheets("Correlations").Activate
Range(Cells(6, 173), Cells(16, 173)).Select
```

```
Selection.Copy
Sheets("New Plant 1").Activate
Range("C16").Select
Selection.PasteSpecial Paste:=xlPasteValues, Operation:=xlNone, SkipBlanks _
    :=False, Transpose:=True
For i = 1 To 1000
Sheets("Correlations").Activate
Cells(5 + i, 171).Select
Selection.Copy
Sheets("New Plant 1").Activate
Range("G6").Select
Selection.PasteSpecial Paste:=xlPasteValues, Operation:=xlNone, SkipBlanks _
    :=False, Transpose:=False
Range("C21").Select
ActiveCell.Value = 0
Range("C26").Select
ActiveCell.Value = 0
Calculate
Range("C49").Select
Selection.Copy
Cells(65 + i, 2).Select
Selection.PasteSpecial Paste:=xlPasteValues, Operation:=xlNone, SkipBlanks _
    :=False, Transpose:=False
Next i

ElseIf Cells(3, 5).Value = "1" And Cells(3, 7).Value = "7" And Cells(3, 9).Value = "0"
And Cells(3, 11).Value = "3" Then
Sheets("Correlations").Activate
Range(Cells(6, 174), Cells(16, 174)).Select
Selection.Copy
Sheets("New Plant 1").Activate
Range("C16").Select
Selection.PasteSpecial Paste:=xlPasteValues, Operation:=xlNone, SkipBlanks _
    :=False, Transpose:=True
For i = 1 To 1000
Sheets("Correlations").Activate
```

```
Cells(5 + i, 171).Select
Selection.Copy
Sheets("New Plant 1").Activate
Range("G6").Select
Selection.PasteSpecial Paste:=xlPasteValues, Operation:=xlNone, SkipBlanks _
    :=False, Transpose:=False
Range("C21").Select
ActiveCell.Value = 0
Range("C26").Select
ActiveCell.Value = 0
Calculate
Range("C49").Select
Selection.Copy
Cells(65 + i, 2).Select
Selection.PasteSpecial Paste:=xlPasteValues, Operation:=xlNone, SkipBlanks _
    :=False, Transpose:=False
Next i

ElseIf Cells(3, 5).Value = "1" And Cells(3, 7).Value = "8" And Cells(3, 9).Value = "0"
And Cells(3, 11).Value = "3" Then
For i = 1 To 1000
Sheets("Correlations").Activate
Range(Cells(i + 5, 124), Cells(i + 5, 134)).Select
Selection.Copy
Sheets("New Plant 1").Activate
Range("C16").Select
Selection.PasteSpecial Paste:=xlPasteValues, Operation:=xlNone, SkipBlanks _
    :=False, Transpose:=False
Range("C21").Select
ActiveCell.Value = 0
Range("C26").Select
ActiveCell.Value = 0
Calculate
Range("C49").Select
Selection.Copy
Cells(65 + i, 2).Select
```

```
Selection.PasteSpecial Paste:=xlPasteValues, Operation:=xlNone, SkipBlanks _
    :=False, Transpose:=False
Next i



ElseIf Cells(3, 5).Value = "1" And Cells(3, 7).Value = "1" And Cells(3, 9).Value = "1"
And Cells(3, 11).Value = "4" Then
For i = 1 To 1000
Sheets("Correlations").Activate
Range(Cells(i + 5, 148), Cells(i + 5, 158)).Select
Selection.Copy
Sheets("New Plant 1").Activate
Range("C16").Select
Selection.PasteSpecial Paste:=xlPasteValues, Operation:=xlNone, SkipBlanks _
    :=False, Transpose:=False
Sheets("Correlations").Activate
Range(Cells(i + 5, 40), Cells(i + 5, 50)).Select
Selection.Copy
Sheets("New Plant 1").Activate
Range("C21").Select
Selection.PasteSpecial Paste:=xlPasteValues, Operation:=xlNone, SkipBlanks _
    :=False, Transpose:=False
Sheets("Correlations").Activate
Range(Cells(i + 5, 28), Cells(i + 5, 38)).Select
Selection.Copy
Sheets("New Plant 1").Activate
Range("C26").Select
Selection.PasteSpecial Paste:=xlPasteValues, Operation:=xlNone, SkipBlanks _
    :=False, Transpose:=False
Calculate
Range("C49").Select
Selection.Copy
Cells(65 + i, 2).Select
Selection.PasteSpecial Paste:=xlPasteValues, Operation:=xlNone, SkipBlanks _
    :=False, Transpose:=False
Next i
```

```
ElseIf Cells(3, 5).Value = "1" And Cells(3, 7).Value = "3" And Cells(3, 9).Value = "1"
And Cells(3, 11).Value = "4" Then
For i = 1 To 1000
Sheets("Correlations").Activate
Range(Cells(i + 5, 148), Cells(i + 5, 158)).Select
Selection.Copy
Sheets("New Plant 1").Activate
Range("C16").Select
Selection.PasteSpecial Paste:=xlPasteValues, Operation:=xlNone, SkipBlanks _
    :=False, Transpose:=False
Sheets("Correlations").Activate
Range(Cells(i + 5, 64), Cells(i + 5, 74)).Select
Selection.Copy
Sheets("New Plant 1").Activate
Range("C21").Select
Selection.PasteSpecial Paste:=xlPasteValues, Operation:=xlNone, SkipBlanks _
    :=False, Transpose:=False
Sheets("Correlations").Activate
Range(Cells(i + 5, 28), Cells(i + 5, 38)).Select
Selection.Copy
Sheets("New Plant 1").Activate
Range("C26").Select
Selection.PasteSpecial Paste:=xlPasteValues, Operation:=xlNone, SkipBlanks _
    :=False, Transpose:=False
Calculate
Range("C49").Select
Selection.Copy
Cells(65 + i, 2).Select
Selection.PasteSpecial Paste:=xlPasteValues, Operation:=xlNone, SkipBlanks _
    :=False, Transpose:=False
Next i

ElseIf Cells(3, 5).Value = "1" And Cells(3, 7).Value = "5" And Cells(3, 9).Value = "0"
And Cells(3, 11).Value = "4" Then
For i = 1 To 1000
```

```
Sheets("Correlations").Activate
Range(Cells(i + 5, 148), Cells(i + 5, 158)).Select
Selection.Copy
Sheets("New Plant 1").Activate
Range("C16").Select
Selection.PasteSpecial Paste:=xlPasteValues, Operation:=xlNone, SkipBlanks _
    :=False, Transpose:=False
Sheets("Correlations").Activate
Range(Cells(i + 5, 88), Cells(i + 5, 98)).Select
Selection.Copy
Sheets("New Plant 1").Activate
Range("C21").Select
Selection.PasteSpecial Paste:=xlPasteValues, Operation:=xlNone, SkipBlanks _
    :=False, Transpose:=False
Calculate
Range("C49").Select
Selection.Copy
Cells(65 + i, 2).Select
Selection.PasteSpecial Paste:=xlPasteValues, Operation:=xlNone, SkipBlanks _
    :=False, Transpose:=False
Next i


ElseIf Cells(3, 5).Value = "2" And Cells(3, 7).Value = "3" And Cells(3, 9).Value = "1"
And Cclls(3, 11).Value = "4" Then
For i = 1 To 1000
Sheets("Correlations").Activate
Range(Cells(i + 5, 160), Cells(i + 5, 170)).Select
Selection.Copy
Sheets("New Plant 1").Activate
Range("C16").Select
Selection.PasteSpecial Paste:=xlPasteValues, Operation:=xlNone, SkipBlanks _
    :=False, Transpose:=False
Sheets("Correlations").Activate
Range(Cells(i + 5, 64), Cells(i + 5, 74)).Select
Selection.Copy
Sheets("New Plant 1").Activate
```

```
Range("C21").Select
Selection.PasteSpecial Paste:=xlPasteValues, Operation:=xlNone, SkipBlanks _
    :=False, Transpose:=False
Sheets("Correlations").Activate
Range(Cells(i + 5, 28), Cells(i + 5, 38)).Select
Selection.Copy
Sheets("New Plant 1").Activate
Range("C26").Select
Selection.PasteSpecial Paste:=xlPasteValues, Operation:=xlNone, SkipBlanks _
    :=False, Transpose:=False
Calculate
Range("C49").Select
Selection.Copy
Cells(65 + i, 2).Select
Selection.PasteSpecial Paste:=xlPasteValues, Operation:=xlNone, SkipBlanks _
    :=False, Transpose:=False
Next i


ElseIf Cells(3, 5).Value = "2" And Cells(3, 7).Value = "4" And Cells(3, 9).Value = "1"
And Cells(3, 11).Value = "4" Then
For i = 1 To 1000
Sheets("Correlations").Activate
Range(Cells(i + 5, 160), Cells(i + 5, 170)).Select
Selection.Copy
Sheets("New Plant 1").Activate
Range("C16").Select
Selection.PasteSpecial Paste:=xlPasteValues, Operation:=xlNone, SkipBlanks _
    :=False, Transpose:=False
Sheets("Correlations").Activate
Range(Cells(i + 5, 76), Cells(i + 5, 86)).Select
Selection.Copy
Sheets("New Plant 1").Activate
Range("C21").Select
Selection.PasteSpecial Paste:=xlPasteValues, Operation:=xlNone, SkipBlanks _
    :=False, Transpose:=False
Sheets("Correlations").Activate
```

```
Range(Cells(i + 5, 28), Cells(i + 5, 38)).Select
Selection.Copy
Sheets("New Plant 1").Activate
Range("C26").Select
Selection.PasteSpecial Paste:=xlPasteValues, Operation:=xlNone, SkipBlanks _
    :=False, Transpose:=False
Calculate
Range("C49").Select
Selection.Copy
Cells(65 + i, 2).Select
Selection.PasteSpecial Paste:=xlPasteValues, Operation:=xlNone, SkipBlanks _
    :=False, Transpose:=False

Next i

ElseIf Cells(3, 5).Value = "1" And Cells(3, 7).Value = "6" And Cells(3, 9).Value = "0"
And Cells(3, 11).Value = "4" Then
Sheets("Correlations").Activate
Range(Cells(6, 173), Cells(16, 173)).Select
Selection.Copy
Sheets("New Plant 1").Activate
Range("C16").Select
Selection.PasteSpecial Paste:=xlPasteValues, Operation:=xlNone, SkipBlanks _
    :=False, Transpose:=True
For i = 1 To 1000
Sheets("Correlations").Activate
Cells(5 + i, 171).Select
Selection.Copy
Sheets("New Plant 1").Activate
Range("G6").Select
Selection.PasteSpecial Paste:=xlPasteValues, Operation:=xlNone, SkipBlanks _
    :=False, Transpose:=False
Range("C21").Select
ActiveCell.Value = 0
Range("C26").Select
ActiveCell.Value = 0
```

```vba
Calculate
Range("C49").Select
Selection.Copy
Cells(65 + i, 2).Select
Selection.PasteSpecial Paste:=xlPasteValues, Operation:=xlNone, SkipBlanks _
    :=False, Transpose:=False
Next i




ElseIf Cells(3, 5).Value = "1" And Cells(3, 7).Value = "8" And Cells(3, 9).Value = "0"
And Cells(3, 11).Value = "4" Then
For i = 1 To 1000
Sheets("Correlations").Activate
Range(Cells(i + 5, 148), Cells(i + 5, 158)).Select
Selection.Copy
Sheets("New Plant 1").Activate
Range("C16").Select
Selection.PasteSpecial Paste:=xlPasteValues, Operation:=xlNone, SkipBlanks _
    :=False, Transpose:=False
Range("C21").Select
ActiveCell.Value = 0
Range("C26").Select
ActiveCell.Value = 0
Calculate
Range("C49").Select
Selection.Copy
Cells(65 + i, 2).Select
Selection.PasteSpecial Paste:=xlPasteValues, Operation:=xlNone, SkipBlanks _
    :=False, Transpose:=False
Next i

ElseIf Cells(3, 5).Value = "1" And Cells(3, 7).Value = "7" And Cells(3, 9).Value = "0"
And Cells(3, 11).Value = "4" Then
Sheets("Correlations").Activate
```

```
Range(Cells(6, 174), Cells(16, 174)).Select
Selection.Copy
Sheets("New Plant 1").Activate
Range("C16").Select
Selection.PasteSpecial Paste:=xlPasteValues, Operation:=xlNone, SkipBlanks _
    :=False, Transpose:=True
For i = 1 To 1000
Sheets("Correlations").Activate
Cells(5 + i, 172).Select
Selection.Copy
Sheets("New Plant 1").Activate
Range("G6").Select
Selection.PasteSpecial Paste:=xlPasteValues, Operation:=xlNone, SkipBlanks _
    :=False, Transpose:=False
Range("C21").Select
ActiveCell.Value = 0
Range("C26").Select
ActiveCell.Value = 0
Calculate
Range("C49").Select
Selection.Copy
Cells(65 + i, 2).Select
Selection.PasteSpecial Paste:=xlPasteValues, Operation:=xlNone, SkipBlanks _
    :=False, Transpose:=False
Next i

ElseIf Cells(3, 5).Value = "3" And Cells(3, 7).Value = "1" And Cells(3, 9).Value = "1"
And Cells(3, 11).Value = "1" Then
For i = 1 To 1000
Sheets("Correlations").Activate
Range(Cells(i + 5, 176), Cells(i + 5, 186)).Select
Selection.Copy
Sheets("New Plant 1").Activate
Range("C16").Select
Selection.PasteSpecial Paste:=xlPasteValues, Operation:=xlNone, SkipBlanks _
    :=False, Transpose:=False
```

```
Sheets("Correlations").Activate
Range(Cells(i + 5, 40), Cells(i + 5, 50)).Select
Selection.Copy
Sheets("New Plant 1").Activate
Range("C21").Select
Selection.PasteSpecial Paste:=xlPasteValues, Operation:=xlNone, SkipBlanks _
    :=False, Transpose:=False
Sheets("Correlations").Activate
Range(Cells(i + 5, 28), Cells(i + 5, 38)).Select
Selection.Copy
Sheets("New Plant 1").Activate
Range("C26").Select
Selection.PasteSpecial Paste:=xlPasteValues, Operation:=xlNone, SkipBlanks _
    :=False, Transpose:=False
Calculate
Range("C49").Select
Selection.Copy
Cells(65 + i, 2).Select
Selection.PasteSpecial Paste:=xlPasteValues, Operation:=xlNone, SkipBlanks _
    :=False, Transpose:=False
Next i

ElseIf Cells(3, 5).Value = "3" And Cells(3, 7).Value = "3" And Cells(3, 9).Value = "1"
And Cells(3, 11).Value = "1" Then
For i = 1 To 1000
Sheets("Correlations").Activate
Range(Cells(i + 5, 176), Cells(i + 5, 186)).Select
Selection.Copy
Sheets("New Plant 1").Activate
Range("C16").Select
Selection.PasteSpecial Paste:=xlPasteValues, Operation:=xlNone, SkipBlanks _
    :=False, Transpose:=False
Sheets("Correlations").Activate
Range(Cells(i + 5, 64), Cells(i + 5, 74)).Select
Selection.Copy
Sheets("New Plant 1").Activate
```

```
Range("C21").Select
Selection.PasteSpecial Paste:=xlPasteValues, Operation:=xlNone, SkipBlanks _
    :=False, Transpose:=False
Sheets("Correlations").Activate
Range(Cells(i + 5, 28), Cells(i + 5, 38)).Select
Selection.Copy
Sheets("New Plant 1").Activate
Range("C26").Select
Selection.PasteSpecial Paste:=xlPasteValues, Operation:=xlNone, SkipBlanks _
    :=False, Transpose:=False
Calculate
Range("C49").Select
Selection.Copy
Cells(65 + i, 2).Select
Selection.PasteSpecial Paste:=xlPasteValues, Operation:=xlNone, SkipBlanks _
    :=False, Transpose:=False
Next i


ElseIf Cells(3, 5).Value = "3" And Cells(3, 7).Value = "1" And Cells(3, 9).Value = "1"
And Cells(3, 11).Value = "2" Then
For i = 1 To 1000
Sheets("Correlations").Activate
Range(Cells(i + 5, 188), Cells(i + 5, 198)).Select
Selection.Copy
Sheets("New Plant 1").Activate
Range("C16").Select
Selection.PasteSpecial Paste:=xlPasteValues, Operation:=xlNone, SkipBlanks _
    :=False, Transpose:=False
Sheets("Correlations").Activate
Range(Cells(i + 5, 40), Cells(i + 5, 50)).Select
Selection.Copy
Sheets("New Plant 1").Activate
Range("C21").Select
Selection.PasteSpecial Paste:=xlPasteValues, Operation:=xlNone, SkipBlanks _
    :=False, Transpose:=False
```

```
Sheets("Correlations").Activate
Range(Cells(i + 5, 28), Cells(i + 5, 38)).Select
Selection.Copy
Sheets("New Plant 1").Activate
Range("C26").Select
Selection.PasteSpecial Paste:=xlPasteValues, Operation:=xlNone, SkipBlanks _
    :=False, Transpose:=False
Calculate
Range("C49").Select
Selection.Copy
Cells(65 + i, 2).Select
Selection.PasteSpecial Paste:=xlPasteValues, Operation:=xlNone, SkipBlanks _
    :=False, Transpose:=False
Next i

ElseIf Cells(3, 5).Value = "3" And Cells(3, 7).Value = "3" And Cells(3, 9).Value = "1"
And Cells(3, 11).Value = "2" Then
For i = 1 To 1000
Sheets("Correlations").Activate
Range(Cells(i + 5, 188), Cells(i + 5, 198)).Select
Selection.Copy
Sheets("New Plant 1").Activate
Range("C16").Select
Selection.PasteSpecial Paste:=xlPasteValues, Operation:=xlNone, SkipBlanks _
    :=False, Transpose:=False
Sheets("Correlations").Activate
Range(Cells(i + 5, 64), Cells(i + 5, 74)).Select
Selection.Copy
Sheets("New Plant 1").Activate
Range("C21").Select
Selection.PasteSpecial Paste:=xlPasteValues, Operation:=xlNone, SkipBlanks _
    :=False, Transpose:=False
Sheets("Correlations").Activate
Range(Cells(i + 5, 28), Cells(i + 5, 38)).Select
Selection.Copy
Sheets("New Plant 1").Activate
```

```
Range("C26").Select
Selection.PasteSpecial Paste:=xlPasteValues, Operation:=xlNone, SkipBlanks _
    :=False, Transpose:=False
Calculate
Range("C49").Select
Selection.Copy
Cells(65 + i, 2).Select
Selection.PasteSpecial Paste:=xlPasteValues, Operation:=xlNone, SkipBlanks _
    :=False, Transpose:=False
Next i



ElseIf Cells(3, 5).Value = "3" And Cells(3, 7).Value = "1" And Cells(3, 9).Value = "1"
And Cells(3, 11).Value = "3" Then
For i = 1 To 1000
Sheets("Correlations").Activate
Range(Cells(i + 5, 200), Cells(i + 5, 210)).Select
Selection.Copy
Sheets("New Plant 1").Activate
Range("C16").Select
Selection.PasteSpecial Paste:=xlPasteValues, Operation:=xlNone, SkipBlanks _
    :=False, Transpose:=False
Sheets("Correlations").Activate
Range(Cells(i + 5, 40), Cells(i + 5, 50)).Select
Selection.Copy
Sheets("New Plant 1").Activate
Range("C21").Select
Selection.PasteSpecial Paste:=xlPasteValues, Operation:=xlNone, SkipBlanks _
    :=False, Transpose:=False
Sheets("Correlations").Activate
Range(Cells(i + 5, 28), Cells(i + 5, 38)).Select
Selection.Copy
Sheets("New Plant 1").Activate
Range("C26").Select
Selection.PasteSpecial Paste:=xlPasteValues, Operation:=xlNone, SkipBlanks _
    :=False, Transpose:=False
```

```
Calculate
Range("C49").Select
Selection.Copy
Cells(65 + i, 2).Select
Selection.PasteSpecial Paste:=xlPasteValues, Operation:=xlNone, SkipBlanks _
    :=False, Transpose:=False
Next i


ElseIf Cells(3, 5).Value = "3" And Cells(3, 7).Value = "3" And Cells(3, 9).Value = "1"
And Cells(3, 11).Value = "3" Then
For i = 1 To 1000
Sheets("Correlations").Activate
Range(Cells(i + 5, 200), Cells(i + 5, 210)).Select
Selection.Copy
Sheets("New Plant 1").Activate
Range("C16").Select
Selection.PasteSpecial Paste:=xlPasteValues, Operation:=xlNone, SkipBlanks _
    :=False, Transpose:=False
Sheets("Correlations").Activate
Range(Cells(i + 5, 64), Cells(i + 5, 74)).Select
Selection.Copy
Sheets("New Plant 1").Activate
Range("C21").Select
Selection.PasteSpecial Paste:=xlPasteValues, Operation:=xlNone, SkipBlanks _
    :=False, Transpose:=False
Sheets("Correlations").Activate
Range(Cells(i + 5, 28), Cells(i + 5, 38)).Select
Selection.Copy
Sheets("New Plant 1").Activate
Range("C26").Select
Selection.PasteSpecial Paste:=xlPasteValues, Operation:=xlNone, SkipBlanks _
    :=False, Transpose:=False
Calculate
Range("C49").Select
Selection.Copy
```

```
Cells(65 + i, 2).Select
Selection.PasteSpecial Paste:=xlPasteValues, Operation:=xlNone, SkipBlanks _
    :=False, Transpose:=False
Next i



ElseIf Cells(3, 5).Value = "3" And Cells(3, 7).Value = "1" And Cells(3, 9).Value = "1"
And Cells(3, 11).Value = "4" Then
For i = 1 To 1000
Sheets("Correlations").Activate
Range(Cells(i + 5, 212), Cells(i + 5, 222)).Select
Selection.Copy
Sheets("New Plant 1").Activate
Range("C16").Select
Selection.PasteSpecial Paste:=xlPasteValues, Operation:=xlNone, SkipBlanks _
    :=False, Transpose:=False
Sheets("Correlations").Activate
Range(Cells(i + 5, 40), Cells(i + 5, 50)).Select
Selection.Copy
Sheets("New Plant 1").Activate
Range("C21").Select
Selection.PasteSpecial Paste:=xlPasteValues, Operation:=xlNone, SkipBlanks _
    :=False, Transpose:=False
Sheets("Correlations").Activate
Range(Cells(i + 5, 28), Cells(i + 5, 38)).Select
Selection.Copy
Sheets("New Plant 1").Activate
Range("C26").Select
Selection.PasteSpecial Paste:=xlPasteValues, Operation:=xlNone, SkipBlanks _
    :=False, Transpose:=False
Calculate
Range("C49").Select
Selection.Copy
Cells(65 + i, 2).Select
Selection.PasteSpecial Paste:=xlPasteValues, Operation:=xlNone, SkipBlanks _
    :=False, Transpose:=False
```

```
Next i


Else: Cells(3, 5).Value = "3" And Cells(3, 7).Value = "3" And Cells(3, 9).Value = "1"
And Cells(3, 11).Value = "4"
For i = 1 To 1000
Sheets("Correlations").Activate
Range(Cells(i + 5, 212), Cells(i + 5, 222)).Select
Selection.Copy
Sheets("New Plant 1").Activate
Range("C16").Select
Selection.PasteSpecial Paste:=xlPasteValues, Operation:=xlNone, SkipBlanks _
    :=False, Transpose:=False
Sheets("Correlations").Activate
Range(Cells(i + 5, 64), Cells(i + 5, 74)).Select
Selection.Copy
Sheets("New Plant 1").Activate
Range("C21").Select
Selection.PasteSpecial Paste:=xlPasteValues, Operation:=xlNone, SkipBlanks _
    :=False, Transpose:=False
Sheets("Correlations").Activate
Range(Cells(i + 5, 28), Cells(i + 5, 38)).Select
Selection.Copy
Sheets("New Plant 1").Activate
Range("C26").Select
Selection.PasteSpecial Paste:=xlPasteValues, Operation:=xlNone, SkipBlanks _
    :=False, Transpose:=False
Calculate
Range("C49").Select
Selection.Copy
Cells(65 + i, 2).Select
Selection.PasteSpecial Paste:=xlPasteValues, Operation:=xlNone, SkipBlanks _
    :=False, Transpose:=False
Next i
End If
Application.ScreenUpdating = True
```